VETS UNDER SIEGE

Also by Martin Schram

Running for President, 1976: The Carter Campaign

The Great American Video Game: Presidential Politics in the Television Age

*Speaking Freely: Former Members of Congress
Talk About Money in Politics*

Cell Phones: Invisible Hazards in the Wireless Age (with Dr. George Carlo)

Avoiding Armageddon: Our Future, Our Choice

Edited by Will Marshall and Martin Schram

Mandate for Change

VETS UNDER SIEGE

How America Deceives
and Dishonors
Those Who Fight
Our Battles

Martin Schram

Thomas Dunne Books

St. Martin's Press   New York

THOMAS DUNNE BOOKS.
An imprint of St. Martin's Press.

VETS UNDER SIEGE. Copyright © 2008 by Martin Schram. All rights reserved.
Printed in the United States of America. For information, address St. Martin's Press,
175 Fifth Avenue, New York, N.Y. 10010.

www.thomasdunnebooks.com
www.stmartins.com

Library of Congress Cataloging-in-Publication Data

Schram, Martin.
    Vets under siege : how America deceives and dishonors those who fight our battles / Mar-
tin Schram.
        p. cm.
    ISBN-13: 978-0-312-37573-7
    ISBN-10: 0-312-37573-5
    1. Veterans—Services for—United States.   2. United States. Dept. of Veterans
Affairs—Rules and practice—Evaluation.   3. Veterans—Government policy—United
States.   4. Disabled veterans—Medical care—United States—21st century.   I. Title.
    UB354.S37 2008
    362.860973—dc22   2008001833

First Edition: July 2008

10   9   8   7   6   5   4   3   2   1

To my in-laws, a military veteran's family, with grateful thanks for their love and inspiration:

The late George Clifton (Cliff) Morgan, who joined the U.S. Army to fight in World War II, rose to the battlefield rank of captain, participated in the landing at Normandy, the Battle of the Bulge, the crossing of the Rhine at the Bridge at Remagen, and the liberation of the Nazi concentration camp at Buchenwald; and spent the rest of his years shielding his loved ones from the wartime events, horrific and heroic, that surely seared his service in the battles he fought for us all.

And Grace Gordon Morgan, whose strength, wisdom, and values of goodness and decency shaped their family while her husband was at war and after he returned home. Her daily example provided a foundation for their children, Bruce, Diana, and Patricia, who became my wife and instilled those sound values in our sons, Kenneth and David.

Contents

Acknowledgments

The men and women of the United States military who fought battles in distant lands gave their country and fellow citizens the gifts of their service and, too often, their lives. Now it is up to the rest of us to do more than just acknowledge their gifts; we need to honor their service and their lives by making sure that we do all we can to provide both respect and restitution for their sacrifices and those of their families.

I am grateful for the brief opportunity I had to talk with one solider who fought and sacrificed, William C. Florey, shortly before he lost his battle to cancer after being exposed to the fallout from Iraqi chemical weapons. He was proud of his service and patriotic about his country; even when he was disheartened to learn in his last days that he had been denied service-related benefits by the Department of Veterans Affairs. At a time when his disease and medications made speaking painfully difficult, he had only good things to say about the nation and government that, it seemed to me, had let him down. I had been put in contact with Bill by his good friend, Francesca Yabraian, who told me about his plight. When Bill died, it seemed clear that we should not let the memory of his sacrifice die, nor that of so many thousands of others who were similarly disrespected and dishonored by their government; we should let their stories live so that we could fix the system that had not done right by the thousands of Bill Floreys who fought our battles while we remained at home, much as children of most presidents, vice presidents, cabinet officers, senators, and representatives had stayed home while others fought our wars. Bill's family made available his military service records. Francesca became a researcher with a mission. And as the full magnitude of our national disservice to our military veterans became clear, the idea of this book became an imperative.

At that point, the contributions of others became crucial. My longtime agent and friend, Ronald L. Goldfarb, quickly championed this project and once again gave me the benefit of his steady counsel and encouragement. Thomas Dunne, editor and founder of the Thomas Dunne Books imprint of St. Martin's Press, was quick to see the importance of this book and became both its publisher and advocate. Senior editor Rob Kirkpatrick proved to be an invaluable and insightful teammate; his every instinct made this book better.

The more this project was researched, the more it became apparent that elements of the story of veterans dishonored and deceived had been around for many years—many decades, in fact. Authors Paul Dickson and Thomas B. Allen told the powerful story of *The Bonus Army,* and in reading their account of the veterans' Washington protest during the Hoover presidency, I found that they in turn had drawn upon news coverage written by several prominent journalists who had covered the clashes as young reporters in Washington. Among them were *The Christian Science Monitor*'s Richard L. Strout and Joseph C. Harsch,

and *The New York Time*'s John D. Morris—men I'd gotten to
know during their last years as journalists, when I arrived decades later to begin working as a Washington correspondent for
Newsday. (By then Strout was writing the famous TRB column
for *The New Republic.*) They had great stories to tell about
events they'd covered that I only knew through history books;
unfortunately, I never had the wit to ask any of them about the
Bonus Army. (I even discovered that my longtime next-door
neighbor in suburban Washington, the late Sam Brightman, had
a bit role to play, when as publicity director of the Democratic
National Committee he published a special tabloid newspaper
in 1952 to remind voters that Dwight Eisenhower had been part
of the Army's routing of the protesting veterans two decades
earlier. Of course, I never thought to ask Sam about that, either.)

In 2005, Knight Ridder newspapers' Washington correspondents Chris Adams and Alison Young wrote an important series
of articles about ways in which the U.S. government has been disserving military veterans; Adams continued to do ground-
breaking stories about veterans' affairs when the Knight Ridder
newspaper chain was bought by the McClatchy newspapers.
More recently, *The Washington Post*'s Dana Priest and Anne Hull
reported and wrote an excellent series detailing the poor condition
of the Walter Reed Army Medical Center's outpatient facilities
and followed up with articles detailing shameful mistreatment of
veterans "Beyond Walter Reed"—journalism that stung official
Washington into taking some corrective action.

Most of all, I am grateful to the veterans who, although proud
and private individuals, were willing to tell their stories in the
hopes that their government would take notice and then take action to right a system that has clearly gone wrong.

VETS UNDER SIEGE

Prologue

There are times when a device, though not new, works perfectly—even if it has not always worked perfectly before. And this is a perfect time to use, once again, the Two Americas device. It was used, rather controversially, back in 1968 by a presidential commission on midsummer inner-city violence: "Our nation is moving toward two societies, one black, one white—separate and unequal." It has been used, unevenly, by politicians pushing populist themes: "There are two Americas. One pays the taxes, the other gets the tax breaks." And so on.

But after looking at what has gone so wrong with the way we treat our military veterans, we see this much is indisputably true: We *are* two Americas: One fights our nation's wars. The other pays those who go to war so the rest of us, our children and our grandchildren, won't have to.

The burden falls upon all of us who don't go to be willing to pay the price for providing care and benefits for those who do. The category of those Americans who don't go to war is wide and deep: It includes presidents and vice presidents who chose not to go to war in distant lands, as well as their children who also chose not to go when they reached military age. It also includes those in public office at all levels, and those who write books and those who read them.

For decades, we have known at some level of consciousness that the men and women who serve in the military are too often dishonored and disserved by our government once they return home. In this book, we will be reminded of things we have overlooked, forgotten, or shoved aside: that for decades we have been reading and hearing about government failures in veterans' affairs—detailed revelations by government investigators and investigating journalists. We will see that the Department of Veterans Affairs—the VA—has failed to fix the bureaucratic backlogs and unconscionable delays that have deprived veterans of the aid they deserve. Yet when nothing was done about it, nobody sounded cries of outrage and demands for action.

Part of the problem of official inaction in the wake of these revelations stems from the way Washington really works—and too often doesn't work. Over the years, many excellent journalists from outstanding news organizations based in the heartland of America have reported on the cruel and dishonoring treatment of military veterans by government agencies; but revelations that are published outside Washington seem to produce few changes inside Washington. In 2005, two reporters from the Knight Ridder Washington Bureau, Chris Adams and Alison Young, produced a major investigative report of VA shortcomings. The series, entitled "Discharged and Dishonored," won a number of professional honors but sparked few political results. A number of other news organizations also produced excellent reports detailing the government's unfair treatment of veterans. But they achieved few results. However, when *The Washington Post* published a powerfully reported series by correspondents Anne Hull and Dana Priest that focused on a small part of the problem—the deplorable conditions at the Walter Reed Army Medical Center in Washington—something finally happened. Because the *Post* series was on the breakfast table of every bigwig in the nation's capital, politicians rushed to do what they do best. The capital echoed with their cries of shock and outrage. Republicans and Democrats dashed to the television studios and cranked out press releases demanding an end to the squalid conditions our military heroes were forced to endure. President George W. Bush vowed decisive action. (In contrast to his mounting woes in Iraq, the Walter Reed crisis was small, manageable, solvable—and positive results could be seen at a glance on the television news.) Naturally, heads rolled, including that of the secretary of the army. A presidential commission was smartly convened, hearings were held, and recommendations were presented—a series of targeted reforms that were designed to be doable.

But bigger, more egregious problems remain unaddressed. These problems are systemic, endemic, and cultural; they are rooted in all levels of the federal government and reach down into our core values. As a society, we have passively tolerated unacceptable decisions that were the results of a flawed mind-set that has developed and festered in both the top echelons and the catacombs of a government that has lost its way. The Department of Veterans Affairs starts from a basic assumption that our nation's veterans must be required to fight new battles even after they have been honorably discharged and sent back home. They have to battle their own government to win basic rights to benefits and care that they earned serving their country. Moreover, it is an unfair fight. Veterans must fight these battles individually against an opponent with superior numbers and far greater firepower. They are forced to battle legions of government attorneys, medical and scientific experts, and bureaucrats who know how to tiptoe around the rules and slip through the labyrinth of loopholes in the law.

To be sure, many veterans who are in need are very well treated by their government. They get excellent hospital treatment and fairly prompt resolution of their claims for benefits. These are the ones who have come back from war with obvious severe injuries; our hearts go out to them as soon as we see them. They are missing limbs; they have traumatic physical injuries that now confine them to wheelchairs or beds. Increasingly, in the Iraq War, many suffer from devastating traumatic brain injuries caused by roadside bombs. We see these badly injured veterans and we know they were in the best of health when they went off to war and we want to thank them for their sacrifice. But we don't want to intrude upon their privacy, so we often we keep our thoughts to ourselves and say nothing at all to them. These are the military veterans our government is quickest to thank for their sacrifice, and treat their wounds, and respond to their needs and benefits claims. The VA has been very good at doing that most of the time—but not always.

But there are other categories of war casualties whose problems are not always seen at first glance. Thousands suffer from posttraumatic stress disorder, a term that is recent to describe a disorder that is as old as war itself and can be devastatingly crippling in its own way; in World War II, and far more recently as well, it was given generic labels such as battle fatigue or shell shock or just nerves. It is a very real casualty caused by the horrors of war, and it leaves its victims often unable to resume the lives they led.

But there are vast numbers of veterans who have been suffering, yet have been disserved and dishonored by the government organization that was created specifically to care for their needs. They file claims for service-related disability benefits only to find that their cases are delayed, their records are lost, and eventually their benefits claims are denied. This has happened over the decades to veterans who fell ill after exposure to hazardous substances such as the Agent Orange defoliant that was used in Vietnam, or the Iraqi chemical weapons that were inadvertently detonated into the battle zone atmosphere in the Persian Gulf War. Those were instances in which government experts were unable to prove or disprove contentions that there appeared to be a connection between the military's exposure to those substances and their subsequent illnesses. The government's reflexive response was not to doubt that the troops were suffering ill effects—but to rule that since there was no scientific proof that the exposure caused those specific problems, claims for service-related disability benefits were denied. Claims were routinely denied not because they were disproved but because there was no proof, just doubt. Never mind that there was no doubt that something was wrong with those veterans who had no such problems when they joined the military. The official government position came down to this: it was up to the individual veterans to prove what the government experts said they could not—to provide conclusive scientific and medical evidence that these substances caused service-related disabilities. No such proof? Claim denied.

VA officials have long operated as if their motivational mission was to deny the veterans the most costly government benefits—unless absolutely forced to provide them due to indisputable evidence amassed by individual veterans.

The Department of Veterans Affairs proudly posts, on its official Web site, www.va.gov, a recently redrafted "Mission Statement" that resonates with warmth and reassurance for veterans who are about to have their first dealings with the VA:

Our goal is to provide excellence in patient care, veterans'
benefits and customer satisfaction. We have reformed our

department internally and are striving for high quality,
prompt and seamless service to veterans. Our department's
employees continue to offer their dedication and commit-
ment to help veterans get the services they have earned.
Our nation's veterans deserve no less.

But thousands upon thousands of veterans came away as dis-
satisfied customers, having discovered that the VA gave them
less than they deserved. The pages of this book are a com-
pendium of American military veterans who experienced unconscionable delays, mind-numbing incompetence, and coldhearted
rejections of claims for care and benefits that had been earned
long ago and were clearly deserved. These veterans, who will-
ingly and unquestioningly went to war, came away convinced
that the de facto motto of the VA was, and still is: First, create
doubt. Second, when in doubt, deny.

There is no doubt about who is to blame: everyone. Presidents, secretaries of defense and veterans affairs and their underlings, and members of Congress who serve on the veterans
affairs committees have all contented themselves with uttering
the right rhetoric but failed to follow through and actually fix
what they knew was wrong. But the blame does not rest with
government officials at all levels. The rest of us must bear a
share of the blame as well, for we have failed to demand that our
representative government do what is fair and decent for those
who volunteered to serve in the military. Part of the cost borne
by a nation that goes to war is for its citizens to be willing to pay
the price for providing benefits and care for those who volunteered and went into battle, only to discover later in life that they
needed our help.

We know the fate that awaits the hardware of war: When bat-
tleships and other weapons become obsolete or are irreparably

damaged, they are mothballed, shunted to the side, abandoned and ignored. When men and women who fought our wars with that hardware become obsolete or damaged, we as a society dare not consign them to a similar fate. Sadly, this book shows that too often, that is what happens. Perhaps what you have in your hands can be seen as not only a book but a bugle—an instrument for sounding a call to arms. This time we can all volunteer—to join the battle and fight alongside those who once fought for us.

PART ONE

The Unending Battles of
War and Peace

1

The Wartime Battles of Bill Florey

E4 SPC, U.S. Army, 82nd Airborne, Persian Gulf War

It was four in the afternoon of March 10, 1991, when the first explosion of the day reverberated through the weapons depot at Khamisiyah, Iraq, propelling a column of gray-white smoke into an already hazy sky. There would be many more explosions that day, as the U.S. Army was deliberately destroying by detonation what was once a major part of Saddam Hussein's arsenal before his Iraqi military had been defeated and he had accepted President George H. W. Bush's cease-fire. Each explosion launched a column of smoke skyward above Khamisiyah, and the columns rose side-by-side, like fingers of a gray glove against a hazy blue-gray sky. Soon the fingers merged into what would become infamously known, years later, as the Plume.

Bill Florey had parked his Army truck after a long morning's work, hauling here and there. Florey, an army E4 Specialist, was given the rest of the day off because the top brass had figured out, after seeing what had happened four days earlier, during the March 6 midday explosions, that there would be debris—metal, masonry, munitions—raining all over the Khamisiyah compound.

Florey figured he'd wait it out near his tent; then after a while when the dust and debris got so bad, he moved inside his tent; and then, when the dust and bad air seeped into and filled the tent, he pulled a tarpaulin over his head, hunkered down, and waited for the Plume to move on. Unglamorous, as wartime poses go; but war in any place is just about surviving day by day, and it was that way even now that Saddam Hussein, who had tested the world by invading neighboring Kuwait, had been quickly defeated and accepted the terms of a cease-fire.

When the rain of metal, masonry, and munitions bits seemed to have tapered off, Florey emerged from under the tarp, stepped out of the tent and into a much hazier haze. After a while, he glanced up and saw that the Plume was taken elsewhere by a moderate wind that was blowing from north-northwest to south-southeast—but he didn't think much about it that day. He just walked to his truck and got to work.

It would be one year after the Khamisiyah explosions before United Nations officials first reported that the U.S. Army had detonated some of Saddam Hussein's chemical weapons—including the deadly nerve gas sarin—that were stored at Khamisiyah. The U.S. Army's official position at the time was that it had no such information.

It would be five years after the Khamisiyah explosions before the Pentagon would officially acknowledge that the army had in fact detonated Iraqi chemical weapons, including sarin, at Khamisiyah and that some troops may have been exposed.

It would be six years after the Khamisiyah explosions before Department of Defense (DOD) officials, under fire from Congress, would get around to sending out the first letters officially informing twenty thousand soldiers that they may have been exposed to hazardous materials, including sarin nerve gas, at that arsenal in March 1991. By then the plume had been cited in congressional hearings and scientific studies as the possible cause of unexplained illnesses and ailments suffered by Gulf War veterans: chronic fatigue, aching joints, headaches, insomnia, diarrhea. Their cases were eventually given a catchall label: Gulf War syndrome.

It would be eleven years before the Defense Department would issue its final report on the 1991 unpleasantness at Khamisiyah: "Case Narrative: US Demolition Operations at Khamisiyah. Final Report. April 16, 2002." The report reads like a mix of officialese and satire. The Pentagon stated that at the time of the demolition, the army didn't know Iraqi chemical weapons, including sarin, were stored at Khamisiyah. The CIA issued a statement acknowledging that it *did* have information that sarin and other chemical agents were stored at Khamisiyah—but that it had failed to tell the army what it knew. The CIA later amended its position when it discovered that it had indeed sent a memo to the army stating that chemical agents were apparently stored at Khamisiyah; and the army amended *its* position, stating that its people had apparently filed the CIA memo but never followed up on it or passed it along through proper channels. Now this: New evidence, discovered in researching this book, raises new questions about just what the army engineers on the ground in Khamisiyah did know on the day they conducted the demolition.

In 2002, the Pentagon recalculated the size and path of the Plume and sent more letters, this time informing 101,763 soldiers that they might have been exposed to hazardous environmental agents at Khamisiyah. The Pentagon still took the passive position that soldiers who felt okay didn't need to take any action; but if they felt ill they should consult a doctor. The Pentagon decided against the more costly recommendation: a physical exam for all exposed soldiers to check for possible problems, or at least a medical baseline to help detect changes. Also that year, a Pentagon–Veterans Affairs epidemiological study found that Gulf War veterans were twice as likely as veterans based elsewhere to develop amyotrophic lateral sclerosis (ALS), also known as Lou Gehrig's disease—the most devastating disease linked to Gulf War service to date.

Bill Florey really did not pay much attention to the government twists and twirls of that tumultuous decade. His time in Iraq seemed like distant history and he was getting on with his life. But in 2003, Florey learned that the plume and the Khamisiyah explosions that created it may have been the defining event of his life— a life that, by then, was devolving into a series of sad, even hideous medical crises. He was diagnosed with a rare cancer, a crisis compounded by bureaucratic bungling, late diagnoses and misdiagnoses that left him horribly disfigured on the right side of his face even as the cancer aggressively burrowed deep into his brain and throughout his body. And near the end, when he reached out for a bit of financial help, this quiet, young man was also rejected by the U.S. government he had so unhesitatingly served in battle years before. The VA coldly and bureaucratically denied his request for modest service-related disability compensation. It didn't even bother to check its own data, which would have proved the merits of his request.

There is no way of knowing, let alone proving, whether Florey's sad outcome might have been averted by quicker and better treatment. But it is indisputable that he honored and served his government—and in the end his government dishonored and disserved him.

Bill Florey's story needs to be told not because he was special or exceptional, but because he was every soldier. He was as average as an individual soldier can be—and in that sense, he was also the best of what we want our soldiers to be. He was a teenager from a small town in Oregon who volunteered to join the U.S. Army in 1987 because he thought his country needed him. If going to war meant driving a truck—not firing a rocket or a gun—well, he'd do whatever job needed doing. He was not a complainer, never one to ruffle eagle feathers or be a crusader. He would never push his story before our eyes, which is why it is important that we see through his eyes how our government systematically dishonors and disserves so many who fight our battles so the rest of us won't have to go to war.

Florey's story shows us that the blame for all of this falls not just upon a government that has become unbearably bureaucratic and legalistic to the point of being antagonistic to the men and women it sends off to war. Blame also falls upon our society—all of us—for our silent acceptance of the way we dishonor veterans who went to war so that we, our children and our grandchildren could stay home.

Khamisiyah is a worthy starting point for taking the measure of Bill Florey's life, and of our own responsibility for what happened to him.

KHAMISIYAH, IRAQ: MARCH 1991

In the days leading up to the order to demolish the arms arsenal at Khamisiyah, soldiers from the 37th Engineer Battalion and the 307th Engineer Battalion conducted random inspections of the bunkers. They were searching for possible chemical weapons that might be stored there. According to the detailed 2002 Pentagon report, the soldiers were told to look for boxes with various colored markings and lettering in Cyrillic or Arabic that would indicate chemical weapons. Soldiers opened a sampling of boxes and, finding no chemical weapons, concluded that all boxes similarly labeled contained no chemical weapons.

"We were to look for yellow bands on the ammunition for chemical," the report quoted one of the soldiers as saying. "I went in bunkers specifically looking for that and didn't find any." It was on that basis that senior officers concluded there were no chemical weapons at Khamisiyah and ordered the destruction of the arsenal. The first series of explosions occurred at a closed bunker on March 4. The second occurred on March 10, this time in an open area known as the Pit. It was that explosion that produced the Plume that officials would conclude eleven years later had been a chemical cocktail cloud—one that may have exposed more than one hundred thousand soldiers to chemical weapons including sarin.

At 2:05 p.m. on March 4, 1991, the first explosion of the closed munitions bunker shook Khamisiyah. "Within minutes of the first detonation debris and 'flyouts' [munitions that were thrown out from the explosion without detonating] began to fall among the soldiers at the observation points and elsewhere, posing a significant hazard," the Defense Department report said. "The explosions created huge columns of dust and smoke, which the prevailing winds carried away from the soldiers at the observation points. The debris was thrown several kilometers in all directions. . . . Munitions continued to explode throughout the evening."

It is clear from the DOD report that in their zeal to complete their mission army experts failed to heed a number of flashing caution lights and even ran some red lights. Forty minutes after the first arsenal was detonated, the report noted, a chemical detection alarm sounded. "At 2:45 PM, an M8A1 chemical detection alarm sounded in Company B, 37th Engineer Battalion's area of the observation point," the report said. "On hearing the alarm, the soldiers in Company B immediately put on their chemical protective clothing, as did some soldiers from other units around the observation point. Others only put on their masks."

The report continued: "By this stage of the Gulf War, the soldiers' experiences . . . taught them that many things common to their environment, such as blowing dust and vehicle exhaust, frequently caused the alarms to sound. Therefore, they generally did not regard the sounding of the chemical alarm as proof of the presence of chemical agents."

Four engineer companies performed tests using their chemical agent detection kits. "All chemical detection tests yielded negative results for chemical warfare agents [i.e., no chemical warfare agents detected], except for the following two instances." In both of those cases, initial tests were slightly positive for chemical warfare agents, but retests then produced negative results.

The warning signs came in various forms but were all ignored: "The intelligence staff NCO [noncommissioned officer] of the 37th Engineer Battalion and his assistant reported that shortly after the explosion they saw 'a dog running across [an] open area [that started] circling and dropped dead.'" By the time Pentagon officials reinterviewed those same battalion members, the two individuals had found a way to explain what they witnessed in a semipositive light: "In follow-on interviews, the two individuals said that the dog did not display any symptoms consistent with nerve agent exposure." In that spirit, the Pentagon report optimistically noted that other dogs didn't die: "The 37th Engineer Battalion videotape of the March 4, 1991, demolition shows several dogs running across the terrain without any obvious health effects from the ongoing explosions."

The Pentagon report provided the conclusion that more than one hundred thousand veterans had waited more than a decade to receive: "We have assessed that chemical warfare agents were

present at Khamisiyah and US soldiers definitely destroyed
many, but not all, of the chemical agent weapons in the Pit and
Bunker 73. It is likely that the demolition of rockets in the Pit
exposed some US units to very low levels of chemical warfare
agents." That exposure occurred mainly from the March 10 explosions, the report concluded. The assessment also noted that the
engineering battalion experts did not have state-of-the-art chemical detection equipment: "US forces did not have chemical warfare agent detection equipment that could distinguish intact
chemical warfare agent-filled munitions. Properly employed,
chemical warfare agent detection equipment possibly can prevent the accidental destruction of munitions containing chemical warfare agents."

The report's second major finding was less than satisfying to
those veterans who had been classified with Gulf War syndrome
and had long awaited this Pentagon task force study: "No evidence exists that any soldiers at Khamisiyah exhibited symptoms consistent with exposure to a chemical warfare agent."

For years, the U.S. government's official pronouncements con-
cerning the army detonations at Khamisiyah were marked by
profound confusion and contradiction. Official assurances and
official denials were issued, only to be rescinded.

The army claimed that it had no intelligence that Iraqi chemical weapons were stored at Khamisiyah at the time of the 1991
explosions—and in fact, had no such information until 1996. In
the early years after the explosions, the CIA took the official
blame, admitting that well before the detonations, it did have intelligence information that Saddam's chemical weapons were
stored at Khamisiyah, but had failed to tell the army.

But in 1997, that explanation was modified, muddled and
muddied. A Pentagon internal investigation discovered that the
CIA *had* sent the army two memos in November 1991—eight

months after the detonations—stating that chemical weapons apparently had been stored in Khamisiyah. One of the memos specifically warned of "the risk of chemical contamination" of the soldiers based there. However, the Pentagon didn't officially follow up on this CIA alert. Indeed, the Pentagon continued for years to state that it had no information that soldiers could have been exposed to chemical agents at Khamisiyah.

But through all of those conflicting statements and denials, the army's central assertion that it had no knowledge of chemical weapons being stored at Khamisiyah stood basically unchallenged. Until now.

Now new information has surfaced about what the U.S. Army officials knew, and when they knew it. It comes from an interview I conducted with a military policeman who was patrolling the compound and was stunned to discover that his beat had taken him into the heart of the demolition zone just as the first explosions shattered the stillness of Khamisiyah.

A NEW DISCLOSURE

U.S. Army Military Police team leader Eric Adams, then a rank E4, had been in his Humvee on a routine patrol with several other MPs along the Khamisiyah perimeter on the afternoon of March 4, 1991. "Just chasing Shiites," he told me in an interview years later. "They'd be driving in these white Toyota pickups, looking for ammo. They were helping our guys take on Saddam's troops and apparently some of our guys had apparently told them they could help themselves to whatever they found lying around. But our job was to drive them away. Keep the perimeter clear." Adams kept in radio contact with the other Humvee on patrol with them and also with their base: his radio was a bulky

VRC 46 radio left over from Vietnam. There was no unusual radio chatter that day, certainly no indication of what was about to happen.

Adams and his team had returned from the perimeter and were on a dirt road, well inside the first checkpoint, about three kilometers from the paved road. At 2:05 p.m., the silence was blown away by the first explosion, which seemed to be very close. Too close.

"They gave us no warning that we'd be having this explosion," Adams recalled. "Chucks of metal were flying around. We could hear them hitting the metal roof of our Humvee, denting it. Took the paint off right down to the black. It was amazing." The MPs figured they were alone and possibly in a dangerous place when Adams looked up the dirt road and saw several other Humvees stopped on the hardtop. He sped toward them, then slowed, stopped and got out. A number of soldiers had gotten out of the parked Humvees—they had their guns drawn and pointed at the MPs. "They were locked and loaded and ready to shoot us," Adams said. "I was a little scared. It was very tense." These were members of one of the engineer battalions that were detonating the weapons depots.

"What are you doing here?" asked the lead engineer, a lieutenant, the top-ranked soldier at the scene. "Where are you guys from?" Adams figured he and his patrol mates first had to prove they were MPs and, second, prove they were doing their assigned jobs, not goofing off. "We gave them the . . . password of the day," said Adams.

Things had calmed a bit. The engineers couldn't believe the MPs hadn't gotten word that the detonations were scheduled and this zone was off limits. The MPs couldn't believe it either. But what happened next is important to remember because it calls into question all of the official government assertions and denials that would wash through Washington in the years that followed. Adams, a savvy MP, had always figured that some of those ammo depot buildings he and his pals had patrolled contained chemical weapons. He said, when interviewed for this book, that it was hardly a blind assumption: he figured it out from the way that some of the buildings were painted and the insignias stenciled on the walls. "Some of the buildings were painted a bright blue and had little symbols that looked like a gas mask and some lettering," Adams said. "We figured those were the ones that had Saddam's chemical weapons inside."

That led Adams to ask the lieutenant what he figured was only a logical question: Aren't there Iraqi chemical weapons in some of those buildings? And doesn't that mean that they all could be in danger of being contaminated by these same weapons, which Saddam had previously used against some of his own people and may have been prepared to use against U.S. troops?

Based upon all the official statements that the DOD, the army, and the CIA issued in the decade that followed, one would naturally expect the lieutenant to have replied that his engineers were confident that there were no Iraqi chemical weapons in the buildings. But no, the lieutenant said nothing of the sort.

"Oh, don't worry about that," the engineer responded, according to Adams. The army lieutenant explained that he understood there were chemical weapons stored there, but that the Iraqi chemical weapons were binary devices and that the precursors and agents weren't mixed together—"So it won't be a problem." That statement by the engineer battalion lieutenant, made at Khamisiyah in 1991, seems to be a version that is significantly different from all those official assertions, assurances, and denials from the Pentagon.

This latest disclosure raises new questions about the government's official decisions, made on the scene in Khamisiyah, to begin the detonation of the Iraqi arsenal. It also calls into question the accuracy of the official pronouncements by various layers of military and civilian senior officials ever since—all of which may well have affected the lives of 101,763 members of the U.S. military who were belatedly notified by the Pentagon, six years after the fact, that they may indeed have been exposed to chemical weapons in March 1991 at Khamisiyah, Iraq.

2

The Peacetime Battles of Bill Florey

E4 SPC, U.S. Army, 82nd Airborne, Persian Gulf War

It was in 1995—two years before the Pentagon would first inform Bill Florey that he may have been exposed to chemicals in Khamisiyah—that he had the first indication of a health problem. Florey had been honorably discharged from the army and moved back home to Oregon. A skilled computer technician, Florey had initially decided to go to work in a way that he could still serve his country and his military colleagues: he went to work part-time for the Department of Veterans Affairs in Eugene while he was also studying at the University of Oregon. But money was tight, so he took a full-time job in the Veterans Affairs office in Denver. In 1995, he went to a private physician in Denver for a physical exam. The doctor told him he had some sort of problem that caused swelling on the right side of his neck; swollen glands and perhaps lymph nodes were involved. The doctor told Florey he ought to get them removed some time, but that it wasn't urgent and he need not worry about it. The VA was just then working on its next budget. It was crunch time at his office and the deadline was near; Florey's VA supervisor told him he needed Florey on the job. The ex-soldier concluded that his work was too crucial to take a medical leave, so he did not have the procedure done. Then the situation seemed to stabilize and Florey stopped thinking about it. He left the VA in 1996, moved to Dallas, and eventually went to work for Stream International, a computer help-desk contractor for various companies, including Dell Computers.

In early 2003, Florey noticed a suspicious growth on the right side of his neck. He figured it was probably a reoccurrence of that infection the doctor in Denver had told him about. He thought the lump was growing larger, but then again, maybe he was just imagining it. He asked a good friend and coworker at Stream International, Francesca Yabraian, to take a look at it. Yabraian, a young woman who would become Florey's most staunch advocate, told him it was indeed the size of a silver dollar and that he absolutely had to go to a doctor. Florey called the VA hospital in Dallas for an appointment. He was told a doctor would be able to see him, but not for several weeks, Yabraian recalled.

Florey got the results of his biopsy in early July 2003. "I have cancer," he told Yabraian. The diagnosis was cancer of the parotid gland, the largest of the salivary glands. The National Cancer Institute Web site notes that this is a rare form of cancer; 80 percent of the tumors of the parotid gland turn out to be benign. It was also supposed to be a very slow growing cancer; but Florey's cancer would turn out to be unusually aggressive. The good news was that the doctors thought an operation would get it all. He wasn't going to tell his parents or grandparents in Oregon; he didn't want to worry them. The doctors scheduled an operation for later in July. But then the VA called to say the operation had to be pushed back to late August.

While awaiting his cancer surgery, Florey reached out for the first time to the government he had served in wartime. He made copies of the letters he had received from the Defense Department warning him that he may have been exposed to hazardous chemical agents at Khamisiyah, clipped them to copies of his medical report warning that he had developed cancer of the parotid artery, and attached the packet to a form in which he requested that the Department of Veterans Affairs begin providing him with service-related disability compensation for his illness and the loss of income it caused. He estimated the claim would provide him with $2,000 a month, which wasn't a lot but would certainly help. He sent in his claim in the second week of August 2003 and awaited a reply.

On August 28, Florey underwent twelve and a half hours of surgery at the VA hospital in Dallas. Doctors said later they were surprised at how far the cancer had spread. They cut out the right side of his jawbone, removed his salivary gland, removed a nerve on the right side of his face, took a nerve from his right arm and inserted it into the right side of his face. The nerve damage from the cancer and the operation meant that Florey lost the ability to close his right eyelid but retained the nerve and muscle function that allowed him to keep the lid open. Doctors put a tiny four-gram gold weight in his eyelid so that, with the assist of gravity, he could close his eye and thus sleep; he could open it and even blink.

There was more: doctors grafted skin from Florey's stomach and leg to cover the hole in his neck that was left from the surgery. But the grafted flap fell off after just one week. Doctors told Florey they could not repair it, that another patch would simply fall off again. The former soldier would live the rest of his life with an exposed hole in his neck, covered only by a thick gauze pad. Unclosed, unhealed, the wound in his neck would have to be cared for and cleansed every day for the rest of his life.

Florey had been home from the hospital for four days when Yabraian stopped by to see how he was doing. She saw that he was doing about as well as could be expected—and then she saw that Florey had another lump, this time on the right side of his head, up near his temple. It hadn't been there before the surgery, she and Florey later agreed; but it was there and visible now. "I didn't think much of it because it was so tiny—maybe the size of a dime," she later recalled.

The doctors who were handling Florey's cancer case were ear, nose and throat specialists at the VA. According to Florey's medical file, on September 29, 2003, a month after his surgery, Florey saw a VA dentist, Preeti Naik. Florey had major dental problems as a result of his surgery, in which part of his jaw had been removed, yet his doctors had not insisted that he see a dentist immediately. Naik wrote: "Pt. [patient] was never referred to dental by ENT [Ear, Nose and Throat] and pt. now has severe malalignment of teeth." The dentist told the thirty-four-year-old Florey he might have to have a number of his teeth extracted. Florey said he wanted to keep his teeth and would live with the consequences.

Florey's next appointment with his primary VA doctor (an ENT specialist) was for October 17. Yabraian went with him to make sure that the doctor examined that new bump on the side of his skull—even if Florey didn't mention it.

Francesca Yabraian is a most determined young woman, someone you very much want as a friend, especially when you very much need a friend. She has long, dark hair that is thick and curly; she has dark eyes that can glisten like stars when she is happy and glare like lasers when she is girding for battle. Her stature is a bit shorter than average, her smile far wider and brighter than average. Her speaking voice is a bit louder than average, and also firm. Except when she is in a battle; then it is very loud and very firm. When Yabraian drove Florey to the VA hospital on the day of the appointment, she was determined to make sure that nothing was overlooked; he was thinking he did not want to make any problems for the hardworking folks at the VA.

At the doctor's office, Florey was his characteristically quiet self, letting the doctor do his work. Yabraian was her characteristically direct and determined self. And so, after watching the doctor do his examination, she pointed to the bump that was clearly visible near Florey's right temple and asked: "Doctor, what is this lump on the side of his head?"

"Oh, it's just an infection," said the doctor, according to her recollection of the episode. To which Yabraian responded with the determination of an old-school reporter asking an old-style press conference follow-up question: "Well, shouldn't you test it?"

"No, no need for that," she recalled the doctor replying. "We'll just inject it with penicillin." And that's what they did at the VA hospital in Dallas, that day and on subsequent visits. Meanwhile, the lump clearly seemed to be growing larger—"at an unbelievable rate," said Yabraian when I asked her about it three years later.

On the next visit, they were greeted by a new doctor: the doctor who'd been treating Florey had been reassigned. Yabraian told the new doctor she thought her friend ought to have a CT scan or an MRI, whatever it was that would best show what was really going on. The doctor said he'd do a biopsy and make an MRI appointment, but that there was quite a backlog and it would be one month before the MRI could take place. "He needs it sooner," she told the doctor, to which she recalled him replying: "That's all we can do."

On November 19, 2003, as Yabraian drove Florey to the VA

for his MRI appointment, she said, "You know, if they tell us again that they won't give you that scan, well, I'll have to say something." Florey wanted no ruckus: "Try to be professional." When they arrived at the hospital, Yabraian told Florey's doctor they were there for his MRI appointment. "I didn't make a MRI appointment for him," the doctor said. He explained that he didn't remember saying a MRI would be scheduled; he would order one now, but they still didn't have enough machines and it would be at least a couple of weeks until—

Yabraian cut him off. Her voice was loud and strong and mainly very angry. "I am not leaving this room until you get on the phone and order an MRI—for today!" There were no doors on these consulting rooms, just privacy curtains, and Yabraian admits that her voice surely echoed up and down the halls and probably brought work to a stop in all directions. She continued: "And if you don't do it right now, you will have to drag me out of this hospital!"

At this, the VA doctor picked up his telephone and ordered the scan. It would be done that day, he promised. She and Florey went to the MRI waiting room. It was midmorning and they waited there until 6 p.m., but Florey got his scan. But Thanksgiving came and went with no results, and the lump grew larger. Finally, on December 3, the telephone call came and Florey was told to come in that day for a consultation. Yabraian and Florey drove in silence; the ride seemed to take forever. At the VA hospital, his doctor gave him the results of the MRI and the biopsy: cancer. The tumor had penetrated his skull and was lodged deep in his brain.

"They said it was a very aggressive cancer," Yabraian recalled. "They said they couldn't operate. It was too late." Florey's face fell, but he betrayed no other emotion. Yabraian was determined not to cry, "because then Bill would just come over to console me. So I never cried in front of him. Never."

Florey was told he had two options: radiation therapy to try to kill the tumor, or chemotherapy, which meant he'd have to stay in the hospital throughout the treatment.

Yabraian drove Florey to his home, or more precisely to the house in which he was renting a room. They drove in silence until they got there. Then Yabraian told Florey he had to telephone his parents, Dick and Coni Florey, and his grandparents, Bill and Laura Harrison, who were next-door neighbors in Medford, Oregon. He had to tell them what was going on, the sad news. Florey's grandparents flew to Dallas the next morning and stayed there with him throughout his radiation treatment. The tumor protruding from the right side of his head grew outward and started to fall off. It left a hole in his head, a hole that had to be cleaned every day.

In February 2004 Florey moved to Medford, Oregon, to live with his grandparents, who had the space to accommodate his needs and the time to care for him, day and night if necessary (which it often was). His parents, next door, had little time during the daylight hours, as they both worked from sunup to sundown in the fields of their modest farm.

The Veterans Administration had a rehabilitation facility in White City, Oregon, which was just minutes away from Medford, but they didn't have the capability to treat Florey's case. Radiation hadn't been very successful, so the doctors said he had to have chemotherapy. Florey hated the thought of having to be a virtually permanent patient in the hospital; his grandmother, Laura, agreed. She said Florey would live at their home and she would care for him and clean his wounds day and night. Florey's grandfather agreed to drive him 272 miles to the VA hospital in Portland.

It was a tough ten-hour drive round-trip for a patient in such constant pain and dire condition.

But for a while it seemed that getting there was not going to be Florey's greatest problem. Getting an appointment was. When Florey called the Portland VA hospital, he was told that they couldn't schedule him for chemotherapy for six months. His grandmother telephoned a friend who worked for the VA rehab facility in White City, and the friend called the Portland VA, and this time an appointment was scheduled right away. His treatments started immediately.

At the Portland VA hospital, the doctors were frank: Florey's cancer was more than unusual—it was rare. "Unfortunately, due to the rarity of his tumor and its aggressive nature, there is no accepted standard chemotherapy," Dr. Ella Rutledge Vining wrote in Florey's VA medical records on March 5, 2004. That month, doctors told Florey that the cancer had spread to his lung.

"Billy was always so patient," said Laura Harrison. "He never complained." At the Portland VA hospital, doctors, nurses, and staff were impressed at the way Florey was not just uncomplaining but cooperative and, in fact, downright appreciative of anything that his caregivers did for him. On March 12, 2004, Dr. Bobak Ghaheri was moved to write a patient history summary that went beyond the minimum professional notation:

SUMMARY
HISTORY OF PRESENT ILLNESS

*Mr. Florey is a very unfortunate 34-year-old gentleman . . .
urgently referred to us from White City, after he presented
there with a rapidly enlarging tumor on his right side. He
had a previous resection of a carcinoma explemorphic ade-
noma in Dallas, Texas, in addition to radiation therapy,
and despite this treatment, the tumor has rapidly grown. . . .*

After noting that the extent of this tumor was quite
large . . . it was decided that this patient has little chance
of long-term survival.

Francesca Yabraian kept in touch with Florey by phone in the
first months of 2004, but in the spring, as his prognosis worsened, she told her boyfriend in Texas that she felt she needed to
go to Oregon to help care for her friend. She was there on May
26, and they celebrated Florey's thirty-fifth birthday. The next
day, a VA chaplain, Catherine Elia, came by the house to see
how Florey was doing. "Pt. [patient] was having wound care
when I attempted to visit today," the chaplain wrote in a report
that is part of Florey's official VA medical record. "Pt.'s grandmother was in room with pt. According to his [grand]father and
friend (caregiver) from Dallas, Texas, pt. had a very busy day
yesterday celebrating his birthday. They said he hadn't been as
active as he was yesterday in a long time."

But those fleeting good times were tempered by medical reality,
as can be seen in another report on the same page in Florey's medical file. It was as grim as the birthday notation right above it was
uplifting. A VA outpatient service rep who had come by to check
the open wound had written: "Wound is still very odorous and
filled with yellow slough. . . . Upper area of wound is painful."
Another report, from a chemotherapy treatment in Portland a
month before, focused on one of the most gruesome aspects of his
physical condition: "While patient received chemotherapy, it was
noted that his right ear was filled with maggots."

Not only did Florey never complain, but his grandmother
found a way to maintain a cheerful disposition as she went about
this most difficult daily task of cleaning his gruesome cancer
wound. "I'd always wanted to be a doctor," she later explained.
"If he wasn't complaining, I sure wouldn't." Indeed, Florey tried

to keep as busy as he could in his weakened condition. "He was unbelievable," said his grandmother. "He designed a waterfall in our yard. And he got all of these computer parts and built us a computer. It just thrilled him to get these packages delivered with all of these computer parts. So he built more computers." Florey liked to be on the back porch when he built the computers. He loved the fresh air. But, as always, every upside seemed to have a downside too. "I'll never forget the day we found those maggots in his ear. I had these big thick gauze pads that covered over the hole—but I went out there and saw that flies had wiggled through the gauze to lay their eggs in that wound. I couldn't get him upset about it. So I just got my tweezers and picked them out, one by one. But I'll tell you, Billy hated the thought of that. Hated it."

There soon came a time when he couldn't stand up to build computers anymore. But when he'd go to the clinic in White City or for chemotherapy at the hospital in Portland, Florey worked on the hospital computers for the doctors and nurses. "One of the doctors told me that she had learned more from Billy than she had in all her years in medicine," said Laura Harrison.

One day, Yabraian asked Florey what he thought about his Gulf War service, given the way things had turned out. "He said he'd do it all over again and wouldn't make any different choices," she later told me. "He said he was proud that he had served his country." Still, she said, she could see in his expression that he was hurt—devastated, in fact—because the government had turned him away when he asked for just a bit of help in the form of service-related compensation.

Through all of his agony and travails, this Gulf War veteran never showed a trace of anger or uttered a word of complaint at the fate that had befallen him. He did wonder why he had never

heard back from the VA about that claim he had sent in for service-related disability compensation. He knew it had been received by the VA on August 13, 2003—two weeks before his first
cancer surgery and three months before he had been diagnosed
as suffering from inoperable brain cancer, a rare and extremely
aggressive form of it.

The VA got back to Florey in a form letter dated February 26,
2004: "Service connection for right parotid carcinoma is denied."
He picked up the telephone and called Francesca Yabraian. "I
have some bad news," he said. "They denied me my benefits."
His voice was flat, void of feeling. "I was heartbroken," said his
grandmother, recalling the moment.

Why did the VA deny Florey's claim? "We have received your
claim for service connection for right parotid carcinoma due to
exposure to chemicals and other environmental factors during
your service in the Gulf War," the VA said. "Service connection
for the diagnosed condition of right parotid carcinoma is not
supported since there is no evidence of treatment or diagnosis of
the condition during military service or shown within one year
of separation." The literature on cancer states that it can take a
decade or more after exposure for cancerous cells to appear, a
fact that the VA made no mention of.

The letter of denial made one other point. The VA had requested an opinion from one of its doctors who treated Florey.
That opinion only focused on Florey's parotid gland cancer. But
it was issued on the very day that the VA doctors gave Florey the
MRI test that revealed his rapidly growing and inoperable brain
tumor—a tumor that developed eleven years after he was exposed to sarin and other chemical agents at Khamisiyah.

The VA doctor who issued that opinion made no mention of
this new tumor. Instead, he narrowed his opinion to the parotid
cancer and then went on to give the VA just enough of a medical

and legal fig leaf to save the government a bit of money. "It should be noted that current medical literature does not support an association or a relationship between environmental hazards found during the Gulf War and mucoepidermoid carcinoma of the parotid gland," wrote the doctor at the VA's Dallas hospital; and he followed that up with this sentence in which the operative phrase was in all capital letters: "Therefore, it is my opinion that IT IS LESS LIKELY THAN NOT that his current mucoepidermoid carcinoma of the parotid gland is related to his military service, particularly to environmental hazards during Gulf War service."

Less likely than not. The words sound as if they were written not by an expert in medicine or science, but by a classically trained lawyer adept at crocheting loopholes. Understand what has happened here: the VA has placed upon the individual veteran the burden of proving a causal relationship between the chemical agent sarin and brain cancer. But this is a burden that should have been borne by the VA and the Department of Defense. For they and they alone possessed the data that could have been used to determine whether there was evidence that would support or refute Florey's benefits claim. In fact, as we will see later, they did indeed have information that, when run through a computer analysis, would have authoritatively buttressed Florey's case.

But as we wade into the legalisms, keep in mind that there is also a larger issue at play here, and it is the one that is fundamental to all that is wrong with the way the U.S. government has chosen to treat the men and women who fight its battles. The government operates on the basic assumption that veterans are not due any benefits unless they themselves can prove that they are entitled to such benefits—even if the decision hinges on scientific or medical research of a highly technical nature. Veterans *as individuals* are required to marshal the resources to do battle with legions of government lawyers, doctors, scientists, bean counters, and bureaucrats.

Florey, his body so destroyed by his illness but his mind still sharp, had two things going for him as he contemplated how to fight yet another battle, this time for minimally fair treatment from his government and the agency where he had once worked. A national services officer on the sixteenth floor of the VA offices in Portland, Daryl Testone, had taken an interest in Florey's case. Testone had no pull on the inside; his job was to help veterans who were lost in the labyrinth of the VA to find their way. He began to work on Florey's appeal—and having someone with knowledge on how the VA works had to help.

In addition, Florey had a powerful champion at his side, Francesca Yabraian. I first met this remarkable woman in an entirely different context. During the last weeks of 2002 I had been working on a book and documentary for PBS about weapons of mass destruction and terrorism—both titled *Avoiding Armageddon*—when I experienced every author's worst nightmare: just weeks before my deadline, my computer crashed. My telephone calls to Dell's help desk got me outsourced to techs in India who only seemed to know how to make a bad problem infinitely worse. Finally, in desperation, I telephoned Michael Dell's executive offices, and minutes later I was talking with a very capable and confident executive help-desk technician named Francesca Yabraian. She solved the problem in a few hours. Thus avoiding my Armageddon, I was able to get the book and TV documentary to the public as scheduled. Now, in the summer of 2004, I received a telephone call in Washington from a woman with a wonderful voice I could never forget—only this time she seemed quite shy. She began by saying that she was sure I wouldn't remember her, so before she could say her name

I interjected: "Francesca, how many people do you think I have had save my book that was trapped in a crashed computer?"

This time, she was the one with the crisis and I was the one who was going to be her Washington help-desk tech. Francesca told me the story of her friend, Bill Florey—right up to the VA's "less likely than not" denial. She wanted to know how she could come to Washington to fight for his rights, since he was too sick to fight his own battle. To a journalist, this was a story worth pursuing; even more so to a grateful journalist. Since one of Florey's home state senators, Kay Bailey Hutchison, a Republican from Texas, was a member of the Senate Veterans' Affairs Committee, I set up a meeting for us with the senator's veterans' affairs staff specialist, figuring he would know the best procedure for getting a fair shake for his senator's constituent. He thought Florey had a very legitimate case and gave Yabraian some sound advice: First, obtain copies of Florey's military entrance medical exam showing that he was in excellent health when he went into the army. Second, obtain Florey's army and VA medical records over the years. Third, contact Dr. Robert Ware Haley, a noted epidemiologist at the University of Texas Southwestern Medical Center in Dallas, who had done pioneering studies on the effect of sarin on Gulf War veterans and problems involving the brain.

Yabraian set out to gather Florey's complete army and VA medical records. This turned out to be a bigger problem than it ought to have been. What transpired is not a rare occurrence, but an infuriatingly common one, as thousands of military veterans can attest. Acting on Florey's behalf, Yabraian contacted the military's National Personnel Records Center (NPRC) in St. Louis and submitted his official request for a copy of his military records, including the vital record that would show he was in excellent health the day he entered the military. About sixty days later, Florey's family received a letter stating that the VA regional office in Oregon had his military records. So Yabraian contacted the VA regional office in Oregon and asked them to retrieve a copy of his medical records. The VA in Oregon faxed her a form for record retrieval; she filled it out for him and sent it to the VA. Florey's family got another letter, this time stating that his records had been sent back to NPRC in St. Louis. So Yabraian contacted NPRC in St. Louis once again—and they told her, no, the records were still in Oregon.

"I was ping-ponged back and forth between the VA in Oregon and NPRC in St. Louis," Yabraian said. "Not just once or twice but several times. Finally an NPRC person told me over the phone that his records had been lost. It was an infuriating experience."

Yabraian and Florey's grandmother, Laura Harrison, also set about obtaining Florey's VA hospital medical records. Harrison had tried once before to get copies of Florey's VA medical records; she had filled out the VA form as instructed and given it to the VA, but she never got any records. This time she contacted her friend who works in the VA clinic at White City. Her friend handled it from the inside and the copies of Florey's VA records were in her hands in short order.

DR. HALEY'S EPIDEMIOLOGIC KEY

The next move was both important and instructive: Following up on the suggestion of Senator Hutchison's staff assistant, I contacted Dr. Haley. He had done pioneering studies of the effects of sarin on Gulf War veterans and was working on yet another study. Haley went through the list of brain damage problems that have been attributed to sarin exposure, noting

that earlier in 2004, the VA and the Defense Department had acknowledged the connection between brain damage and sarin exposure in some Gulf War veterans. So, just because there has
been no scientific proof that sarin can cause cancer does not
mean that Florey's exposure to sarin could not have been instru-
mental in the cancer. Dr. Haley explained that while the VA calls
the various Gulf War syndrome ailments "undiagnosed illnesses,"
the government actually has key evidence in its files that, when
properly assembled, could show whether Gulf War veterans
who were exposed to sarin have actually suffered greater inci-
dences of brain cancer and other illnesses than military veterans
who were never in that combat zone.

At that very moment, Dr. Haley explained, the VA had the capability of merging its records and those of the Defense Department in order to undertake such an epidemiological analysis. The
VA and the Pentagon could take a sample of the hundred thousand veterans who were exposed at Khamisiyah to see if they
reported specific health problems in the last decade—and then
compare that result with a control group of veterans who were
based elsewhere. Then, said Dr. Haley, the government could at
least render its decision regarding disability claims on the basis of
fact—for cases of brain cancer, Lou Gehrig's disease, or any other
illness.

That should have been the bare minimum that the VA demands of its bean counters, bureaucrats, and barristers in making decisions that will honor or dishonor the men and women
who risked their lives for their country.

Here is where the VA's misconduct in this matter becomes
even more maddening: at the very moment that the VA was sending Florey his routine claims denial, the top-level VA officials and
many lower down knew that the very study that Dr. Haley said
was possible had indeed been done. It had been funded by the

Army and conducted by VA experts, and the results had already been collated and were being peer-reviewed.

On New Year's Day, 2005, William Michael Florey, a "very unfortunate" young man, soldier who loved and honored his country more than his country loved and honored him, lost the last battle of his life. Bill Florey had lived just long enough to know that his government had coldly turned away from him— treated him like some sort of freeloader—when he had swallowed his pride and had asked only for the disability benefits he had earned when he went to war.

Just six months and twenty-five days after Florey died, on July 25, 2005, the news broke: "Brain Cancer Linked to Nerve Agent," said the headline in *USA Today*. The story, by correspondent Liz Szabo, reported: "For the first time, a study has found an increase in brain cancer deaths among Gulf War veterans who might have been exposed to the nerve agent sarin by the destruction of Iraqi weapons in 1991. . . . According to the study, soldiers inside the 'hazard area' were about twice as likely as those outside it to die from brain cancer."

The study, done under the auspices of the Institute of Medicine and published in the *American Journal of Public Health,* focused only upon soldiers who had died of various causes in nine years following the explosions at Khamisiyah. It compared the results for 100,487 Gulf War army veterans who had been inside the hazardous weapons depot area when the sarin and other chemical weapons were detonated with 224,980 Gulf War army veterans who were not in the exposed area. The total numbers of deaths were small, the study noted, but the epidemiological conclusions were nevertheless valid.

Importantly, the study made no effort to compare veterans who may have been diagnosed with brain cancer or any other ailments, but were still alive at the end of nine years. That may well have produced even more alarming figures. As the Defense Department's deputy director for deployment health support, Dr. Michael Kilpatrick, noted when the study was made public, the length of time before exposure to a carcinogen and the development of a tumor "is generally 15 to 20 years for brain cancer."

Infuriatingly, Kilpatrick's point makes a mockery of the VA's initial letter of denial to Florey, which based its decision on these two points: Florey's brain cancer was not diagnosed before he was discharged from the army in 1991 (just months after the Khamisiyah incident); and it wasn't diagnosed within one year of his honorable discharge. Given Dr. Kilpatrick's own explanation that it can take fifteen to twenty years for brain cancer to develop, how could the VA possibly have denied Florey's claim?

As for the VA's ear, nose, and throat specialist in Dallas, whose "less likely than not" opinion became the basis for denying benefits to Florey, he simply did not know: the VA had never bothered to inform its doctors that a study was underway investigating the effects of sarin exposure. Those at the VA who knew of the study never sent out an alert telling adjudicators to hold off on deciding cancer-related claims linked to Khamisiyah until the study was done. Indeed, at that moment, all of the statistics had been gathered and analyzed and were being sent out for peer review. The statistical conclusion of that analysis was that it was *twice as likely as not* that the brain cancer that ultimately killed Florey was related to his exposure to the plume at Khamisiyah: The study concluded: "When we looked at specific diseases as well as major disease groupings, there was only 1 disease for which exposed veterans were at a statistically increased risk. Compared with unexposed veterans, exposed veterans had an almost twofold increased risk of brain cancer–related deaths."

Had the VA consulted its own data and granted Florey's request, he would have received an estimated $2,000 a month that would have been paid retroactive to when his claim was filed, August 13, 2003—roughly $33,000 in service-related compensation that would have been paid to him until the day he died. But Veterans Affairs rules say that a veteran's claim dies when the veteran dies, whether it is valid or not. If the veteran wasn't paid what he or she was entitled to receive before the death certificate was signed—well, that is officially tough luck for the veteran's survivors.

After Florey died, his grandmother, Laura, contacted the VA advocate, Daryl Testone, to tell him the news and thank him for all he'd done. She later told me, "Daryl was very upset—upset that the VA didn't do more for Bill and several of the other veterans. Daryl said to me, 'I just can't take this anymore. They're not doing right by the veterans. I'm leaving.' And he resigned from the VA and I was told he had moved to Arizona."

Slowly, painfully, and often tragically so, Washington eventually catches up with reality, and September 25, 2007, was one of Washington's catch-up days. The Senate Veterans' Affairs Committee convened to hear testimony from James Binns, chairman of the Research Advisory Committee on Gulf War Veterans' Illnesses, a special advisory composed of scientists and veterans and mandated by Congress to tell it information that it wasn't getting from the Pentagon or the VA. (Note that it is called the committee on Gulf War Veterans *Illnesses:* the committee has found a more substantial name for that catchall label, Gulf War syndrome, which was coined back when Washington's wiseheads were stuck in the sands of denial.) Binns testified about the persistent and increasing occurrences of Lou Gehrig's disease and brain cancer—the disease that Veterans Affairs officials had blithely claimed was *"less likely than not* to have been caused by Florey's exposure to sarin at Khamisiyah.

Binns testified in language that made sure that this time Washington would hear about reality from an official who would tell it like it is. The McClatchy newspapers' Washington correspondent Les Blumenthal filed a report that began with Binns's hearing testimony disclosure that sixteen years after the Gulf War, more than one in four of veterans who fought there are still "seriously ill with medical problems ranging from severe fatigue and joint pain to Lou Gehrig's disease, multiple sclerosis and brain cancer." The article reported Binn's assertion that the departments of Defense and Veterans Affairs remain in virtual denial about the causes of Gulf War Veterans Illness and that the government has been slow to provide treatment for the Gulf veterans who are still ill. "This is a tragic record of failure, and the time lost can never be regained," the McClatchy article quoted Binns as testifying. "This government manipulation of science and violation of law to devalue the health problems of ill veterans is something I would not have believed possible in this country until I took this job."

Binns testified that out of the 700,000 U.S. troops who were deployed in the Gulf War, some 170,000 to 200,000 are still ill. Officials from the Defense Department and Veterans Affairs sought to defend the slow-motion manner of dealing with the illnesses that were by then clearly associated with Gulf War service; they maintained they were funding research and were making sure that Gulf War veterans who needed care received it. Dr. Michael Kilpatrick, still DOD deputy director for force health protection and readiness programs, testified: "Veterans who report health problems are definitely ill. However, they do not have a single type of health problem. Consequently, these veterans have to be evaluated and treated as individuals."

That is the way things are said in Washington by officials who are always at pains to put things into their most comfortable context. But the key witness, research chairman Binns, chose his words artfully to make sure the senators had no false illusions about the situation. When a committee member noted that Pentagon and VA officials have long linked Gulf War Veterans Illness to battlefield stress and other related psychological disorders, Binns's response was succinct: "That's garbage." He said the government had cut important research programs for Gulf War illness.

In wartime, Florey performed the role of the ordinary soldier, unheroic perhaps by a Hollywood glamour-and-glory definition, but unflinchingly patriotic: he always did all that was asked of him. It was in peacetime, in his dying days, that Florey became an American hero, in his own way. He was courageous and considerate, optimistic yet realistic, patriotic and unquestioningly supportive of his government, even after he had received his government's devastating and unjust rejection of his dying request.

Bill Florey left behind a legacy of respect and a lesson for us all. As a nation and as a society, we must fix what has gone so wrong with a government of officials who fail to hold themselves responsible and accountable when they dishonor those who deserve our very best.

Engraved in gold letters on a plaque outside the entrance to the Department of Veterans Affairs in Washington is a quotation from President Abraham Lincoln's second inaugural address: "to care for him who shall have borne the battle and for his widow, and his orphan."

Too often, the Department of Veterans Affairs has demonstrated that its chances of fulfilling that noble goal are less likely than not.

PART TWO

The Shaping of
a National Mind-set

3

The Bonus Army

The Sad Summer When the Veterans Invaded Washington

They had fought in the Great War and come home in 1918, and in 1924 their appreciative government had promised that they would be paid bonuses of one dollar for every day they had served in the military plus 25 cents more for every day they had served overseas. They were issued genuine paper service certificates assuring them that the government would pay them the money they had earned and deserved. But not until 1945.

Nobody reckoned on the collapse of Wall Street in 1929 and the onset of the Great Depression. By 1932 millions of Americans felt that they were in their darkest of days; unemployment was nearing 25 percent, and even that didn't tell just how grim life had become. For many veterans of the World War, pride was long gone; desperation and starvation were their everyday reality. So the veterans took to derisively calling their certified bonus the "Tombstone Bonus" because the only way these soldiers could get their money was to die. Only then would their government pay their next of kin the money these veterans had earned—as a death benefit. But the veterans needed their money and they needed it now, not later. Indeed, many wondered if there would even be a later.

The story of how thousands of U.S. military veterans came to march on the government and camp on the mall just west of the Capitol to demand immediate payment of the money they had been promised is one of the early chapters in the sad history of the way America has treated its veterans.

It is a story in which towering figures of politics and the military played crucial and emotionally wrenching roles. President Calvin Coolidge had opposed the bonus payments for the veterans. His successor, Herbert Hoover, did too; he ordered U.S. Army troops to oust the encamped veterans from the mall. His orders were carried out by three relatively unknown military officers who a decade later would become military legends: General Douglas MacArthur, the army chief of staff, who was determined to act forcefully; and his two subordinates, Majors George S. Patton Jr. and Dwight D. Eisenhower.

This was a time when America was indeed in conflict with itself, with its patriotic and political values and its concept of honoring military veterans who had fought for our freedom and now needed our help—all balanced against the limited resources of a nation in distress. The conflict within went public in June 1932, when, as protesting veterans were arriving in Washington, members of Congress moved to provide them with army cots, blankets, tents, surplus clothing, medical and mess facilities—only to have the War Department say no. Writing in the journal *Military Affairs* in the summer of 1962, Dr. John W. Killigrew of American University noted that providing these basic supplies to demonstrators, even veterans, "violated the 'basic principles' of the War Department and the Army hoped that there would be no further discussion of the matter."

But that, of course, was not what was at the heart of it. As Killigrew wrote:

In the opinion of the Army the motley assemblage of veterans congregating in Washington was hardly worthy of aid and comfort; indeed, the War Department was concerned with the possibility of serious disturbances and some anxiety that the development of close relationships between the bonus marchers and the troops would have a deleterious effect on the reliability of the latter in case they were called out for riot duty. According to one officer who participated in the eviction of the bonus people this factor made some impression on the War Department: "Initially, the relations between the troops and the Marchers were so good as to cause some concern among War Department staff officers who, unlike the officers on duty with the troops, were somewhat doubtful about the reliability of the troops if their services were needed."

As the army chief of staff, General MacArthur was among the most senior officials in Washington that summer who were concerned that an upheaval on the streets of Washington, especially one against U.S. war veterans, might spark incidents nationwide. And there was yet one more concern in this time of economic strife and political uncertainty. As Killigrew wrote: "Early in June the Chief of Staff wired all corps area commanders that in case any bonus marchers passed through their respective corps areas it should be determined if any communist elements were present. The corps area commanders were directed to 'report in secret code' to Washington indicating the presence of communist elements and the names of the leaders of the bonus marchers with 'known communistic leanings.'"

In the end, it was President Hoover who gave the order and General MacArthur who implemented it. What happened can be noted briefly: MacArthur brought in tanks, teargassed the veterans, and torched their shantytown. A violent and bloody confrontation ensued as the U.S. Army routed the veterans and drove them out of town. But that misses the impact of what that long-forgotten summer of 1932 represented to this still young nation in a struggling time.

A year after the conflict the commander of the movement that called itself the Bonus Expeditionary Force, former army Sergeant W. W. "Hot" Waters, told his story to the journalist William C. White, who put it between hard covers as their book, titled *B.E.F.: The Whole Story of the Bonus Army*. In reviewing it for *The New York Times,* John Chamberlain captured wonderfully what the moment and the era were really about. For Washington was a place where the powerful and well-connected mainly got their way, leaving it up to the people to fend for themselves. In this case, those being asked to fend were the ones who had defended in the World War the very freedoms that were celebrated daily beneath the gleaming Capitol dome, and within the gleaming White House, and for that matter in those profundities chiseled long ago on the walls of Washington's gleaming monuments to its better self. In his review, Chamberlain explained why we care: "If democracy is the political expression of the great game of all living off each other, then the Bonus Army was in the American tradition and rhythm. To direct moral indignation against it, while at the same time extolling American institutions is a social non sequitur; for better or worse, the Bonus Army was expressing an American institution."

Actually, more for the better than the worse, the Bonus Army was in a tradition that vastly predated the United States and its institutions. As long as there have been civilizations there have been soldiers who have gone into battle for purposes deemed worth fighting and dying for. And when the battle was done, those civilizations turned away from the needs and pleas of their soldiers. The Romans set up the *aerarium militare* to deal with former soldiers who wanted payment for their services and treatment for their wartime wounds. That was the first veterans' bureau, authors Paul Dickson and Thomas B. Allen, note in their impressive history, *The Bonus Army: An American Epic.* In England, during the richly gifted era of William Shakespeare, soldiers home from war ended up begging in the streets and robbing citizens. That led London authorities to declare martial law, and a royal proclamation warned that mariners and soldiers would be executed if they remained in London.

In the American colonies the concept from the outset was that wounded soldiers were to be well treated when the war was done. In Plymouth Colony, a 1636 proclamation declared that any soldier who was maimed in war "shall be maintained competently by the Colony during his life." In the Revolutionary War, disabled soldiers and families of those slain received pensions under provisions of the Continental Congress. That was the intent. But in 1783, after the end of the war, soldiers belonging to the Pennsylvania Line had not been paid and marched to the new nation's capital in Philadelphia to demand what they said they were owed. The soldiers thrust their muskets through the windows of the State House, where the Congress was meeting at the time. The Congress, which included James Madison and Alexander Hamilton, fled to Princeton, New Jersey. Weeks later, with the soldiers still camped on the site in Philadelphia, George Washington ordered some fifteen hundred troops to force the protesting soldiers to leave and go home.

So there has been ample precedent for these disputes between soldiers and their own governments—and almost always the disputes were rooted in controversies about money the troops felt they were owed. When the Civil War erupted in 1861, as Dickson and Allen wrote, the nation already had eighty thousand pensioners from as far back as the War of 1812. When the Civil War ended four years later, almost 2 million veterans were receiving pensions. And in 1914, at the outbreak of World War I, more than four hundred thousand Civil War veterans and tens of thousands of veterans of the Spanish-American War were receiving pensions.

When the United States became involved in World War I, President Woodrow Wilson proposed and the Congress unanimously approved a war-risk life insurance program. Both the president and Congress assumed that those who returned from war uninjured would not seek further compensation than the dollar a day they had been paid. But the veterans by then had groups that served as their advocates—the American Legion and the Veterans of Foreign Wars—and they pressed Congress to pay the returned soldiers and sailors more fairly. In 1924 the Congress finally approved a plan to grant World War veterans "adjusted universal compensation"—the so-called bonus.

When President Coolidge vetoed the measure, reasoning that "we owe no bonus to able-bodied veterans of the World War," Congress overrode his veto. Because the federal budget was severely strained after the war, the congressional measure provided that only those veterans who were owed up to $50 were paid immediately. All who were owed more got certificates that could not be redeemed until 1945.

Veterans were pressing to speed up the payment process when, in 1929, the stock market crashed and the Depression descended with a vengeance. Congressional efforts to speed veterans' pay went nowhere. In Portland, Oregon, on March 15, 1932, William Waters, the unemployed former sergeant, spoke up at a meeting of veterans and urged everyone to head to Washington via freight train to demand the money the government owed them. As Congress continued to bury the veterans' help proposals, Waters began working his veteran colleagues one by one. On May 11, about three hundred hopped an empty livestock freight car in Portland and headed to Washington. They had a banner that read: "Portland Bonus March—On to Washington."

As they traveled slowly across the country, the Portland veterans made news and gained support. They also made controversy. By the time they had reached St. Louis, officials of the Baltimore & Ohio railroad confronted Waters and showed him a court order that barred the veterans from using the railroad's boxcars. On Saturday, May 21, Waters located a veteran who had a truck and was willing to take food, cooking supplies, and so on. Then the veterans set out to march on foot; they crossed the bridge over the Mississippi River into East St. Louis. They had a motorcycle escort, courtesy of the Illinois State Highway Police. They paraded through East St. Louis and the mayor welcomed them. The veterans figured that in Illinois, they would once again board a B&O train for the trip to Washington. But the railroad wouldn't carry the veterans and the veterans wouldn't leave the trains, and nothing was moving.

The veterans amassed some trucks and cars and continued their trek to Washington by motorcade. Along the way they picked up more veterans and much more attention from the national news media. The famed radio newscaster Lowell Thomas told his nationwide audience: "The march of the Bonus Army on Washington, D.C., becomes more promising of excitement every day."

The word spread. The cause of the veterans had become, in every sense, an American cause célèbre. Naturally, America's foremost current events humorist got into the act. "This country is not broke," observed Will Rogers, referring to the debt the nation owed the veterans. "If we owed it to some Foreign Nation, you would talk about honor and then pay it."

Veterans throughout the United States, desperate for money and furious that they couldn't cash in their modest bonus certificates, began to make their own way to Washington. Still others joined the Portland vets' caravan en route; as it wound eastward through Indiana, Ohio, and then Pennsylvania, veterans all along the way joined the procession.

At the Maryland state line, Maryland National Guard trucks showed up and brought the veterans across the headwaters of the Potomac River and into the picturesque city of Cumberland, Maryland, where they spent the night in an old skating rink, sleeping on the floor. The next morning, the Guard drove the Portland contingent of veterans all the way into the center of Washington.

And there they found thousands of other veterans. They lived in anything—tents, of course, but also wooden crates and cardboard boxes—anywhere they could find space. Some lived on the land where the National Gallery is today, on the mall, just west of the Capitol. The largest group wound up in a shantytown set up on the flats of the Anacostia River in southwest Washington. The vets bathed in the river, near a sewage pipe. Many had brought their wives and children with them. Around the country, shantytowns where homeless men and women found shelter had become known derisively as Hoovervilles. Anacostia's flats, where at least fifteen thousand veterans and their families bedded down, had become the nation's largest Hooverville.

President Hoover had decided that it was time for the army to evict the veterans from downtown Washington. He later gave MacArthur specific orders not to cross the Anacostia River bridge and not to drive the veterans out of their shantytown on the Anacostia flats (it is unlikely that the president chose to call it Hooverville). But MacArthur ignored Hoover's order and ordered his troops to clear out the Anacostia site.

Richard L. Strout, correspondent for *The Christian Science Monitor* was up on the roof of the Ford Building on July 22. Dickson and Allen tell the story of what happened next from Strout's perspective. He looked down and saw the soldiers mobilizing, their bayonets fixed. An officer stood in the middle of Pennsylvania Avenue—where the inaugural parade passes every four years—and shouted that the veterans had three minutes to leave. The soldiers put on their gas masks; somebody threw a stone. "Then the riot started." Soldiers started lobbing tear gas grenades at the veterans. A cavalry unit charged down the street, and soldiers on horseback galloped into the crowd. "Men and women were ridden down indiscriminately," wrote *The Baltimore Sun*'s J. F. Essary. "Nothing like this cavalry charge has ever been witnessed in Washington."

Joseph C. Harsch of *The Christian Science Monitor* reported: "Most of the marchers gave way and fell back. In front of me, one stood his ground. A saber flashed in a swinging arc and grazed the cheek of the marcher. Blood flowed. The marcher backed away, holding a hand to his bleeding ear."

Then the soldiers started torching the shanties. "I watched the soldiers moving from hut to hut, starting the blaze," wrote Strout. The shanties blazed and with them the clothes and belongings of the veterans and their families.

Then MacArthur gave the order for his troops to cross the Anacostia bridge and clear out the shantytown on the flats—violating the order of his commander in chief, President Hoover. The infantry crossed the bridge with bayonets fixed. The crowd booed the troops. MacArthur ordered the torching of the Ana-costia shanties, and one by one they were set ablaze.

In a sad epilogue, in 1934 many veterans were moved into Federal Emergency Relief Administration camps in the Florida Keys, on Matecumbe Key, to build a bridge to connect the upper keys with Key West—only to be caught in the devastating hurricane of 1935. Many were killed. Witnesses reported seeing bodies tossed into the trees, partly buried in the sand, some with no skin, "literally sand-blasted to death," according to one witness. Ernest Hemingway had rushed down to the Keys. He wrote about finding sixty-nine bodies, including two women who had been tossed into the trees. Hemingway was furious, contending that these Bonus March veterans had been shipped down to south Florida to keep them away from Washington, lest they start another march on the nation's capital when Roosevelt was seeking reelection. "It was as bad as the war," Hemingway told a friend.

On May 22, 1935, President Roosevelt vetoed a congressional bill that would have provided immediate payment of those bonus service certificates. Like his Republican predecessors, Coolidge and Hoover, he too had chosen to hold the line on government spending as his overriding priority. He offered his rationale in his veto message, which in a rare act he traveled to Capitol Hill to deliver in person in a speech broadcast nationally. He drew a sharp distinction between veterans maimed in war and those who returned physically healthy. "I hold that able-bodied citizens should be accorded no treatment different from that accorded to other citizens who did not wear a uniform during the World War. . . . The veteran who is disabled owes his condition to the war. The healthy veteran who is unemployed owes his troubles to the depression."

But almost a decade later the president who declared his outright opposition to special treatment for some citizens just because they once wore a military uniform famously reversed his position. In 1944, Roosevelt affixed his signature to one of the landmark pieces of legislation in American history, and certainly the nation's grandest program of special assistance for military veterans: the GI Bill of Rights. The program paid the college tuition for millions of veterans. And loans from the GI bill financed 11 million of the 13 million houses that were built in the United States in the 1950s. The shameful specter of the era when the nation defeated its own Bonus Army veterans no doubt contributed mightily to a national sense that this time those who fought to keep the world free would be honored and helped.

For a limited time in the years that followed, partisans with admittedly political purposes occasionally sought to rekindle a sense of outrage over what was done to the veterans of the Bonus Army. One of those moments came in the last days of the 1952 presidential election campaign when the Democratic strategists sought to stave off the coming landslide defeat of their nominee, Governor Adlai Stevenson of Illinois, by seeking to remind Americans that just two decades earlier, the Republican candidate had played a role that was, well, anti-veteran. The notion would prove a hard sell given that Dwight D. Eisenhower was the symbol of all that Americans were still celebrating in the heroes who had only seven years earlier fought the war that saved the world.

"Eisenhower Scored on '32 Bonus 'War,'" said the headline in *The New York Times* on October 25, 1952. Followed by the subhead: "Democrats Put Out Newspaper with Photo Captioned 'Gen. Ike Helps Rout Vets.'" The article, by *The Times*'s Washington correspondent John D. Morris straightforwardly covered the news: The Democratic National Committee had published five million copies of a tabloid-sized newspaper that was being distributed throughout the country in an effort to remind voters that General Dwight D. Eisenhower had played a role in the army's forceful 1932 eviction from the Washington Mall of some seven thousand protesting bonus march military veterans. The Democrats' newspaper published a news photograph showing Eisenhower alongside General MacArthur, with a caption stating that the two men were discussing "the battle tactics they will use to drive the Bonus Army out of Washington." Next to that photo was another captioned "Army Attacks Veterans," showing troops wearing gas masks and advancing on the protesting veterans with bayonets fixed.

The *Times* article also identified the Democratic strategist who had overseen the production of this one-time-only campaign newspaper: "The tabloid was prepared under the direction of Sam Brightman, the [Democratic National] committee's director of publicity. He was asked if one purpose was to imply that General Eisenhower shared responsibility for the handling of the bonus marchers. 'The content of the tabloid speaks for itself,' he replied. 'We are not trying to blame Eisenhower for the attack on the bonus marchers. But we are not averse to pointing out that General Eisenhower's experience had been in the military rather than in civilian life.'"

It wasn't that Americans had forgotten what had happened to the veterans of the Bonus Army—it had been only twenty years since the U.S. Army had routed those men who had once worn its uniform but were now out of money and luck. But already, in 1952, the Depression seemed to be a bygone era. Today, it would also be incorrect to say that Americans have forgotten about the Bonus Army episode—because most Americans have never even heard about that microdot of our history. But we all recognize the modern-day manifestations of that narrow mind-set that spread easily through Washington during hard times past. It always seems to fester just below the surface of political Washington, turning veterans into casualties of our economically challenged peacetime wars.

4

Old Soldiers Sometimes Die—Waiting

After a Lifetime of Delays

The Bikini Atoll was always in its glory at sunrise and sunset. The Pacific sky would light up in a brilliant orange that began and ended at the opposite ends of the earth, where the water met the sky. The vivid spectacle was a paint-chart match for the bright orange color the U.S. government had painted the USS *Nevada* so that on July 1, 1946, the pilot of the B-29 could spot the target ship in a cluster of vessels moored off the atoll. Michael Stanco was one of forty-two thousand American seamen stationed on nearby support ships. Stanco, who had been wounded when the Japanese attacked Pearl Harbor and again in the Philippines, was about to become part of Operation Crossroads, the United States' post–World War II testing program designed to assess the impact of a nuclear bomb by exploding one at this tranquil atoll in the Pacific. Back in the United States, the event Stanco was embarking upon was being declared the "Greatest Show on Earth" by *Newsweek*, which also trumpeted "The Good That May Come from the Tests at Bikini."

At midday on July 1, 1946, B-29 droned over the bright orange target ship and dropped its payload, an atomic bomb the size of the one dropped on Nagasaki. The mushroom cloud rose—first dark, then a mix of orange, brown and pink from the nitrous oxides. Half a world away, *Newsweek*'s coverage grew purple: "Man, pygmy that he is in the endless stretch of time, set off his fourth atom bomb this week. Trembling, he waited once again to see if he had wrought his own destruction. . . . Yet, as the macabre cloud of his fourth explosion rose majestically from Bikini's environs . . . he could sigh with relief. Alive he was; given time and the sanity of nations, he might yet harness for peace the greatest force that living creatures had ever released on this earth."

At Bikini, Geiger counter needles went off the scale. Four days later, nearby ships carrying naval and government bigwigs turned around and tried to outrun a radiation that was much worse than anticipated. But Stanco and his fellow sailors didn't know about that and of course no one told them. They had their own jobs to do. Seven and a half hours after the blast, Stanco's unit pulled into the lagoon. He was a machinist's mate, one of sixty-two seamen who boarded the USS *Nevada*. He and the others went about their assigned tasks and ate the food that was in the *Nevada*'s refrigerator.

"We became deathly ill after eating. I remember being so ill along with the others," Stanco said in an interview at his home in New Port Richey, Florida, that was published in the *Atomic Veterans' Newsletter* in autumn 1980. Eventually the navy had to sink the USS *Nevada* because the radioactivity remained at levels that were unacceptable. The bitter irony of the government's conclusion was not lost on Stanco: The contamination caused damage that was unacceptable for its vessel but not for those who manned it or for the divers who inspected its hull in waters that were fouled with oily substances that leaked from the bombed ships. "If this ship was sunk for reasons of contamination," said

Stanco, "what effects do you think it had upon the 60 men who ate and slept aboard it? And what about the divers who sank to their armpits in ooze—and the other 42,000 men that also participated?"

Years later, Stanco's health was bad and getting worse. He had multiple cancers; his body was failing him. But when he filed a claim with the Veterans Administration for service-related disability in 1976, saying his health problems were due to his exposure to plutonium at Bikini Atoll, he found his government was failing him too. It turned out that he was a member of a very large club: between 1946 and 1962 more than two hundred thousand members of the military based in the Pacific and stateside had been ordered to do tasks that put them into target areas where they were exposed to radiation from atomic tests. The government maintained that the troops had been exposed only to very low levels of radiation. Until the 1970s, the federal government did no epidemiological tests or follow-up on the health of the troops who had been exposed to radiation and placed in harm's way by their government.

In 1979, the Veterans Administration's general counsel, Guy H. McMichael III, testified before the Senate Veterans' Affairs Committee about how difficult it was to make a definitive connection between exposure to radiation from an atom bomb and the onset of cancer or other illness. "There are serious difficulties inherent in the adjudication of claims involving more lengthy post-exposure development of cancer, when there is no pathological evidence to indicate that the disease process began in service." The VA's unstated policy was already clear by then: don't pay the vets any compensation unless the link between their service assignment and their later illness is absolutely irrefutable— as clear as a grenade taking off a limb. If you can't see that it happened, then you can claim there is insufficient proof—and cheat tens of thousands of deserving veterans out of their just compensation. Using legalistic language, McMichael noted "that radiation-induced cancers have no unique pathological characteristics to distinguish them from cancer due to 'natural' factors. This makes it impossible to determine with certainty whether such a disease would have occurred regardless of the radiation exposure."

This was the government mindset that would be applied to any number of cases where the military had ordered a member of the service into a situation that clearly harmed him—at the time or in later years. The government would deny that causality could be proven until the individual veteran found a way to do so. Veterans saw it in the Vietnam War with Agent Orange, in the Gulf War with the Gulf War Disorders and the exposure to chemical nerve agents at Khamisiyah, and in all wars where troops came home with what is now diagnosed as post-traumatic stress disorder. Perhaps most incredibly, this official state of denial extended even to the U.S. military personnel that Uncle Sam had placed smack in the middle of radioactive fallout zones. Even then Uncle Sam recognized no injury except those that could be proven with 100 percent certainty. A better, healthier national mind-set—and the only truly patriotic one—would have been to say from the start: We put the troops there, so we'll pay them for their ordeal.

For decades, the official position of the Department of Defense and the Veterans Administration was that there had been no health problems caused by the nuclear contamination at Bikini, but the military personnel who were there all knew better. In time they formed their own advocacy group, the National Association of Atomic Veterans, composed of those in the military who had suffered medical problems after being exposed to radiation from nuclear tests conducted in the Pacific and, later, in the deserts of the United States.

There was Jack Leavitt, a 22-year-old sailor based in California. He followed orders and climbed aboard the USS *Pensacola*, a heavy cruiser in the targeted area at Bikini Atoll. His team began "to scrub down the decks to wash off any radioactive fallout. . . . At no time did I or anyone working with me—that is, naval personnel—have a Geiger counter, nor any other testing device to measure danger of radiation." Leavitt spoke in a Mesa, Arizona, interview that appears in the 1982 book, *Killing Our Own: The Disaster of America's Experience with Atomic Radiation* by Harvey Wasserman and Norman Solomon, with Robert Alvarez and Eleanor Walters. "I had diarrhea for some time after the test, but was told it was emotional and would go away. I had accompanying pain in the lower abdomen, and in the right side. And have had since. I have had stomach trouble since 1946." The authors wrote that Leavitt later suffered from colitis, bleeding of the bladder, obstructive lung disease, and "malfunctions of organs vulnerable to internally absorbed radioactive particles."

The Veterans Administration would not cover Leavitt's medical treatment, according to the account in *Killing Our Own*. Instead the VA asked him to submit to a number of tests, but never agreed to pay for his treatment, let alone any service-related benefits. Said Leavitt: "I am bitter because I have lost my ability to work, to take care of myself. I collect five hundred thirty-four dollars and ten cents Social Security. I am totally disabled. . . . There must be thousands still suffering, and loved ones left behind prematurely by early death to veterans who have passed on with claims pending, and some could still be alive today if proper treatment was given, and the responsibilities accepted by those responsible in the first place."

Frank F. Karasti was on the target ship the day after the atomic blast at Bikini Atoll. His job was to put out fires. Initially he suffered severe nausea and then hypertension. And later: "My skin is deteriorating on my whole body and it is possible to wash off parts of it while bathing. . . . I have been aging ahead of my time and should I use any physical effort, I get ill for three days after."

Occasionally—usually when there was extensive media attention to the case—the VA would grant a service member's claim for benefits. But it was always an isolated case, and it was never granted in a way that could be seen as setting legal precedent. The authors of *Killing Our Own* noted that, as of 1981, "the VA has turned down more than 98 percent of radiation-based claims for atomic veterans' service-connected benefits." In the summer of 1980 the Pentagon issued a widely circulated press release that stated: "The average exposure of atmospheric nuclear test participants is about *one-tenth* of the level that is generally agreed as an acceptable annual exposure for radiation workers." The Pentagon statement said that "approximately one fatal cancer per 20,000 individuals" would result from the nuclear test exposure. It made no mention of an analysis by the Centers for Disease Control a year earlier that had found that soldiers exposed to nuclear tests in Nevada suffered twice as many leukemia occurrences as a similar nonexposed population—and that was a measurement only of that one cancer, not any of the others that should have been examined.

A case filed by the founder of the National Association of Atomic Veterans proved a major turning point. Former army sergeant Orville Kelly was commander at Japtan, in the Marshall Islands, in the 1950s. During the twenty-two nuclear test explosions he witnessed, he wore a film badge, a device that measured gamma radiation. In the 1970s, suffering from lymphocytic lymphoma, he took on the VA. For five years Kelly's claims and appeals were denied, but in November 1979, he won. The Board of

Veterans' Appeals ruled in favor of the *plausibility* of his claim that his exposure caused his cancer. The VA board maintained that this was a one-case decision and not a precedent. But it was of course far more than that. Kelly died in June 1980.

As more veterans began pressing their cases, the DOD became more defensive than ever. The Defense Nuclear Agency's spokesman, Colonel Bill McGee, said famously in a 1980 interview: "We're not in the health effects business—we're in the defense business."

Meanwhile, Michael Stanco's case was still bouncing back and forth through the VA in 1985 when he died at age seventy. "His body was riddled with cancer," said his wife, Dorothy, in an interview with the *St. Petersburg Times*. She vowed to continue fighting his cause and his case and did both. She became a state commander of the Disabled American Veterans Ladies Auxiliary.

In 1997, Michael Stanco won his case—twenty-one years after he first filed it and twelve years after he died. The VA gave Dorothy Stanco $71,000. She told the *St. Petersburg Times* she believed they won their case only because then-VA secretary Jesse Brown came to Florida to give a speech and she confronted him directly.

She also believed the VA had been deliberately stalling her case and those of all the other old veterans, hoping they would grow weary and quit fighting, or die. "It took all this while because they made 46 mistakes in my case," she said. "They deliberately stall the veterans off by making mistakes. . . . They're just waiting for the veterans to die, and the widows. It's just sad."

On September 28, 2001, Dorothy Stanco, who finished the fight her husband began, died at home.

Alfred Brown's voice remains forever firm, his cadence carefully measured for posterity. After decades of being bounced up and down on the VA's legal trampolines, this World War II veteran from Dry Ridge, Kentucky, talked into a tape recorder about the essentials of his case. He spoke with unmistakable purpose, so that everyone who might someday hear his voice would be sure to understand all the ways he had been wronged by the VA over the past four decades. Brown's tape-recorded words became public in 2005, in an award-winning newspaper series by Knight Ridder Washington correspondents Chris Adams and Alison Young.

Brown's problems began in 1945. It was less than a year since the GI Bill of Rights had been signed into law in Washington, but that was the furthest thing from his mind. It was an ocean away and, it seemed, a lifetime away. Brown was a nineteen-year-old soldier serving in Italy when an explosive shell fragment ripped through the right side of his abdomen and lodged in his chest wall. He was administered last rites on two occasions.

He was operated on and sent home to Kentucky with an honorable discharge from the U.S. Army. He received only a modest benefit from the Veterans Administration and, in time, he came to believe he'd been shortchanged—bureaucratically cheated out of the money he had earned in the service of his country: "This treatment of my case by the Veterans Administration . . . is just one more example of the apparent indifference by the VA and its personnel to 'he who has borne the battle.' I have never been given a fair shake by the VA in anything I have asked for," said Brown.

It would get worse. His case would make him a poster vet for bureaucratic wrongs, showing that the government runs on a treadmill of red tape that can make a bad situation much worse and an unfair situation unconscionable.

The comprehensive Knight Ridder investigation, entitled "Discharged and Dishonored," showed how the VA is failing the men and women who once served in the military and have now been discharged into civilian life. Indeed, the McClatchy Washington bureau (Knight Ridder's successor after McClatchy bought the rival chain) has become the capital's leading news organization in covering and exposing ways in which the U.S. government disserves its military veterans, as Chris Adams has continued to pursue the VA's underperformance. Yet in the infuriating way that Washington works—and so often doesn't work—the McClatchy coverage, published widely but not in Washington, had little influence on government officials, who seem to respond only when kicked in their career aspirations—a Washington-fueled clamor demanding that they change their ways. (We will later take a hard look at the failure of the Senate and House Veterans Affairs' Committees to move aggressively to fix all that was wrong.)

In 1981, three and a half decades after his discharge, Alfred Brown discovered that he had not been receiving all of the benefits he was due for his injuries. The problem seemed merely bureaucratic: Brown knew he had been discharged in 1945, but the VA papers said he had been discharged in 1946, and that made a big difference in the benefits he was eligible for, due to the medical problems he later suffered. Here is Brown's view of it, spoken into a tape recorder for posterity: "The VA is twisting and dodging and doing everything they can to use a phony date of July of 1946 [as the discharge date]. . . . Something really stinks about this date."

For the next twenty-one years, Brown battled the VA for his back pay. He calculated that he was owed about $30,000. When Senator Strom Thurmond, a Republican from South Carolina, got involved, the VA responded at the highest level but with the lowest form of logic, calling it a "harmless" error. "The secretary of the VA, in a letter to Senator Strom Thurmond concerning my case . . . alleges that it was harmless error in their overlooking all of my injuries," Brown said. "It is not harmless error when 30 percent of your disability is taken from you."

The VA assesses disability on a scale ranging from 0 percent, for no disability, to 100 percent, for total disability. A veteran's eligibility for a wide range of services, from health care to vocational rehabilitation, is determined by this disability rating. Basic service-related disability payments range from $103 a month for a disability rated at 10 percent to $2,163 for a disability rated at 100 percent; the ratings are set in increments of 10 percent. Brown's position was that his disability was underrated and that he was also owed a year's worth of benefits because the government had erroneously listed his discharge date as 1946 instead of 1945. It would seem that such relatively basic issues could have been resolved in just a few minutes once appropriate records were put on the table. But it didn't turn out that way.

Instead, the VA fought Brown through the courts. In 2001, Brown wrote the top veterans' affairs judge a letter that is part of his publicly available case file: "As a member of the so-called 'Greatest Generation,' I am well aware of the large numbers of us passing away. I am prepared to meet our Creator. My fear is that your court will not make a decision in my case."

The next year, Alfred Brown died, and so did his case. In its final decision, the Court of Appeals for Veterans Claims notes that Brown died on September 11, 2002, adding that: "an appellant's disability compensation claims . . . 'die with him.'" According to VA rules, a veteran's case dies when he dies, unless he or she has a qualifying spouse or dependent children. In that event, the case can be pursued by those who are entitled to compensation if the VA's final adjudication supports the veteran's claim. But if the veteran dies before the claim is paid and there are no immediate dependents, then the veteran's estate and non-dependent beneficiaries are out of luck—even if the veteran would have received a sizable sum of money had he or she lived. Thus, to Uncle Sam, a veteran's death can literally be money in the bank.

But the chief judge of the court of appeals, Kenneth Kramer, went out of his way to write a lengthy separate assessment of Brown's "underlying claim." He detailed the shattering injuries Brown had suffered in Italy and their later ramifications, all endured because he had gone to war for his country. In complexity and length, the carefully framed opinion read like a medical emergency room textbook. Judge Kramer concluded that "it appears that the [1947 reviewing officer] . . . erred in failing to award a 50% rating for the [1945] injury." Moreover, that initial rating became the basis for subsequent low ratings; Judge Kramer calculated that Brown had deserved a rating of 80 percent disability all of those years. He also found that the Board of Veterans' Appeals ruling supporting the original review was "arbitrary, capricious, an abuse of discretion, or otherwise not in accordance with law." He concluded: "Had the appellant not died, I believe that the Court would likely have so held, thereby reversing the February 8, 1996, BVA [Board of Veterans' Appeals] decision . . . and remanding the matter to the Board for payment of past-due benefits."

For decades, adjudicators, medical analysts, and lawyers had bounced this case up and down the VA system, which seemed determined to do all it could not to pay this one veteran his due. Judge Kramer's extraordinarily caring opinion reads like a lawyer's version of Alfred Brown's tape-recorded message: that he had "never been given a fair shake by the VA."

Veterans who have had dealings with the Department of Veterans Affairs (and the Veterans Administration before that) know that there will be delays and lost files, then more delays and more lost files. To the veterans it begins to seem as though the bureaucrats are dancing the VA Two-Step. To the younger veterans it is infuriating. To the older veterans, it is often far more desperate as they fight to outlive their VA appeals.

May, 15, 2000, was the saddest day for World War II veteran Donald Hart's family. That was the day the Fort Worth, Texas, veteran won his long battle with the Department of Veterans Affairs for disability benefits back pay—the day the VA finally admitted that from 1997 to 1999 it had indeed been underpaying him by as much as $3,000 each month for injuries he'd suffered in a parachute jump, injuries that had cost him the use of his legs later in life.

May 15, 2000, at 4:15 P.M. was also the day Donald Hart died. According to the 2005 Knight Ridder series, Hart's lawyers had estimated he was due some $63,000. He had also incurred about $50,000 in medical bills. His estate had to pay for the twenty-four-hour medical care he needed in his last years. The VA did not have to pay his estate the bills it owed for his service to his country.

The case of Belie Bowman, a Vietnam veteran from North Carolina, was a classic example of how bureaucratic delays can so dishonor and disserve veterans. Like many, he had gone to war as a healthy young man and had returned with a disordered personality. The Knight Ridder report said he was "skittish, quick to anger, uneasy in crowds." He applied twice for service-related benefits due to "nerves" and was twice denied, in 1971 and 1995. Then he got an attorney and filed papers showing that he suffered from post-traumatic stress disorder. His case went through six time-consuming rulings. After he had contracted pancreatic cancer, the VA Board of Veterans' Appeals agreed, on June 16,

2004, that he had proved his case: it was basically the same one he had filed years earlier. By then his cancer had worsened and his treatment had stopped—and at the VA, things somehow slowed a bit more. On June 21, Bowman's attorney was talking to the VA every couple of hours. The next day the attorney was told all they needed were a couple of additional signatures before the check for $53,784 could be prepared. It was in the computer system, Bowman's attorney was told.

That night, Bowman died and the VA never cut his check.

But there are times when the VA can cut through its own red tape and move quickly, as it did in the case of George Wilkes, a World War II sailor who was disabled due to a spinal cord injury. The New Orleans veteran had fought the VA for years over the amount he was being paid in benefits, contending that his disability rating was far too low. Finally, in April 1997, he won his case. The VA notified him that it concurred and that he would be paid $109,464 in back compensation.

It was the veteran sailor's last victory. He had been suffering from pneumonia and died four days later. The VA wired the money directly into Wilkes's bank account six days after he died. When the officials of the VA realized Wilkes had died before the money was deposited in his account, the agency pounced and took back its money. Although Wilkes had no immediate dependents, his nephew and niece had cared for him for years so he could remain in his own home. There was no way the government was going to let them keep the money, even though it may well have been the sailor's last wish.

The misfortune of a missed fortune happens far more often than one might assume. Naturally, this falls mainly on the aging veterans of World War II. The original Knight Ridder analysis of

VA appeals records showed that more than 13,700 veterans had died during the time that their cases were being appealed.

In 2003, then VA secretary Anthony Principi told Knight Ridder reporters that he was "stung" when he learned just a few years before how frequently veterans die while their cases are still being appealed. "It's not acceptable," said Principi. "We need to do something about it."

We need to do something about it. Understand what the secretary of veterans affairs was really saying and you will grasp the essence of the problem we face as a country and as a culture. Principi had learned about the problem a few years earlier, yet he had let years pass without being sufficiently outraged to do something about it. And he was the top gun for veterans' affairs policy. This is the essence of what is wrong in Washington in so many areas. It is not that there is a master plan somewhere in which top policy makers or midlevel bureaucrats set out to deliberately and systematically dishonor those we sent into war. It is just that there is no outrage—no finely honed fury in those who make and administer our policies.

5

Decades of Waste

How the System Spent Decades Making a One-Day Decision

Life is tranquil in the Atlantic coast city of Stuart, midway down the Florida peninsula, and on his good days, when the back pains weren't bad, Irving Levin could enjoy life and forget about his battles—those battles of more than a half century ago and the battles he was still being forced to fight in the twenty-first century. But like most octogenarian soldiers, especially ones who get around by using a walker for short distances and a wheelchair for longer ones, Levin didn't relish combat anymore. Especially not when the adversary he was combatting was his own government, whose uniform he wore proudly as a young army air corps flight engineer on a B-29 in the Pacific during World War II.

On April 13, 1945, Levin and his mates flew a mission over Tokyo. They dropped their bombs on their assigned target, turned around, and headed home, when they were attacked by Japanese fighters; Japanese gunfire tore a hole in the left wing and set the plane on fire. The B-29 barely made it to Iwo Jima, where it crash-landed. The impact threw Levin against the bulkhead, and a flying metal object, later thought to be a water or coffee jug, hit his head. His injuries mended, the war ended, and Levin went on with his stateside life, building a career as a researcher at the Massachusetts Institute of Technology. It was a few years after the war that the problems began. "They were nebulous problems at first," Levin told me in a 2007 telephone interview, "but they got worse." Doctors said it was some sort of neurological problem; in 1965 he began experiencing numbness and coldness in his arms and left leg. But it wasn't until four decades after that crash landing that a physician made the causal diagnosis that he had suffered spinal damage. "I've had three operations on my cervical spine," he said. His first operation was in 1967.

In April 1988, Levin first filed his claim for service-related injury compensation with what was then the Veterans Administration, the noncabinet agency that a year later would become the present cabinet-level Department of Veterans Affairs. He contended that the crash landing had caused his spinal damage. The VA denied his claim in January 1989 on the grounds that it found "no evidence relating the veteran's alleged neck injury in service, and the development of his cervical spine problems in 1965." Levin appealed. He had no idea that this was but the start of another long war, one that would be fought with medical records against endless red tape.

"Initially I had faith in my government," Levin said. "I didn't think it was an adversarial process—but it is. I had to dig up for myself all of my information. Every hospital report. Every single one of them. The help I got from the VA was next to nothing. I thought they were supposed to be on the side of the veterans."

Almost two decades after filing his initial claim, Levin was still battling multiple levels of the government and those who make its decisions at low levels, apparently in the belief that they are doing precisely what the officials at the top want and expect them to do: Safeguard the money and not the vets. In a 2006 interview, Levin explained why he was not willing to surrender to what had been a long and exhausting appeals process. In an interview with Cory Reiss of the Lakeland, Florida, *Ledger*, Levin said: "I felt that if it was happening to me, it was happening to other veterans. So I decided to stick with it. Never give up."

Levin was at war not just with the government and its bureaucrats but with the system. At Veterans Affairs, the system, as it applies to benefits claims, is a hodgepodge of rules, red tape and mind-set that functionally work against the individual veteran. The system, as it has evolved, is counterproductive and counterintuitive: it makes no sense at all. And Irving Levin's case would eventually demonstrate precisely that, with infuriating clarity.

Levin's appeal eventually was decided in a court that operates in virtual anonymity in the federal legal system. It is the U.S. Court of Appeals for Veterans Claims, an independent court that did not even exist before 1988 and whose proceedings are rarely, if ever, covered by the mainstream news media. The sole purpose of the court is to hear appeals from veterans whose claims have been denied by the Board of Veterans' Appeals. Prior to 1988, that board, an arm of the VA, was the final arbiter. This meant that the VA was the only federal agency that had no independent judicial review: it ruled on veterans' claims, then reviewed its own decisions.

The way The System works is that when this Court of Appeals for Veterans Claims gets an appeal, the case is sent back to the VA to work its way through the process again. Levin's case was sent back once, twice and then a third time, finding fault with the decisions of the VA's Board of Veterans' Appeals.

The VA denied his claim in 1991 on the grounds that his

service record contained no evidence that he was treated for cervical spinal damage. (Levin had been hospitalized for observation a few weeks after the crash landing.) Levin appealed. In 1995, the board again denied his claim, saying an "injury to the cervical spine was not demonstrated in service." Levin appealed. In 1997, the Court of Appeals for Veterans Claims told the VA to get a medical opinion as to whether his injury could have been caused by the events of the crash landing. The court specifically noted: "In May 1997, a private neurologist . . . concluded that 'it is possible that the airplane accident with the initial shock-like sensation into both arms did represent a significant neck injury. It also is quite clear from the patient's medical record and his history that he had symptoms [in the] years prior to the minor motor vehicle accident in 1967, and therefore this accident could not have caused his lower extremity symptoms.' He concluded that it was possible that the appellant's cervical spondylosis was directly causally related to the 1945 airplane crash."

The VA case history contains a voluminous collection of testimony from medical experts, adjudications, appeals, reviews, remands from the appellate court to the Board of Appeals, and so on. Anyone who reads through the case record will come away with the conclusion that this is an idiotic waste of time and money. The pattern was established early and ran true to form for a decade: the VA and its reviewers seemed determined to find some way of denying payment of service-related benefits to Levin and the appellate court kept saying the lower-level reviews had not shown that it was impossible that the veteran's claim was accurate.

Through it all, the debate pivoted on a reprehensible lawyer-driven turn of phrase that is all too familiar: A VA neurologist reviewed Levin's current cervical spinal problem and submitted expert testimony in April 2003: "I would state that it is less likely than not the result of his service related injury." The Court of Appeals for Veterans Claims noted that the same VA neurologist "provided an addendum in May 2004, stating that '[the appellant's] cervical spine disability or any portion thereof is, less likely [than] not, the result of cerebral injuries sustained in the service as documented multiple times before in his records by various neurologist[s].'"

That led the court to send the case back to the Board of Veterans' Appeals on July 11, 2003, with pointed instructions that turned the VA's favorite phrase on its legal ear. The court stated that the VA examiners should "render a single, collaborative supplemental opinion . . . as to whether the veteran's documented post-service cervical spine disability, or any portion thereof, is a[t] least as likely as not the result of injury sustained in service . . . notwithstanding the absence of specific documentation of the alleged in-service injury."

Back at the lower level, in 2005, the VA's board of appeals seemed to disregard the remand instructions of the court of appeals, issuing the same ruling again finding no proof that Levin sustained his cervical injury in that crash because he wasn't treated for a cervical spine injury at the time. The board had relied upon opinions given by VA doctors, so that decision was appealed once again by Levin and his lawyer.

In July 2007—nineteen years after his first claim was filed—Irving Levin won his case. He was eighty-four years old. The Court of Appeals for Veterans Claims ruled in his favor, rejecting the VA board's decisions and admonishing the board for its faulty reasoning. The court said that the medical opinions the board relied upon "are inadequate because they were based on the inaccurate premise that it was necessary for the appellant to have documentation of a cervical spine injury dating back to the appellant's military service."

The court opinion continued: "The Board relied on both of these opinions, even though the first was based on the flawed factual predicate that, in order to relate the current condition to an injury sustained in the plane crash, contemporaneous medical records documenting a cervical spine injury at the time of the crash were necessary to substantiate the occurrence of a cervical spine injury. The absence of contemporaneous medical records is not dispositive in cases where the purported in-service injury occurred in combat, as the Board acknowledged was the case here."

The court said the board should have rejected the addendum that contended it was "less likely than not" that the injury was caused by the crash for not providing a sufficient rationale for the conclusion. The court sharply admonished the board for having "failed to ensure compliance with its July 11, 2003, remand order," that the VA examiners should state "whether the veteran's documented post-service cervical spine disability, or any portion thereof, is a[t] least as likely as not the result of injury sustained in service . . . notwithstanding the absence of specific documentation of the alleged in-service injury."

The more you read these VA case histories, the more you come away thinking that layers of VA lawyers have apparently made this phrase, "less likely than not," part of the departmental mantra of denial: a one-size-fits-all argument. The VA's in-house ear, nose, and throat doctor used it as his basis for concluding that Bill Florey should not be granted benefits. Now the same phrase has surfaced in the case of Irving Levin. It was used repeatedly by the VA's in-house experts, then cited repeatedly by the VA's claim adjudicators—only to be rejected and condemned by the independent Court of Appeals for Veterans Claims.

Anyone reading these case histories begins to develop a clear understanding of at least one major problem in the VA process.

The problem is a basic mind-set that seems to permeate the VA—a mind-set that has as its core the notion that veterans are out to bilk the system. (And of course some of them may well be; but there are also many honest veterans who have fallen into a real crisis, have a legitimate need, and long ago earned our grateful help.) Yet this mind-set, which seems to be held by many within the VA, holds that because some veterans may be trying to get benefits they don't deserve, all veterans must be held to a sometimes impossible standard of proof of service-related and service-caused disability before they can be paid benefits. Even when it has been proved that they now have a severe health crisis and that a hazardous combat situation could indeed have caused their present life-threatening crisis. If detailed evidence was not kept in the war zone, while bullets were flying and bombs were falling, then decades later it just might be tough luck for a deserving veteran. His or her case may be summarily rejected on the claim that it is "less likely than not" that the veteran's problem today was caused by that combat crisis long ago. That is the view from one end of the VA mind-set.

Then, at the opposite end of the spectrum, there are appellate judges in the independent Court of Appeals for Veterans Claims. Read their opinions and you come away thinking they seem to understand that, first, that war is hell; and, second, that sometimes injuries sustained in wartime won't immediately cripple a twenty-year-old youth but can in time become crippling when the veteran reaches middle age or beyond. These appellate judges also seem to accept the fact that the full extent of combat injuries may not be certified in battle-area treatment, so they call upon the lower reviewers to at least investigate, not whether there is a way to deny this claim, but whether it is possible that the present medical crisis could have been caused by a combat incident.

In Irving Levin's case, the court of appeals ruled that "it does not matter that the appellant was not diagnosed with a cervical spine injury while he was in service; what matters is that he has demonstrated that he suffered an injury in service, and that, as discussed immediately above, competent medical evidence links his current condition to that injury."

"I was very lucky," Levin said. "I got a very sharp lawyer through the DAV [Disabled American Veterans]. He knew what we needed to do."

Levin's case is a window into the state of disarray at Veterans Affairs—and especially the distorted mind-set that underlies all that has gone wrong there. Consider the context of the times and the conditions at the VA. When Levin filed his first claim in 1988, the VA was already under fire for being overworked and understaffed and unable to handle the increasing backlog of claims for benefits at the end of the Vietnam War. Through the 1990s it would get much worse as veterans of the Gulf War began filing their claims for all manner of injuries that were plainly visible, plus those so-called Gulf War illnesses.

Then came the surge of benefits claims from the newly minted veterans of the Afghanistan and Iraq wars. By the end of 2004, there were 5,800 appeals awaiting decisions—twice as many as there had been two years earlier. The number of appeals of VA claim denials filed each month had increased by 50 percent, and that number was climbing ever higher, ever faster.

Now consider what happened in Irving Levin's case. The ruling that was issued by the Court of Appeals for Veterans Claims on the last day of the last appeal in July 2007 was the same ruling as when Levin first filed his claim nineteen and a half years earlier. How many VA employee hours were spent trying to find a way not to pay Levin's benefits? The VA sought to discredit him for claiming he was injured, and the doctors he brought in who said he was injured. No one doubts that he had three operations and gets around now either by a walker or by wheelchair. The case was simple and the facts that eventually decided the case were beyond dispute from the outset: Levin fought for his country, and while in the military he was in an airplane crash landing— and suffered the sort of injury that some doctors said could have caused his subsequent spinal health problem.

The amount of time wasted through this process is disheartening. According to the Disabled American Veterans office in Washington, during fiscal 2004, for example, 7,140 cases were remanded to the Board of Veterans' Appeals; at the end of that year, the board had a total of 31,645 cases that had already been decided but were appealed and then remanded for additional consideration. The DAV concluded: (1) most of the delay in these unreasonably protracted appeals processing times is at the field office level, (2) far too many cases must be remanded more than once, and (3) multiple remands add substantially to the workload of Board of Veterans' Appeals.

In 2004, the Board of Veterans' Appeals allowed 17.1 percent of the cases it decided, and approximately one-quarter of those claims it approved had been remanded previously. The board remanded 56.8 percent of the cases it reviewed in 2004 for further consideration, and of those, 18 percent had been remanded at least once before. What this indicates is that the field office adjudicators were not fulfilling the instructions of the board. All totaled, of the board's total decisions in 2004, the board either remanded or allowed 73.9 percent of the claims it decided that year. It only denied 24.2 percent of its cases. The obvious conclusions from this are as follows: Many cases with merit were originally denied at the local level. Many of those cases were denied at the local level without developing adequate records. And the claimants who had appeals without merit constituted only a small percentage of the total.

In the case of Irving Levin, the July 2007 decision of the VA's unique but little-known appellate court was the same one that could have been rendered on day one, more than seven thousand days earlier. If the guiding principles of the Department of Veterans Affairs were really about honoring and serving U.S. military veterans—"to care for him who shall have borne the battle"—then the decision to grant the claim of that army flight engineer who had borne the battle over Tokyo could have been made by one VA employee on the first day. And all the rest of those nineteen years of VA employee hours could have been spent reducing that huge VA claim backlog.

We know well that the human condition produces, in every life category, many who are deserving and some who are not. As the veteran population ages, we know that virtually all veterans develop new health problems, and there is no doubt that some try to claim their new illness or infirmity is service-related when in fact it is not. The challenge faced today by the Department of Veterans Affairs, the Congress, the president, and the public is to forge a systemwide cultural mind-set that will not reward the undeserving but will also not dishonor and disserve those who are genuinely deserving and in need.

6

Veterans at War at Home

DAV vs. DVA

We are dealing with veterans, not procedures—with their problems, not ours.

—GENERAL OMAR BRADLEY,
ADMINISTRATOR, VETERANS ADMINISTRATION, 1947

Washington in August is always sweltering, which is why official Washington rarely sticks around to endure it. Congress vacations, presidents do too. Those who have to stay on the job are not happy about it, so while they rarely wear ties, it doesn't take much for them to get hot under the collar. Sometimes things get so heated that hard truths are spoken in plain English (a rarity most other months in Washington). And that's what happened in August 2005, after David W. Gorman, the executive director of the Disabled American Veterans, read an official policy statement from the Department of Veterans Affairs undersecretary for benefits. He saw things that he couldn't let go unchallenged—he couldn't even let them wait until official Washington returned in September.

One of the things the undersecretary wrote seemed especially objectionable: a suggested rule change that could make it impossible for older veterans such as Irving Levin to ever file a late claim for benefits. The exchange of position papers between the VA undersecretary and the veterans' advocacy group executive shines a beacon on the mind-set of those who run the Department of Veterans Affairs and highlights the chasm that divides the leaders of the VA from the veterans they were hired to help.

The VA's undersecretary for benefits, retired vice admiral Daniel L. Cooper, had written a wide-ranging statement of policy positions and observations for the Veterans' Disability Benefits Commission, a panel created just a year earlier to study the problems with the VA benefits system. Cooper's thrust seemed to be that what was wrong was mainly the fault of others: the Congress, the advocates, the lawyers, and, yes, the veterans. To which Gorman responded with a fifteen-page letter of rebuke and rebuttal addressed to Cooper's boss, Veterans Affairs secretary Jim Nicholson, with copies to the Veterans' Disability Benefits Commission and to Cooper.

"The Undersecretary's statement included several disturbing views that can only be described as insulting to the men and women who have borne or are today bearing the extraordinary burdens of military service," Gorman wrote. The Disabled American Veterans, created after World War I, is one of the leading advocacy groups that stepped in to help veterans deal with the confusing thicket of rules and red tape at the VA. They provide legal advice and navigational advice for their members. Gorman added: "It is all the more objectionable that such attacks on the benefit program for disabled veterans came from the agency whose mission is to 'care for him who shall have borne the battle' . . . the statement has a poorly camouflaged self-serving focus leading to suggestions that are all adverse to veterans. . . . The statement [of the VA undersecretary] attempts to blame this predicament on Congress and veterans themselves and thus suggests changes that would accommodate VA's deficiencies by limiting veterans' entitlements and restricting their access to the system."

The undersecretary for benefits had acknowledged an increase in the backlog of claims and a decrease in timeliness of handling claims, saying this had happened despite VA reforms that had been reducing the time for ruling on veterans' benefit claims. Why had this happened? One of the reasons he gave was that older veterans were being allowed to file claims decades after leaving the service—which is just what the World War II B-29 flight engineer Irving Levin had done when problems apparently caused by his injuries worsened over the years. VA Undersecretary Cooper had told the Commission:

Today, there is no time limit for a veteran to submit an initial claim for disability compensation. He or she can be 18 or 85, have been on active duty for six months or 50 years, and can submit the claim immediately upon leaving the service or decades later. The major question which begs discussion is the effect of age and 'life habits,' over a period of time, on injuries and diseases. What effect does age alone have on health?

The DAV's Gorman countered:

To be entitled to service connection for a disability, the veteran's disability must have been incurred or aggravated during service in the Armed Forces. Once a disease or injury is service connected, subsequent manifestations or residuals are service connected except when attributable to intercurrent causes. Some degenerative and progressive conditions

worsen with age, but the effects of age alone are not a basis
for compensation. The veteran who files a claim at age 18
and immediately upon discharge will be compensated for the
level of disability present at age 85 if it worsens and he or she
seeks reevaluation. The veteran who first files a claim at age
85 will be compensated based upon the degree of disability
present at that time.

Thus the debate was joined between the submarine admiral
who became commander of VA benefits program and the Vietnam veteran who lost both legs in combat and became a leading
veterans' advocate. Neither was advocating compensation for
someone simply because they had once served in war and then
got old and infirm. "Effects of age alone are not a basis for compensation," Gorman had said, emphasizing that the problem
had to have occurred or been made worse during military service. But there was and still is a fundamental disagreement over
whether there should be a time limit on when a veteran can file
for disability. Gorman understood that such a time limit could
prevent some older veterans from ever getting the compensation
they deserved—if, for example, they fell into the category of Irving Levin, who didn't experience major problems from his crash
landing until years later.

The Disabled American Veterans was not the only veterans'
advocacy group to object to the idea of a time limit for filing
claims. In September, the American Legion, the Vietnam Veterans of America, the AMVETS, and the Military Coalition all
strongly objected as well.

Some of the undersecretary's points correctly identified a
problem, even if they missed the mark on workable and equitable solutions. For example, Cooper accurately focused on the

problem of the red tape that was clogging his department's pipelines:

The Disability Compensation Program is an extraordinarily complex, multifaceted, laborious, paperdominated, frequently-modified program which has a long history. Over the years it has had an uneven and frequently disconnected series of enhancements and additions. All the changes have had the single focus of helping veterans; but, as far as I can tell, no change has worked to make the process or the adjudication easier, quicker, or more consistent. . . . The incremental legislative process has had the effect of building an increasingly complex system.

Indeed, he was right in noting that Congress has micromanaged and further complicated a situation that desperately needed simplification. But he then cited as a problem a reform that was smart, simplifying, and streamlining. He wrote: "Our Disability Compensation Program recognizes over 110 diseases that are considered to be presumptively related to special conditions of military service." This referred to an effort by Congress to get the VA to stop trying to prove that an illness was definitely caused by a condition of combat (such as exposure to Agent Orange in Vietnam or chemical weapons in Iraq). Instead, Congress had directed that all the listed diseases should be presumed to have been contracted through direct exposure to a toxic agent during military service—if the member of the military was in the region where the toxin was used.

"Our experience is that presumptions make [the] adjudication process easier, quicker, and more consistent," Gorman wrote in criticizing the undersecretary's reasoning. "We understand that a VA Deputy Assistant General Counsel and the Chief of the Policy Staff of VA's Compensation and Pension Service both told the Commission that presumptions serve to 'simplify adjudications' by eliminating the need to gather evidence and decide complex issues. According to these VA experts, presumptions 'serve to fill evidentiary gaps in cases where it is infeasible or unduly burdensome to obtain direct evidence on an issue,' and they 'promote accuracy and consistency in agency adjudications.'"

One of the policies that Undersecretary Cooper took issue with was the "benefit of the doubt" concept that was pushed by Congress and was intended to stop the VA from making veterans prove that their problem was caused by a specific event during military service. At one point Cooper actually wrote: "We have stressed giving the 'benefit of the doubt' to the veteran, and every regional office has certainly attempted to do that." It is a statement that is flatly contradicted by the case histories of thousands of veterans.

Indeed, the undersecretary went on to cast doubt on his own statements about benefit of the doubt. He brought up concerns about the new policy that says that a Vietnam veteran who was exposed to herbicides in Vietnam and later develops diabetes shall be presumed to have a service-related disability. Cooper notes that diabetes can be caused by many other factors. Of course that is correct, but it misses the point. The presumption of service-related illness was created not to say that this is the *only* way such a thing could have happened, but to give fairness and justice at last to veterans in cases where a causal relationship could not be conclusively documented but did seem scientifically and medically plausible, and even probable.

At the VA, where officials are forever caught in a vise that consists of unyielding budgetary limitations and ever-expanding benefits claims that merit increased payments, there was a built-in inclination to resist benefit-of-the-doubt approaches. There was always a preference for time-consuming and even costly government claims appeals that could produce precedents that would eventually justify cutbacks in claims payments to veterans. The unstated theory was: claims denied mean dollars saved.

Cost effectiveness is rarely a path to fairness. But a benefit-of-the-doubt process can be just that. In the case of Agent Orange most veterans were not able to prove conclusively that they had been exposed to Agent Orange that had been dropped in a specific area at a specific time. They could not prove whether the herbicide remained on plants they later brushed against, or seeped into groundwater or streams in which they waded, or was mixed into the air they breathed. This benefit-of-the-doubt policy—and similar rules and proposals for contamination problems that arose in the subsequent wars in the Persian Gulf, Afghanistan, and Iraq—were never about saving time for the government and the veterans. These rulings were about providing fairness to veterans in cases where the United States had placed troops in situations that science and medicine later concluded were hazardous environments. The significance of this approach was that after years and sometimes decades of rejecting benefits claims of individual veterans on grounds of inadequate scientific and medical proof, the government recognized that the science had changed or been refined, and that individual veterans could not be expected to gather conclusive proof (indeed, scientific and medical experts could not always agree on what constituted sufficient proof). But when veterans had been placed in hazardous environments—and especially when unintended consequences of government actions had created this harm—the government should stop disputing, stop refuting, and start paying what it surely owed to large numbers of veterans.

The downside was that some veterans would indeed receive benefits for problems that perhaps were not caused by their military deployment. The upside was that many thousands of veterans would get benefits they were due but had been unfairly denied by the VA for decades.

Undersecretary Cooper still seemed to doubt the overarching good to this principle: "As public servants, we must also ensure our adjudicators, while treating each veteran fairly, are not pressured to make speedy decisions or to resolve [the] 'benefit of the doubt' prematurely, resulting in an award of benefits despite the lack of fully documented justification."

But the "lack of fully documented justification" is precisely what the benefit of the doubt is all about. "The benefit-of-the-doubt rule is a philosophical foundation of the adjudication process which the Undersecretary apparently finds questionable," the DAV's Gorman wrote.

The years since the attacks of September 11, 2001, have seen a sharp increase in the number of disability benefits claims submitted to the Veterans Benefits Administration. The VBA received 578,000 claims in 2000, 771,000 in 2004, and some 800,000 in 2005. Through that period, the Veterans Benefits Administration saw its budgeted number of full-time employees decrease in 2003 and in 2004.

President Bush's 2005 budget highlights stated that one of the VA's highest priorities was to "improve the timeliness and accuracy of claims processing." And the VA's budget submission made this promise: "As a Presidential initiative, improving the timeliness and accuracy of claims processing remains the Department's top priority associated with our benefit programs." The Bush administration's 2005 Veterans Benefits Administration budget requested 829 fewer full-time employees than were authorized at the end of the 2003 fiscal year; the figure was 540 fewer full-time employees than were authorized for fiscal 2004.

At the Disabled American Veterans, Gorman looked at the problem from the other end of the funnel, where the claims were being reviewed and decided in the heartland. "About two-thirds of our supervisors pointed specifically to overworked VA employees as a serious problem responsible for poor performance," Gorman wrote. "Associated with this inadequate adjudication staff were frequent comments that management pushed for production over quality and that there were timeliness problems in developing and deciding claims, as well as authorizing awards, and completing actions on appeals and remands." The VA's inspector general conducted a survey of VA adjudicators: 65 percent of respondents reported that the staff numbers they had were insufficient to provide quality service in a timely manner.

"The process can be improved, and veterans and taxpayers can be better served," said Gorman, "but the proper solution is not to penalize veterans for VA's mistakes. . . . Attempts to shift blame away from VA to Congress and veterans with the suggestion of changes for VA expedience or to save on Federal spending should greatly concern all citizens who place a high value on the contributions and sacrifices of our veterans. It should concern those dedicated VA employees who understand and appreciate the reasons for the programs. This statement by the Undersecretary begrudges veterans for what they are entitled to and grumbles about everything we do for veterans. . . . We are compelled to strongly oppose such self-serving suggestions and condemn such disdain for America's disabled veterans."

Gorman's message was hard-hitting and in the tradition of his organization. In 1998, the then national commander of the DAV, Harry R. McDonald Jr., saw a nation that was turning away from the needs of its veterans. In a message to fellow members, McDonald wrote: "I used to believe that veterans could be secure in the knowledge that a grateful nation would always be willing to take care of the needs of its defenders of democracy. But time is proving me wrong. Veterans can no longer be assured that this government will fulfill its promises to them."

It is a sad state of affairs when the leader of a national organization of veterans who were disabled in the service of their country would ever feel compelled to make such a statement about his nation's government. It is far sadder to realize that, in the years since, he has repeatedly been proven right.

7

The Mystery Caller

VA Help Lines Are Often Helpless,
Hapless, Hopeless

MYSTERY CALLER: My father served in Vietnam in 1961 and 1962. Is there a way he can find out if he was exposed to Agent Orange?

VA SERVICE REP: He should know if they were spreading that chemical out then. He would be the only one to know. OK. (*Hangs up laughing*).

In 2002, and then again in 2004, the Mystery Caller dialed the VA help line 1,089 times. The Mystery Caller was indeed a mystery to the Veterans Service Representatives at fifty-seven VA regional offices whose job it is to answer the telephone and serve as the first and perhaps only live human contact a veteran may have with the federal department that is officially supposed to care for his or her best interests. But the Mystery Caller was no mystery to the VA's top brass.

The "Mystery Caller Telephone Service Quality Assessment" study of 2002 and a follow-up study of 2004 were part of the VA's effort to see how it is doing in fulfilling its mission statement: "Our goal is to provide excellence in patient care, veterans' benefits and customer satisfaction. . . . Our department's employees continue to offer their dedication and commitment to help veterans get the services they have earned. Our nation's veterans deserve no less."

What the VA's own in-house study showed was that, far too often, the veterans are getting much less.

The VA's trained Veterans Service Reps gave the callers "completely incorrect" information 22 percent of the time and "minimally correct" answers 23 percent of the time. They gave "completely correct" answers just 19 percent of the time and "mostly correct" answers 16 percent of the time. Their answers were "partially correct" 20 percent of the time.

On the example of the Mystery Caller who was ostensibly seeking information about whether his father had been exposed to Agent Orange in Vietnam, the VA's evaluation noted that the service representative had been "completely incorrect (gave no information)" and was also "rude and unprofessional."

MYSTERY CALLER: My grandfather is a Korean War veteran who was injured in Korea. When he dies, is he eligible for burial in Arlington National Cemetery?

VA SERVICE REP: I can't answer for Arlington. You can call your congressman. They love doing those kinds of things for their constituents.

VA'S EVALUATION: Completely incorrect (didn't provide the information). Unprofessional; unwilling to help

This brings up another crucial result of the Mystery Caller study. The VA's critics frequently claim that the department is standing still, failing to make the progress it needs to make. But that criticism is not entirely true. The Mystery Caller follow-up study showed that in this area the VA had not stood still at all— it had gotten considerably worse in a number of key areas. A major finding of the 2004 study's Executive Summary stated that "conveying the willingness to help declined significantly from 92 percent in 2002 to 78 percent in this study."

The Veterans Service Representatives' ratings also declined significantly for categories of courtesy, professionalism, and prompt service. Favorable ratings in those categories were listed at 90 percent, which was judged "down significantly from 97 percent in 2002."

MYSTERY CALLER: My brother is being discharged in 2 weeks from the Marine Corps. Are there any veterans' preferences for State or Federal jobs?

VA SERVICE REP: No preference. Everyone is a veteran. With government, you get points if you're a veteran. For a disabled veteran, there's points. Nothing out of the ordinary.

VA'S EVALUATION: Completely incorrect (wrong information). Tone discourteous; unwilling to help

A VA effort to improve its unacceptable 2002 Mystery Caller scores produced results that merit no bureaucratic bragging: 22 percent of the answers given were completely wrong in both 2002 and 2004. Some at the VA might find reason to boast about a sliver of improvement: While only 5 percent of the answers were completely correct in 2002, the completely correct rate improved to 19 percent in 2004. But think about that: The fact that only 19 percent of the VA's help line answers were completely correct is nothing to brag about; the theory of help lines is that *all* of the answers should be completely correct. The rate of mostly correct answers improved just a bit, from 10 percent in 2002 to 16 percent in 2004. But again, think about what that means: in 2004, after the VA spent two years trying to improve its accuracy, the percentage of veterans receiving completely accurate or mostly accurate answers totaled only 35 percent—an abysmal figure. Put another way, the percentage of veterans who telephoned a veterans service representative in need of help in 2004 and received answers that were completely wrong or mostly wrong was a combined total of 43 percent—which is unacceptable. The study reported:

RESULTS	2002	2004
Completely Correct	5%	19%
Mostly Correct	10%	16%
Partially Correct	29%	20%
Minimally Correct	34%	23%
Completely Incorrect	22%	22%

MYSTERY CALLER: My son served in Vietnam, and he just died of lung cancer. I have custody of his 10-year-old daughter. Are there any benefits for my granddaughter?

VA SERVICE REP: Are you claiming his cause of death is due to service? If you can prove the cause of death is service-connected, we can pay DIC. We would need his medical history from the time of his discharge to his death. Do you know his medical history? *(Mystery caller said: He died of lung cancer.)* That's not one of the conditions related to Agent Orange.

VA'S EVALUATION: Completely incorrect (wrong information given—lung cancer *is* one of the conditions related to Agent Orange; also didn't explain what DIC is. It stands for "Dependency and Indemnity Compensation"). Didn't express empathy in recent loss of son.

On October 14, 2004, Undersecretary Cooper sent a memo to the VA's fifty-seven regional offices and attached to it the 2004 Mystery Caller Telephone Service Quality Assessment Follow-up Study. Cooper wrote that all regional offices (ROs) were required to conduct local telephone quality reviews by silent monitoring of the service representatives. "Not all ROs are in compliance," he wrote. "In July, there were five stations that had not conducted any silent monitoring in FY 2004 and eight stations that consistently reported 100 percent accuracy. As of July, the national average accuracy rate reported by ROs through local silent monitoring was 94 percent for FY 2004. This is not consistent with the accuracy rate found during the national 'mystery call' findings (22 percent completely inaccurate responses)."

Time out. Not consistent? Eight of the regional offices said they had monitored and reported that their service reps were 100 percent accurate—and *all* of the regional offices found their service reps were 94 percent accurate. That is so far off from the results of the Mystery Caller study that it seems as though the heartland was trying to con the headquarters. Did the regional offices only monitor top-flight service reps so that they could report excellent ratings? And why would the VA tolerate that five of the regionals in effect told their bosses in Washington to stick their silent monitoring edict in their ears?

MYSTERY CALLER: My dad was killed in a training accident while on active duty just before Desert Storm. Does the VA offer any benefits for me to go to college?

VA SERVICE REP: Was your mother in receipt of benefits from the VA? Was she married to your father? *(Mystery caller said: yes.)* Your mother was not in receipt of benefits? *(Mystery caller said: no.)* Did your father die on active duty? *(Mystery caller said: he did.)* And your mother wasn't getting benefits? Well, if your mother was in receipt of benefits, you would be eligible. But you're telling me that your mother was not in receipt, so you are not entitled.

VA'S EVALUATION: Completely incorrect (he would be entitled if his father died on active duty). Tone was discourteous.

Cooper is a former navy admiral, and yet, considering the poor results of the study, the lackadaisical attitude in some regional offices that went to the brink of insubordination, and a possible attempt to submit inaccurate information, the tone of his memo was remarkably restrained. The memo administered a gentle lashing to the regionals. "The results of the 2004 study are below expectations and are disappointing to the organization," Cooper wrote. "Of special concern is that the excellent and very good responses declined for courtesy and professionalism (from 81 to 69 percent) and for willingness to help (from 76 to 62 percent). Significant improvement, however, was made in prompt service (from 76 to 87 percent). We must be able to provide prompt service and give correct answers with the courtesy and professionalism that our customers deserve."

MYSTERY CALLER: My son hurt his back while he was in the service. I think he is receiving disability benefits for this, but he needs help. He can't do construction work like he used to do before he went in the service. Can you help?

VA SERVICE REP: He can file for an increase. *(Mystery caller indicated that the veteran only knew construction work, and that he had to lie down all evening after returning home from work.)* Yes, uh-huh, well, he can file for an increase.

VA'S EVALUATION: Completely incorrect (didn't answer the question). Unprofessional and discourteous.

Part of what is so astonishing about those low scores is that the VA has set up a structure for training these Veterans Service Representatives. They have public contact team (PCT) coaches and a long list of training materials. Cooper wrote:

There are many training tools available to Public Contact Team coaches for use in training VSRs. The following are some of these tools:

- *VA Pamphlet 80-04-01,* Federal Benefits for Veterans and Dependents, *can be used as a basic training tool for new VA employees and for refresher training.*
- *ADVISOR is a computer-based training program that covers the eight major benefit programs administered by the Department of Veterans Affairs and is readily available on line. Each benefit module includes information on eligibility requirements, application procedures and*

processing, and rates of payment. Scenarios are included as part of the learning process. ADVISOR also features a 'Training Mode of Operation,' which allows participants to keep a record of lesson assessments. Information from individual participant disks can be compiled and used to determine PCT training needs. ADVISOR is available through the Internet and Intranet.

- *Twelve videotapes were sent to each RO in August 2004 for training of employees assigned to the PCT. Eight of the 12 videotapes cover the Education, Vocational Rehabilitation and Employment, Loan Guaranty, and Insurance programs. These tapes can be used to train new employees or for refresher training. There are two tapes for each program. The first tape addresses the overall program, and the second tape includes frequently asked questions and the threshold for transferring calls to the appropriate toll-free number. The four remaining tapes are overviews of the National Cemetery Administration and the Veterans Health Administration benefits and services.*
- *The Compensation and Pension Service Training web page contains the Core Training Curriculum for the Claims Processing Initiative (CPI) Model and includes lesson plans, handouts, and PowerPoint slides for the PCT.*

MYSTERY CALLER: My son served in Vietnam, and he just died of lung cancer. I have custody of his 10-year-old daughter. Are there any benefits for my granddaughter?

VA SERVICE REP: What is your son's Social Security number? *(Mystery caller said: I don't have it.)* Well, I can't help you if you don't give me any information. I can send you an application for benefits, or you can download it from the computer. You can try for benefits. But you say you are now the child's custodian? Well, your income is going to count. What is your monthly income?

MYSTERY CALLER: About $200 a week.

VA SERVICE REP: Well, that sounds like it is awful high, and you wouldn't be eligible.

VA'S EVALUATION: Completely incorrect (didn't address possible DIC—only pension). Very discouraging; didn't express empathy in recent loss of son

. . .

MYSTERY CALLER: My husband just started going to college using the Voc-Rehab program, and I was just wondering how long he has to use this program.

VA SERVICE REP: I don't know. He needs to ask his vocational rehabilitation counselor the next time he talks with him.

VA'S EVALUATION: Completely incorrect (didn't answer the question). Unprofessional and discourteous

. . .

MYSTERY CALLER: My sister's husband served in Vietnam, and their youngest child (age 15) has spina bifida. Is there anything VA can do for them?

VA SERVICE REP: Hang on just a second, and I'll get you to the spina bifida coordinator. Hold on a second. OK, ma'am, hang on a second. Let me track down that phone number. OK, ma'am, guess he's out to lunch. They would have to prove he was in Vietnam and in the area where Agent

Orange was sprayed. I'm not sure how they go about doing that. That's why I wanted you to talk to him. You can either call back after lunch, or I can leave a voice mail and ask him to call back.

VA'S EVALUATION: Completely incorrect (didn't offer any information). Showed unwillingness to help.

• • •

MYSTERY CALLER: My husband served in the National Guard from the late sixties until 1986. He has had a bad back for years, but now it's so bad he can't work. Can he get any help from VA?

VA SERVICE REP: I don't know. He just has to file a claim. (Mystery caller asked: He just has to file a claim?) That's right. He just has to file a claim.

VA'S EVALUATION: Completely incorrect (didn't give answer). Discourteous; unwilling to help.

The results of those two Mystery Caller studies may well point the VA toward a solution that is far different from the one the officials who designed the Mystery Caller survey thought they were targeting. Clearly, the survey designers set out to measure how well the Veterans Service Reps had mastered the complexities of the VA's regulations—and whether the service reps could adequately help the military veterans who of course could not possibly be expected to figure out on their own what they had to do at the VA to get the basic benefits they had earned serving their country.

Perhaps the solution is not to get brainier service reps who can navigate the VA's labyrinthine rules and regulations. What seems clearly needed is a total revamping of the VA rules—a new set of regulations and procedures that will be so clear that even a VA help desk rep can understand them. And in the process, perhaps it is not naïvely utopian to suggest that the new and improved VA rules and procedures be made so straightforward that they could actually be understood by the customers the VA is in business to serve—America's military veterans.

8

A Government History of VA Failures

Decades of Reports About Delays

At the top of the photostat of the old government report there is a printed title: "The Veterans Administration Can Reduce the Time Required to Process Veterans' and Survivors' Initial Claims for Benefits." In the margin just above that, there is an ink-stamped warning: "Restricted—Not to be released outside the General Accounting Office except on the . . . [this part is faded and illegible] specific approval by the Office of Congressional Information." And also on the front page—so that no official reader whose days are hurried could possibly miss it—there is this tight two-paragraph summary of the major conclusions in this forty-page report:

Veterans and their survivors making their initial claims for compensation and pension generally wait months while VA processes their claims. Most of the waiting time occurs while VA obtains additional evidence necessary to properly adjudicate the claims. Some of the data needed is not within VA's control.

> *VA has acted to speed up the claims processing system by developing an advanced computer system to modernize the process. However, more needs to be done to improve processing time, and this report contains recommendations to accomplish this.*

What is important and even infuriating about this analysis and the recommendations contained in the report by the General Accounting Office, the official congressional investigating agency, is not its message about what is wrong with the VA and how to fix it. What is so noteworthy is that this report was written in 1978, and during the more than quarter century that followed, the GAO would revisit, year after year, the same VA problems, reach the same conclusions, and recommend the same solutions. And still the VA would never find the way to right what was wrong.

Today that old GAO photostat and all of the GAO reports that followed are no longer treated as confidential; they are posted on the official GAO Web site.

The date on that old GAO report was December 27, 1978. Perhaps because this was the Christmas-to-New-Year week when nothing harsh happens, the wording of this report was mild; a gently gift-wrapped present to VA officials, a package of findings and solutions. The central conclusion was that military veterans had to wait "months" after making claims before they would get any word back from the VA on whether they would get the benefits they felt they deserved. One "bottleneck" was identified as the delay in processing the physical examinations of veterans, a prerequisite to decisions on whether to award or deny veterans' claims. Here the GAO found that the Veterans Administration was on the case. A new wonder machine, the computer, would soon be operating an "advanced" target system that would "modernize" the claims process. So not to worry.

More than a quarter century and a million or so GAO report words later, it is time to worry. Computers have come and the systems they serve have been refined and then replaced, but as the reports churned out by the GAO have shown, the problems at the VA have just gotten worse. It didn't take long for the GAO to lose the gift wrapping and the gentle words; in time the warnings were blunt and urgent. A common theme ran through these reports: delays. Delays in processing claims, delays in medical treatment, delays in case appeals, delays in paying benefits.

This is not to say there were no changes. The Veterans Administration changed its name to the Department of Veterans Affairs and the General Accounting Office changed its name to the Government Accountability Office. But those were the sort of changes that only officials who plod on the Washington treadmill care about; change the names (carefully pleasing the city of acronyms by keeping the initials the same) and call it progress. But out there at the other end of the funnel, the veterans mainly saw no change at all. Well, that's not quite right. They saw things change from bad to worse.

As we thumb through those reports in this chapter, there is one thing we need to keep reminding ourselves: each of these reports was read at the time it was issued by legions of government officials who could have made a difference but did not. Officials at the VA read them and mainly tried to rationalize their way out of implementing them. Officials at the Office of Management and Budget read them and then continued to short-sheet the VA budget, year after year, administration after administration, Democrat and Republican alike. Officials at the White House, under every president, may have reviewed them but most likely asked underlings to skim them and point out anything that might be political trouble. And if potential political trouble was discovered, someone in the administration would be tasked (that is a government term of art) to draft a letter to veterans' groups assuring them that veterans were indeed a top priority. Then on budget day the veterans would see that, once again, those promises seemed to be written in disappearing ink. And at the other end of Pennsylvania Avenue, up on Capitol Hill, members of the Senate and House Committees on Veterans' Affairs would read these GAO reports closely (after all, they had requested them) and then hold hearings—years of hearings, decades of hearings. But throughout this time, Congress, which holds the purse strings, just fiddled with the fringes while failing to solve the problems or demanding that they be solved by a succession of VA, Pentagon, and budget officials. And presidents.

As we read through this long string of VA failures, the sameness of each investigative report—the same problems and often the same words—becomes both numbing and infuriating. Keep in mind that through all the decades that veterans' claims were being delayed and denied, every top official at the VA was getting his or her paycheck in a timely fashion. And so was every budget bender at the OMB, every political accommodator at every White House, every buck-passer in the bureaucracy, and every windmill on Capitol Hill. They all got paid promptly and grandly. The only ones who didn't get the money they were due were the men and women who went to war and fought our battles so the rest of us could enjoy life at home.

The 1978 GAO report said that the VA's average delay for processing disability compensation claims was 147 days; and for processing death pension claims, 80 days. When benefits were due it would take an additional 25 days to pay them. This was considered unacceptable, so the GAO analysts presented a series of blue-sky recommendations.

*Claim processing delays can be held to a minimum if VA re-
gional offices do the following where appropriate:*

- *Set goals for expeditiously requesting evidence required
  from other sources.*
- *Assess more thoroughly, early in the process, the income
  information submitted by pension claimants to minimize unnecessary delays resulting from piecemeal requests for evidence.*
- *Reassign claims processing workloads to balance the
  work and thereby alleviate backlogs.*
- *Follow up more aggressively on requests for medical information from VA medical facilities to preclude unduly
  long delays.*

The GAO found that claims processing was often delayed at
regional VA offices because the paperwork from VA hospitals arrived late and sometimes was lost. So it made one other recommendation that seems so mild and so obvious that it should have
been instantly implemented.

*VA hospitals also can minimize delays in the claims process
by initiating appropriate supervisory controls to ensure that
medical summaries on claimants treated in those hospitals
are furnished promptly to VA regional offices.*

Yet decades later, similar complaints would be sounded and
similar recommendations would be made.

In 1982, the GAO took the rather unusual step of working
with VA officials and proposing a series of ways in which the VA
could vastly speed up claims processing and cut costs at the

same time. The report, dated July 13, 1982, made two recommendations that could save the VA an estimated $7 million a year. One was a straightforward proposal to eliminate 100 of the 117 VA section chief positions, assigning their duties to other officials. That would save an estimated $3.7 million. But by far the most interesting proposal in the GAO list was a suggestion that the VA should end its policy of reviewing each and every veteran's claim for service-related benefits; instead, it should review 75 percent of them.

"Reducing claims authorizations by using statistical sampling at a 75 percent level could save about $3.4 million," the GAO said in a report sent not to Congress but to the VA. "Authorizing claims on a sample basis could save both calendar and "hands-on" time and free senior adjudicators to perform other processing functions. The Veterans Administration (VA) has about 526 senior adjudicators who authorize (review and approve someone else's decision) all compensation, pension, burial, and initial education claims."

The idea was that the VA would approve the 25 percent of the claims that were never reviewed. GAO analysts said that by reviewing fewer cases, the VA senior adjudicators would reduce their rate of errors. The proposal would also cut the costly and time-consuming number of cases that were reversed by appeals. "Private industry has long recognized that even examining 100 percent of the items produced does not guarantee a l00 percent perfect product," the GAO told the VA.

The idea made sense from a business time-and-motion management perspective, but it ran contrary to the mind-set of the VA. It was never implemented. (A quarter of a century later, with the VA's problems having grown far worse and no workable solution being implemented, the proposal would be revived, modified, and made anew, in 2007 by a professor from Harvard

University, Linda Bilmes. This time, as we will see later, it would receive considerable attention and a good bit of acclaim—including from the Congress that had paid little attention to the idea when it was explored twenty-five years earlier by the Congress's own GAO.)

In June 1986, the GAO delivered to Congress a good-news report titled "VA Disability Benefits: Timely Delivery of Military Service Medical Records to VA." This report stood in stark contrast to others made by the same agency both earlier and later, because the GAO found things at the VA were going well. How did the GAO analysts know? The VA told them so.

One key finding was the assertion that delays had dwindled. "In doing our work between November 1985 and March 1986, we generally found that although there were large backlogs of requests in 1984, VA currently obtains service medical records from military records centers in a timely manner," the GAO reported. "Of its 1985 total of over 95,000 initial disability claims, VA identified 658 requests in process as of November 1985 for service medical records that had not been answered within 6 months and were still pending. This number represents only a small fraction of VA's total annual requests for these types of records. Veterans' service organizations also reported that few disability compensation claims were currently delayed because service medical records were not provided in a timely manner."

The investigators took this good news on faith and didn't bother to investigate further. According to their report: "In doing our work, we relied on data provided by VA to establish the extent of untimely delivery of service medical records. We did not verify the accuracy of the data."

In May 1990, the GAO showed that it had learned a lesson: verify all statistics independently before painting a by-the-numbers rosy picture of the VA. And what these investigators

found were significant delays in the processing of veterans'
claims:

> *In fiscal year 1989, veterans waited a reported 463 days on*
> *average for a Board decision—an increase of 44 days, or*
> *11 percent, over 1988. Untimely appeals can delay finan-*
> *cial, medical, and other benefits to which veterans are*
> *entitled. . . . GAO concentrated on appeals relating to dis-*
> *ability claims because they represent about 82 percent of*
> *all veterans' appeals.*

Moreover, the GAO found that statistics provided by the VA
proved too good to be true—and said so in language that was especially (and necessarily) blunt.

> *The time VA reported to process cases decided by the*
> *Board of Veterans' Appeals was understated. VA did not*
> *include time spent by the regional offices on appeals the*
> *Board returned to them for additional development. The*
> *regional offices spent an average of 282 additional days on*
> *about 5,500 cases that they returned to the Board for a fi-*
> *nal decision in fiscal year 1988. If included, this time*
> *would have increased the fiscal year 1988 average pro-*
> *cessing time from 419 to 457 days. Thus, VA management,*
> *the Congress, and others who use the data have an inac-*
> *curate perception of how long veterans actually wait for*
> *decisions. VA does not gather data nor report the time*
> *spent on appeals resolved in the regional offices—about*
> *45 percent of all appeals. Thus, VA management has no*
> *basis for accurately determining how promptly such ap-*
> *peals are resolved.*

The GAO investigators went beyond the numbers and took note of the human impact of the VA's delays on the lives of individual veterans.

If VA's appeals process takes too long, veterans wait unnecessarily for what could be a key decision in their lives. For example, whether they receive VA benefits could affect their need to pursue alternative sources of income. The Congress, VA, veterans, and service organizations have all expressed concern about the time the VA appeals process takes.

This was a new era for the VA. It had become a full-fledged cabinet-level department the previous year, but it appeared that it was the GAO that had matured the most. The GAO analysts did the VA the favor of taking a new hard look at not just the VA's statistics but the department's assertions that it was fixing what had been wrong before. They found that the VA had problems that led to the delays and growing backlog of claims. And they found that the VA hadn't figured out what its problem was, let alone how to fix it.

Improved management could reduce appeal processing time. In 1988, the average processing time for appeals decided by the Board was 419 days. Some of the processing time is out of VA's control, for example, time taken by veterans to respond to information requests. GAO, however, identified some avoidable delays. Further, significant variations in regional office processing times, combined with a variety of management weaknesses GAO found, indicate that VA could better manage the process and thus improve service to veterans.

VA has not identified the reasons for delays in the appeals process, nor the reasons for the wide variations in processing times among regional offices. It lacked data to identify systemic problems and to identify regional differences. Other management weaknesses that contribute to lengthy processing times included (1) a lack of time standards to measure performance, (2) ineffective guidance and oversight, and (3) a failure to correct known problems. Moreover, VA does not accurately report the time for the appeals process, resulting in a lack of accurate oversight data not only for VA but for the Congress as well. By improving management, VA can improve the time it takes to process appeals and the accuracy of reporting without adversely affecting the quality of decisions.

Under the heading, "VA Does Not Effectively Manage Appeals," this team of hard-hitting GAO analysts reported:

VA needs to better manage the appeals process. Currently VA lacks (1) the necessary data on the regional offices' appeals processing to identify innovative practices or systemic problems to develop corrective action, (2) adequate time standards to provide incentives for regional offices to identify and avoid delays and to promote more uniformity in processing times, (3) effective guidance and oversight of the regional offices, thus some offices established procedures that lengthened the process and some circumvented VA requirements to reduce their reported processing times, and (4) a focal point to ensure that the units involved cooperate to effectively process appeals, so that processing and reporting problems can be resolved promptly.

The GAO investigators also did what the VA could have and should have done for itself at the outset—just look for the points in the system where the delays occur, then require those responsible for causing the delays to mend their ways immediately.

The investigators found three areas where the VA had major delays that seemed fixable. The first involved a regional office that took half a year to answer a veteran's written notice of disagreement with an initial claim denial:

For example, one regional office received a veteran's notice of disagreement on January 13, 1987, but it did not send the statement of the case until July 15, 1987, 183 days later. Regional officials attributed this delay to ineffective case control and inadequate follow-up by the supervisor on a pending case. In another case, a regional office received a medical report, needed to complete the statement, on October 5, 1988, but the statement was not sent until December 22, 1988, 78 days later. Regional officials could not explain the reason for this delay.

The second category of delays that were avoidable involved requests for medical data:

We identified 28 cases, involving 4 of the 6 regional offices, in which the offices took more than 30 days either to request medical data or to use the data once it was received. The processing times for 25 of these cases ranged from 40 to 155 days, and 3 took 225 days or more. In one example, BVA returned a case to a regional office on June 5, 1986, for a special medical examination at a VA medical center. The regional office waited, however, until April 7, 1987, about

306 days, to request the examination. In another example, on November 17, 1986, a regional office determined from a veteran's medical records that the veteran needed a physical examination, but it was not requested until January 28, 1987, 72 days later. Regional officials said these examinations should have been requested much sooner, but they could not explain the reasons for the delays.

The third category of delays that the VA should have easily fixed concerned simply forwarding a veteran's detailed appeal to the Board of Veterans' Appeals. Shockingly, the VA had no standards for what constituted a timely referral and what was to be an unacceptable delay.

VA had no time standards for this step, so we allowed 30 days. We found 14 such cases, involving 4 of the 6 regional offices, in which the offices took more than 30 days to complete this process. The processing times for 12 of these cases ranged from 42 to 134 days, and 2 took 171 days or more. For example, a regional office received one veteran's substantive appeal on October 14, 1987, but the office waited 85 days to request comments from the veteran's service organization, which were required before the office sent the case to BVA. In another case, after the veteran's substantive appeal was received, the office took 77 days to request that the veteran's service organization review the case. Regional officials could not explain the reasons for these delays.

Notice that all three examples ended with VA officials admitting they could not explain the reason for the delays. That of course is because they had not bothered to look for the problems on their own. After all, they had no financial incentive to do so. In these reports, there is never a mention of what, if any, corrective action was taken toward the VA individuals responsible for causing or countenancing these delays. But what if the VA officials and case adjudicators were all paid as most small business proprietors are—they get their money when the customer's order is fulfilled? These delays might dwindle and probably disappear.

The GAO investigators also found that in the Veterans Benefits Administration, the number of veterans submitting claims had remained relatively constant—but the backlog of undecided claims had increased significantly. "The anticipation of judicial review, the officials added, has also resulted in more thorough reviews by BVA board sections, increasing the time spent on each case," the GAO reported. In the years that followed, the degree of judicial review would become further institutionalized, as the U.S. Court of Appeals for Veterans Claims would be created. But the mission and mind-set of the VA would remain the same. Claims reviewers and adjudicators seemed to operate with the assumption that their job was to deny whenever possible and approve only when veterans proved an airtight case. Of course, the only cases that ever reached the court of appeals were those that the VA denied. Thus, the VA's de facto assumptions and the Damoclean sword of judicial review combined to create a self-fulfilling process of delay and an ever-lengthening backlog.

And through all of this, the only ones who paid a price—in the form of income delayed, as life's expenses mounted—were those who had already paid a price in fighting their nation's wars.

None of this was a secret within the VA. Officials there knew of the problems but failed to fix them. In 1994, VA Secretary Jesse

Brown was quoted in the *Atlanta Constitution* as saying that the claims backlog "remains one of the foremost concerns of the VA's Veterans Benefits Administration." Unlike some VA heads who preceded him and followed him, Brown did not sound an optimistic refrain. He said that because claims are getting more complex and legal requirements more demanding, he was predicting that even fewer claims would be processed in the future.

Clearly, it was time for a drastic revamping of the VA's claims system. But that was not happening, nor would it.

By 1995 veterans were enduring long waits for the VA to rule on their claims for benefits and pensions—far longer if they appealed the VA's initial decision. Some four hundred thousand veterans were appealing their initial denials by the VA each year; they could expect to wait more than two years before their claims were decided.

In fiscal 1994, four hundred veterans died while awaiting a final VA decision, the GAO reported in September 1995. In a report entitled, "Veterans' Benefits: Effective Interaction Needed Within VA to Address Appeals Backlog," the GAO investigators told Congress about a VA that was failing to address its appeals problems and warned that things would likely get worse. The GAO report sounded once again what had become the a frequent refrain:

VA's appeals process is increasingly bogged down, and the outlook for the future is not bright. The act [1988 Veterans Judicial Review Act that created a Veterans Court of Appeals] and Court rulings expanded veterans' rights but also expanded VA's adjudication responsibilities. VA is having difficulty integrating these responsibilities into its already complex and unwieldy adjudication process. Since 1991, the number of appeals awaiting Board action has increased

*by 175 percent and average processing time has increased
by over 50 percent.*

Veterans going through the VA's claims decision and appeal process might well feel as if they had been made to run up and down a staircase. A veteran files a claim for service-related benefits at the VA regional office. A regional VA staff member assembles all relevant military service and medical records and decides whether to grant or deny the claim. If the veteran is denied and disagrees, the regional office may reconsider the case or may issue reasons for continuing to deny the claim. Then a veteran can file an appeal and the same regional office will again reconsider it and, if the denial still stands, forward the case to the VA Board of Appeals. The board can then decide the case or, as often happens, remand it back to the regional office with instructions for new considerations. And thus the case can go up and down and back up again. If the board of appeals then denies the veteran's claim, the veteran can appeal that decision to the court of appeals, an independent body not part of the VA. That court can remand the case back to the board (which can send it down to the region yet again) or can satisfy the appellate court's objections. The court of appeals will then issue a ruling. And if the court of appeals approves the veteran's original claim, the system will have wasted vast sums of employee hours as well as the veteran's time and money. The board reported that the cost per case had grown from $400 in 1990 to $1,250 by 1994.

*Over 47,000 appeals were awaiting decisions at the end of
1994, and this backlog is likely to increase. . . . Even more
alarming, almost one-half of the [Board of Veterans' Appeals] decisions are not final; they are decisions to remand
the claim back to the [Veterans Affairs Regional Office].*

Based on recent history, VAROs will again deny three-fourths of these claims and return them to the Board for action.

In other words, after all of those months, or even years, the case would be again denied—which means it would again be appealed, unless the veteran just gives up in disgust. So it was that the VA was functioning in the most wasteful, least productive way imaginable—and also treating veterans in the most degrading and dishonoring way. It was doing nothing to fix what was wrong—except to make excuses and blame the Congress and the courts for its problems. Shockingly, what the VA seemed to object to most of all were the provisions that required it to assist veterans in filing claims. It should not have been necessary for Congress to make such a mandate, since the reason the department was created in the first place—to help veterans get the benefits they were due, not reject them.

VA attributes much of its claims processing difficulties to increased responsibilities placed on it by the 1988 act and Court decisions, particularly the need to explain the "reasons and bases" for decisions and to meet VA's "duty to assist" the veteran in filing and proving a claim. VA officials also said that the act and Court decisions have placed greater emphasis on procedures, resulting in remands for failure to follow technical procedures even though the final outcome was not expected to change.

GAO found evidence that VA organizations are not effectively identifying and resolving intra-agency impediments to efficient claims processing. GAO's limited review identified several instances in which VBA policies and practices were inconsistent with Board decisions. . . . If

VBA and VHA policies and practices are not consistent with Board decisions, the likelihood that the Board will remand claims increases.

Investigators noted that in 1990, the GAO had made a number of recommendations. "Although VA agreed to implement each of these recommendations, it did not do so," the GAO noted. That said, the intrepid investigators tried again: "GAO recommends that the Secretary of Veterans Affairs designate an official to direct efforts to identify and resolve intra-agency impediments to efficient processing of veterans' compensation and pension claims and appeals." The report then noted that the VA had again agreed and had promised to implement the recommendation. But, burned before, the GAO analysts were less sanguine that the VA would keep its word.

The VA had developed a convenient habit of telling investigators what they wanted to hear—then not being able to back up its assertions with real accomplishments. The GAO analysts recounted one such meeting: "In a meeting on August 15, 1995, VA officials concurred with GAO's recommendation and said that the Deputy Secretary sees the identification and resolution of impediments to efficient claims and appeals processing as his responsibility. They said that actions to ensure identification and resolution of problems have been suggested in many past studies and that many of these ideas have been or will be implemented. Officials, however, did not identify any specific planned actions."

The millennium saw the VA succeeding in what might charitably be described as a pursuit of nostalgia. It brought upon itself the same old complaints by veterans and their advocacy groups, triggering the same old investigations by the GAO and occasionally the news media, into the same old topics that featured one word: delays. There were delays in processing veterans' claims,

and delays at every stage of the appeals process that followed instances in which veterans believed they had gotten a raw deal
when their initial claims were denied by low-level VA adjudicators. Veterans who were counting on benefits they were sure they
deserved—money they needed to make ends meet—were forced
to wait half a year, a year, often years and sometimes even a decade or more while their claims were bounced up and down between the initial adjudicators and the Board of Veterans' Appeals.
Their cases would be sent back because the original review was
considered incomplete or the original decision was ruled to be in
error; then these claims would often be denied anew on the same
or other grounds and the process of appeal and delay would begin again. Sometimes after cases were denied at the level of the
Board of Veterans' Appeals they would be bounced still higher,
to a U.S. Court of Appeals for Veterans Claims, where they
would be remanded back down all the way to the original adjudicators with specific instructions to consider evidence that the
government had earlier brushed aside.

All this created a cottage industry of sorts for the Government Accountability Office, which was called upon year after
year (mainly by members of the Senate and House Veterans' Affairs committees) to investigate once more what was wrong at
the VA.

By 2001, complaints about the VA's backlog of initial claims
and appeals were being widely reported (but rarely prominently
played; the stories were usually buried on inside pages of newspapers, beside those ads about storm doors and chain-link
fences). Veterans who thought they would be getting a VA check
for service-related benefits were now learning that their appeals
might outlive them.

Against this backdrop in 2001, President George W. Bush's
new VA secretary, Anthony Principi, told the House Veterans'

Affairs Committee that getting rid of the claims backlog was "one of my top priorities."

The increasing number of errors made by the VA's initial claims adjudicators—and the lengthy delays in the appeals that followed—was cited as a central cause of the VA logjam in a March 16, 2001, article by *The Washington Post*'s respected national correspondent, Edward Walsh. The article noted that VA regional offices too often processed the claims improperly and issued denials based on errors or faulty judgment. This led veterans to appeal their cases, dragging out for years what could have been a simple decision. And every time the VA attempted to speed its claims decision process, it often compounded the problem it was attempting to solve.

Veterans advocates complained that the incentives for good work by VA bureaucrats at all levels were seriously skewed. "They get rewarded on how much paper they move, but never mind whether it's accurate," Richard F. Weidman, the director of government relations with Vietnam Veterans of America, told *The Washington Post*. "So it comes to the [veterans'] court of appeals and gets kicked back. They have to deal with those claims first, so the backlog grows. The managers and supervisors of these offices are not held accountable. It's all been oriented to the needs of the bureaucracy as opposed to the needs of the veterans."

Not only was Weidman right; if anything, he had actually understated what was wrong at the VA: it had lost its compass, lost its way, lost sight of its mission. The Veterans Benefits Administration, headed by Undersecretary Cooper, had adopted the position that it had been holding its own in the battle of the backlog—until 2000, when Congress enacted the Veterans' Claims Assistance Act (VCAA), which required the VA to assist veterans in developing a complete and substantive claim. Before then, while it was the VA practice to help veterans prepare claims, this was done unevenly in various regional and local VA facilities, as staff time and inclination permitted. Then, in 1999, the Court of Appeals for Veterans Claims issued a decision in *Morton v. West* that the VA did not have a duty to help veterans develop their claim unless the claim was "well-grounded." This meant that an existing condition and its connection to military service were clearly established. But years of cases of veterans with problems believed traceable to expose to Agent Orange defoliant in the Vietnam War or who suffered the Gulf War Syndrome maladies that were not precisely defined scientifically led the Congress to conclude that it was the VA's mission to help those who had borne the battle gather evidence that may have been available to the government but not individual veterans and help the veterans prepare their claims for service-related benefits. The new congressional act caused the VA to review ninety-eight thousand cases in which veterans had been denied assistance in preparing their claims. But while the VA blamed that congressional act for its new problems, the records also showed that the VA had a huge claims backlog before the law took effect. From fiscal 1997 to fiscal 2001, the VA's pending workload of ratings-related claims had doubled and its backlog was year after year more than two hundred thousand cases.

Even more mind-numbing was the persistent complaint from within the Veterans Benefits Administration that the top court of appeals was itself a big cause of the backlog—because it kept remanding cases back to the Veterans' Board of Appeals and then down the chain to the regional claims adjudicators. The court of appeals had the audacity to insist that decision errors be rectified and that veterans be given a fair chance to present their best evidence. In so doing, the court was reaffirming the VA's central function: to treat veterans fairly.

In June 2001, the GAO prepared a report for Senator Fred Thompson of Tennessee, the ranking Republican on the Government Operations Committee, that was really nothing more than unfiltered and unverified statements by VA officials about their own performance. The VA gave itself high grades for doing a better job of providing health care for veterans while containing costs: "VA reported that its average cost per patient was 2 percent less than last year. Also, VA reported that performance improved for most of its key measures, including quality indicators, compared to last year." And it gave itself top marks for improvement in job training and job placement for disabled vets: "VA reported that 65 percent of the veterans who exited the Vocational Rehabilitation and Employment (VR&E) program returned to work in fiscal year 2000—an increase of 12 percentage points over its fiscal year 1999 performance."

But when it came to the new VA secretary's priority—those case backlogs and delays—not even the VA could give itself decent marks: "VA reported making little progress towards achieving this key outcome. VA reported that it has decreased the number of days required to resolve appeals of claims. However, VA reported that performance declined with respect to its rating-related claims-processing timeliness and national accuracy rate."

Meanwhile, Veterans Affairs secretary Anthony Principi had created a special task force to review the claims process. It was headed by Undersecretary Cooper, head of the Veterans Benefits Administration, the very organization that presided over all of the backlogs and delays and had failed to solve the crisis for so many years. In the fall, Principi approved the task force's recommendations: On October 3, 2001, the Associated Press quoted Principi as saying: "The president and I promised a top-to-bottom review of our claims process. That promise has been kept, and now is the time to get to work to fix this problem so that veterans get the benefits they earned through their service to this nation. . . . If I leave this town with VBA's problems still under study, I will count my tour here a failure."

The next year, the GAO found that the Veterans Benefits Administration had indeed improved its performance in processing veterans' claims. Secretary Principi had set a goal of reducing the VA's case backlog to 250,000 claims by the end of fiscal 2003. On April 26, 2002, in hearing testimony and a written report to the House Veterans' Affairs subcommittee on benefits, Cynthia A. Bascetta, the GAO's director of health care, veterans' health and benefits issues, noted the progress that had been made during Principi's tenure as VA secretary but went on to cite looming problems.

> *Even if these goals are met, VBA will have difficulty meeting the Secretary's timeliness goal. Improving timeliness depends on more than just increasing production and reducing inventory. . . . For example, VBA needs to continue to reduce delays in the process—in particular, delays in obtaining evidence. In fiscal year 2001, the average age of pending cases was actually greater than the average time to complete decisions. According to officials at some of the regional offices we visited, staff have recently been focusing on completing simpler and less time-consuming cases. Officials told us that focusing on completing simpler cases might result in increases in production and short-term improvements in timeliness. At the same time, it may also result in the office's pending inventory getting even older.*

The GAO official also noted one crucial problem: the high rate of errors made by the VA's low-level claim adjudicators.

In addition to problems with timeliness of decisions, VBA acknowledges that the accuracy of regional office decisions needs to be improved. Inaccurate decisions can also lead to delays in resolving claims when veterans appeal to the BVA. Appeals to BVA can add many months to the time required to resolve claims. In fiscal year 2001, the average time to resolve an appeal was 595 days—almost 20 months. VBA has made progress in improving its accuracy; its accuracy rate for rating-related decisions increased from 59 percent in fiscal year 2000 to 78 percent in fiscal year 2001. Beginning in fiscal year 2002, VBA has revised its key accuracy measure to focus on whether regional office decisions to grant or deny claims were correct. . . .

To hold regional office managers accountable, VBA incorporated specific regional office production goals into regional office performance standards. For fiscal year 2002, regional office directors are expected to meet their annual production target or their monthly targets in 9 out of 12 months.

With the accuracy of the VA's initial claims decisions identified as a key to reducing the backlog, the VA's new effort produced precisely the wrong results: the adjudicators became more inaccurate. In September 2003, a GAO report found that the Veterans Benefits Administration instead placed new emphasis on having claims staff employees increase the number of claims processed per month. The result should have been predictable: the accuracy of the claims decisions declined over this period. (In a quirk that could drive government bean counters back to the bean-fields, the VBA statistics did not reflect this decline in accuracy because the VA altered the way its statistics were processed.)

In its report titled "Veterans' Benefits: Improvements Needed in the Reporting and Use of Data on the Accuracy of Disability Claims Decision," the GAO concluded:

From fiscal years 2001 to 2002, VBA's accuracy of decision-making in the disability compensation and pension benefit programs declined from 89 percent to 81 percent. The agency had reported a slight improvement in accuracy between fiscal years 2001 and 2002—from 78 percent to 80 percent. However, we found that these two annual figures were not comparable because the agency had substantially changed the way it measured accuracy for fiscal year 2002.

A year later, in November 2004, with things no better, the GAO (renamed the Government Accountability Office) added a new verse about the virtues of consistency to its standard accuracy refrain. This time, its report was entitled: "Veterans Benefits: VA Needs Plan for Assessing Consistency of Decisions."

In the past, we have reported concerns about possible inconsistencies in the disability decisions made by the 57 regional offices of the Department of Veterans Affairs. . . . In January 2003, in part because of concerns about consistency, we designated VA's disability program, along with other federal disability programs, as high-risk.

In summary, we found that VA still does not systematically assess decision-making consistency among the 57 regional offices. We also found that data contained in VA's Benefits Delivery Network system, which was designed for the purpose of paying benefits, do not provide a reliable basis for identifying indications of possible decision-making inconsistencies among regional offices.

It was at this point that Knight Ridder's Chris Adams and Alison Young wrote their excellent newspaper series spotlighting the VA's benefits claims problems—the long waits and inconsistent rulings from region to region. While most of Washington never even saw their reporting, the various congressional committees gave themselves protective cover by asking the GAO to investigate the VA claims process and report back. This is the sort of game that Washington's players—elected officials and ensconsed bureaucrats—like to play with each other. The committees knew very well what the truth was—because they'd already heard it from the GAO and others for many years, in reports that sometimes read like copies of the ones they'd received in months and years past. Now the committees asked the GAO to tell them again; and the GAO dutifully did just that. On May 26, 2005, two and a half months after the Knight Ridder series, the GAO report substantiated the problem and looked pessimistically at the future. By now even the GAO's titles were beginning to read like carbon copies. This one was "Veterans' Disability Benefits: Claims Processing Problems Persist and Major Performance Improvements May Be Difficult."

> *The Department of Veterans Affairs (VA) continues to experience problems processing veterans' disability compensation and pension claims. These include large numbers of pending claims and lengthy processing times. While VA made progress in fiscal years 2002 and 2003 in reducing the size and age of its inventory of pending claims, it has lost some ground since the end of fiscal year 2003. For example, pending claims increased by about one-third from the end of fiscal year 2003 to the end of March 2005. Meanwhile, VA faces continuing questions about its ability to ensure that veterans get consistent decisions across its 57 regional*

offices. GAO has highlighted the need for VA to study the consistency of decisions made by different regional offices, identify acceptable levels of decision-making variation, and reduce variations found to be unacceptable. Also, reacting to media reports of wide variations in average disability benefit payments from state to state, the Secretary of Veterans Affairs instructed VA's Inspector General in December 2004 to determine why these variations were occurring.

The answer to that was simple: they were occurring because the top officials in the Veterans' Benefits Administration had all failed to do their jobs. Either that or the VA's top guns had known about the problem but didn't care to do anything about it until the Knight Ridder series made them look inept. Then they rushed to form another ad hoc inquiry to examine themselves. It is the way Washington works—and why it doesn't work at all.

The GAO investigators found that the same old problems were worse.

VA continues to experience problems processing veterans' disability compensation and pension claims. These include large numbers of pending claims and lengthy processing times. While VA made progress in fiscal years 2002 and 2003 in reducing the size and age of its inventory of pending claims, it has lost some ground since the end of fiscal year 2003. . . . Pending claims increased by about one-third from the end of fiscal year 2003 to the end of March 2005, from about 254,000 to about 340,000. During the same period, claims pending over 6 months increased by about 61 percent from about 47,000 to about 75,000.

Similarly, . . . VA reduced the average age of its pending claims from 182 days at the end of fiscal year 2001 to 111 days at the end of fiscal year 2003. Since then, however, average days pending have increased to 119 days at the end of March 2005. This is also far from VA's strategic goal of an average of 78 days pending by the end of fiscal year 2008. Meanwhile, the time required to resolve appeals remains too long. While the average time to resolve an appeal dropped from 731 days in fiscal year 2002 to 529 days in fiscal year 2004, close to its fiscal year 2004 goal of 520 days, but still far from VA's strategic goal of 365 days by fiscal year 2008. . . .

In addition to problems with timeliness of decisions, VA acknowledges that the accuracy of regional office decisions needs to be improved. While VA reports that it has improved the accuracy of decisions on rating related claims from 81 percent in fiscal year 2002 to 87 percent in fiscal year 2004—close to its 2004 goal of 90 percent. However, it is still below its strategic goal of 96 percent in fiscal year 2008.

The GAO report sniffed that the issue of inconsistency of claims decisions made by various regional offices "is not new"— and went on to list its own findings in virtually every year since 2000. Now that Knight Ridder had reported the wide variation in benefits from state to state, the VA looked into itself and found its inconsistency spanned a gap from the lowest payments in Ohio of $6,710 to the highest in New Mexico of $10,851. Thus there was no possible claim of average salaries and cost-of-living factors being at play, for New Mexico was hardly a high-income state. What it really showed, of course, was that the VA had failed to fix its problems year after year and that Congress had failed to hold anyone accountable. All the people who were comfortably placed in top jobs at the VA still had their jobs; and they were all still studying the problem. The GAO noted in 2005:

In November 2004, we reported that to achieve its claims processing performance goals in the face of increasing workloads and decreased staffing levels, VA would have to rely on productivity improvements. . . . It is still not clear whether VA will be able to achieve its planned improvements.

The GAO, having been on the case for decades, also produced a warning call of its own: the VA may never be able to fix its problems without fundamental reforms.

Several factors may impede VA's ability to make significant improvements in its disability claims processing performance. Recent history has shown that VA's workload and performance is affected by factors such as the impacts of laws and court decisions affecting veterans' benefit entitlement and the claims process, and the filing behavior of veterans. These factors have affected the number of claims VA received and decided. Also, to achieve its claims processing performance goals in the face of increasing workloads without significant staffing increases, VA would have to rely on productivity improvements. GAO believes that fundamental reform might be necessary to achieve more dramatic gains in performance.

But the GAO warning call went basically unanswered. After all, Adams and Young's investigative series had only been big news in the heartland, so Official Washington gave the GAO report the business-as-usual response. The congressional committees, the VA, the Office of Management and Budget, and the White House just put it on the shelf with all the others. There would, of course, be more to come.

In 2007, at the request of the Senate Veterans' Affairs Committee, the GAO analyzed the VA's progress in combating its persistent and growing problems with the timeliness and accuracy of disability claims decisions and subsequent appeals. The result was a report dated March 7, 2007, and titled familiarly, "Veterans' Disability Benefits: Long-Standing Claims Processing Challenges Persist."

The GAO report could have dated from almost any year in the past three decades. Most of it was predictable, as in this ho-hummer: "VA continues to face challenges in improving service delivery to veterans, specifically in speeding up the process of adjudication and appeal, reducing the existing backlog of claims, and improving the accuracy and consistency of decisions." There was the standard material that should have been anticipated by everyone: owing to U.S. prosecution of two new wars, in Afghanistan and Iraq, the number of claims filed between 2003 and 2006 increased by half, to 378,000. Except it apparently had not been obvious to the officials at the VA and the Office of Management and Budget. This increase in claims wasn't obvious to those budgeters (who usually move at the command of political string-pullers) because the VA had not initially budgeted for any additional burdens from these wars, which still remained grossly underbudgeted three years later.

But this GAO report had something more. Tucked well into the text was this mind-boggling finding: Veterans who filed appeals for claims denied now had to wait an average of almost two years for a decision! And that was only an average—a complex case could take much longer. The GAO report put it like this: "Meanwhile, appeals resolution remains a lengthy process, taking an average of 657 days in fiscal year 2006."

The GAO added that both its investigators and the VA's inspector general "have identified concerns about the consistency of decisions by VA's regional offices and the Board of Veterans' Appeals (BVA)." President Bush's fiscal 2008 budget provided funding for 450 more full-time Veterans' Benefits Administration employees to work on claims for service-related disability compensation. The GAO investigators said the VA is also working to reduce the time wasted on appeals that were remanded back to the regional adjudicators to correct shortcomings and failures made in their initial decisions. In other words, the same old refrain: end the errors, get it right the first time.

But unlike many GAO reports, this one, submitted to the Senate Veterans' Affairs Committee in the form of testimony by Daniel Bertoni, the GAO's acting director of education, workforce, and income security, issued a call for a fundamental reform of the VA's disability compensation program. "Opportunities for significant performance improvement may lie in more fundamental reform of VA's disability compensation program," Bertoni stated. He pointed to studies that indicated that the VA might find it more profitable—from the viewpoint of staff time wasted—to consider paying lump-sum benefits instead of monthly disability compensation to veterans with relatively lesser disabilities who file claims for increased benefits. It was an old proposal that he urged be considered anew.

In 1996, the Veterans' Claims Adjudication Commission noted that most disability compensation claims are repeat claims—such as claims for increased disability percentage— and most repeat claims were from veterans with less severe disabilities. According to VA, about 65 percent of veterans who began receiving disability compensation in fiscal year 2003 had disabilities rated 30 percent or less. The commission questioned whether concentrating claims processing resources on these claims, rather than on claims by more severely disabled veterans, was consistent with program intent. The commission asked Congress to consider paying less severely disabled veterans compensation in a lump sum. According to the commission, the lump sum option could have a number of benefits for VA as well as veterans. Specifically, the lump sum option could reduce the number of claims submitted and allow VA to process claims more quickly—especially those of more seriously disabled veterans. Moreover, a lump sum option could be more useful to some veterans as they make the transition from military to civilian life. In December 2000, we reported that about one-third of newly compensated veterans could be interested in a lump sum option.

Finally, Bertoni warned that the VA was missing opportunities for significant changes.

VBA and others who have studied claims processing have suggested that consolidating claims processing into fewer regional offices could help improve claims processing efficiency, save overhead costs, and improve decisional accuracy and consistency. . . . VA has not changed its basic field structure for processing compensation and pension claims at 57 regional offices, which experience large performance variations and questions about decision consistency. Unless more comprehensive and strategic changes are made to its field structure, VBA is likely to miss opportunities to substantially improve productivity, accuracy, and consistency, especially in the face of future workload increases.

Looking back at the sad history of the Department of Veterans Affairs and its predecessor, the Veterans Administration, as chronicled by the wonkish historians of the Government Accountability Office and its predecessor, the General Accounting Office, one cannot help but notice an unmistakable pattern of nonachievement. From the 1978 GAO report entitled "The Time Required to Process Veterans' and Survivors' Initial Claims for Benefits" to the 2007 GAO report entitled "Long-Standing Claims Processing Challenges Persist," the VA, by its inability to fix blatant deficiencies, has at least proved itself a model of consistency. In fact, the VA has made itself a Washington monument to government inaction.

9

Outpatient Delays

Diagnosis and Cure

Michael L. Staley is a Veterans Affairs expert who in 2005 was able to accurately diagnose one of the most persistent problems suffered by veterans—and even provide a prescription for curing it. He did it without performing a physical examination on any of the veterans he sought to help. And that is just as well, because Staley is not a physician and the veterans' persistent problem wasn't medical—it was bureaucratic: the delays veterans endured when they tried to schedule appointments for outpatient treatment at their local VA clinic.

Staley was the assistant inspector general for auditing at the Department of Veterans Affairs when VA secretary Anthony Principi asked the IG to investigate the department's hospital and clinic outpatient appointment scheduling. Patients kept complaining about long delays in scheduling appointments at VA Hospitals. But the records kept showing that the VA was scheduling outpatients in a timely manner. Timely, according to the Veterans Health Administration requirement, means that at least 90 percent of outpatients are scheduled for appointments within thirty days of their request; also, patients with service-related disabilities must be given priority. The VA records kept showing the hospitals and clinics coming close to what the rules required.

So the inspector general designed a study that would, as he wrote in his subsequent report to Principi, "determine the accuracy of the reported veterans' waiting times and facility waiting lists." The audit found that the appointment schedulers often were failing to follow proper VA scheduling procedures, failing to give patients the next available appointment—and then providing inaccurate and misleading statistics to the top management at the VA that made their efforts appear far better than they actually were. Moreover, the schedulers were often doing this at the instruction of their immediate supervisors.

"Schedulers did not follow established procedures when selecting the type of appointment and when entering the desired appointment date," Staley wrote in his report to the secretary dated July 8, 2005. "In some cases, supervisors instructed schedulers to create appointments contrary to established scheduling procedures."

In 75 percent of 380 appointments that were audited, "schedulers incorrectly selected" a date other than the "next available appointment date," the IG report said. And only 65 percent of the appointments were scheduled within the VA's stated goal of thirty days. The inspector general's report added:

Because schedulers did not use the correct scheduling procedures, actual waiting times were understated, resulting in medical facility directors being unaware that 2,009 service-connected veterans waited longer than 30 days from their desired date of care. . . . Using the error rate from our sta-

tistical sample, we estimated that this may impact as many as 24,463 veterans nationwide.

While the Veterans Affairs officials like to boast of the advances that their department has made in converting to an all-electronic medical records system, computerized systems can only be as accurate as the information that is fed into them. And the inspector general's audit found that the VA hospital and clinic electronic waiting lists were beset with problems stemming from the inaccurate information that was being fed into the system.

In a section entitled, "Medical Facilities Did Not Have Effective Electronic Waiting List Procedures," the report stated:

VHA [Veterans Health Administration] medical facilities did not have effective procedures to ensure all veterans either had appointments within 4 months of the desired date of care or were identified on an electronic waiting list. At 5 of the 8 medical facilities, schedulers understated their electronic waiting lists by 856 veterans. Using the error rate from our statistical sample, we estimated that the electronic waiting lists could be understated by as many as 10,301 veterans nationwide. We also identified clinics with substantial backlogs of consult referrals where veterans did not have appointments within 7 business days and were not included on the electronic waiting lists.

The auditors also discovered a handful of schedulers left over from the Pleistocene Age of information technology who were apparently determined to resist the arrival of all-electronic data. The report said that 17 out of 247 schedulers who were interviewed said that they kept "informal waiting lists ... of veterans who needed appointments"—data not entered into the electronic listing but kept the old-fashioned way, perhaps on legal pads and yellow sticky notes.

Which brings up the matter of scheduler training. It too was lacking, to a degree that is both shocking and beyond the bounds of bureaucratic professionalism. The IG report stated:

> *VHA did not have an adequate training program for schedulers. Instead, schedulers received most of their training as on-the-job training, which may have contributed to the errors we identified during our review. For example, 2,246 (68 percent) of the 3,298 schedulers who identified themselves as trainers in our nationwide survey did not know how to correctly create an appointment for a veteran who wanted an appointment as soon as possible but did not need urgent or emergent care.*

The results of the initial audit were so jarring that the inspector general's team wanted to measure their findings against a nationwide VA universe. So they placed an in-depth survey on their Web site and asked the VA's 29,818 personnel who deal with scheduling appointments nationwide to respond, and a total of 15,750 did so.

> *The results of our survey confirmed that the findings we identified at the eight VHA medical facilities exist nationwide. According to 7 percent of the survey respondents, managers or supervisors directed or encouraged them to schedule appointments contrary to established procedures. Also, 81 percent of the survey respondents told us they had received no training on the use of the electronic waiting*

*list and only 45 percent of the survey respondents had re-
ceived any formal training on the use of the . . . scheduling
module [the computerized Veterans Health Information
Systems and Technology Architecture, known as VistA].
Survey respondents who identified themselves as trainers
often did not know the correct scheduling procedures.*

The auditors made a series of recommendations to the Veterans Health Administration, which runs all of the VA hospitals and
clinics, to ensure proper scheduling procedures: monitor the work
of the schedulers, provide proper training to the schedulers, and
develop a standard training package. (Unbelievably, this had not
been done before; schedulers learned their craft on the job, in
training that seemed to range from haphazard to ad hoc.)

The audit report ended on a seemingly upbeat note: "The Under Secretary for Health agreed with the findings and recommendations and provided acceptable implementation plans. . . .
The Under Secretary noted that VHA has made significant
progress in improving the outpatient scheduling process." But
those who are skilled at interpreting governmental nuance
might have noticed that the undersecretary for health, Dr.
Jonathan B. Perlin, seemed far more optimistic than the inspector general. Perlin, who had just been confirmed in the job in
2005 after having served as acting under secretary for the previous year, was placing great faith in the newly implemented Advanced Clinic Access (ACA) initiative—a program that the
auditor viewed as underwhelming, based on the results so far.

The IG report first gave Perlin his due, then added its own
less sanguine perspective.

*[Perlin] stated that VHA's Advanced Clinic Access (ACA)
initiative is an ongoing national process to implement*

patient-centered, scientifically based redesign principles and tools in all of its operations. According to the Under Secretary, under the ACA umbrella VHA is vigorously addressing problems with waiting times and scheduling delays and has taken steps to accurately quantify the numbers of patients on wait lists, lengths of waits, and reasons for scheduling delays. He believes that once implemented systemwide, VHA's ACA initiative in conjunction with other planned and ongoing improvements will result in needed scheduling enhancements that are consistently applied by all VHA medical facilities.

We are encouraged by VHA's efforts to improve the scheduling process. However, our review did not evaluate the implementation of the ACA initiative, and therefore, we expressed no opinion or conclusions on its adequacy. We evaluated the accuracy of the reported veterans' waiting times and facility waiting lists and our findings addressed weaknesses in the scheduling procedures used by both clinics that have implemented ACA and by clinics that have not implemented ACA. We found that the schedulers' use of incorrect procedures distorted the reported measurement of veterans' waiting times and facility waiting lists regardless of whether the clinic had implemented ACA.

If the confidence voiced to the auditors by the VA undersecretary for health was well placed, this chapter would end right here, after a quick note of mission accomplished. But this not the case. When the auditors conducted a follow-up review two years later, they found that many of the same problems still existed and most of the recommendations made in 2005 had not been implemented.

This finding did not cause the optimistic Dr. Perlin undue embarrassment every time he walked down the corridors of the gray stone Veterans Affairs building on Vermont Avenue—because he was no longer at the VA. In July 2006, after just one year on the job, the official who had promised that all recommendations would be implemented had twirled out the revolving door and into the private sector, becoming a senior vice president of HCA, the nation's largest for-profit hospital chain, based in Nashville.

There was also a new face at the auditing office of the VA's inspector general—Belinda J. Finn, now assistant inspector general for auditing. Finn authored a straightforward follow-up analysis to Michael Staley's report. The central conclusion: "The conditions we identified in our previous report still exist."

Schedulers were still not following established procedures for making and recording medical appointments. We found unexplained differences between the desired dates as shown in VistA and used by VHA to calculate waiting times and the desired dates shown in the related medical records. As a result, the accuracy of VHA's reported waiting times could not be relied on and the electronic waiting lists at those medical facilities were not complete. Also, VHA has not fully implemented five of the eight recommendations in the July 8, 2005, report.

These audits are usually written in the carefully impersonal style of government-speak, but Finn's report provided a memorable example of how one VA clinic finessed the statistics.

On December 20, 2005, a veteran . . . was seen in the Eye Clinic. The medical provider wrote in the progress notes

that the veteran should return to the clinic in 6 weeks (Jan-
uary 31, 2006). However, over 7 months later, on Septem-
ber 6, 2006, the scheduler created an appointment for the
veteran for October 17, 2006. The scheduler entered a de-
sired date of October 2, 2006, which resulted in a reported
waiting time of 15 days. Based on the provider requested
date of January 31, 2006, the veteran actually waited 259
days, and was never placed on the electronic waiting list.
We saw no documentation to explain the delay and med-
ical facility personnel said it "fell through the cracks."

The inspector general's follow-up report said that in 281 of
600 cases reviewed (47 percent), the veterans had to wait longer
for appointments than the Veterans Health Administration reported. Of that 281, there were 176 who experienced waiting pe-
riods that exceeded thirty days, a violation of the VA's rules.

The report also found that the VA's appointment schedulers
still "lack necessary training" at six medical facilities. "Schedulers and managers told us that, although training is readily
available, they were short of staff and did not have time to take
the training."

But there was one significant difference between this report
and the 2005 audit. This time, the new undersecretary for
health, Michael J. Kussman, strongly disputed some of the inspector general's findings. Kussman, a retired army brigadier
general and a medical doctor who had been confirmed in the job
just four months earlier, contended that appointments were often scheduled later at the patient's request. The inspector general replied that VA regulations required the schedulers to enter
that explanation, but they had not done so. The IG report noted
the undersecretary's "attempts to discredit the audit findings
by comparing the audit results with the results of VA's national

patient satisfaction survey," which showed that 85 percent of responding veterans said they got appointments when they needed them. But, the auditor replied, the two surveys could not be validly compared: "To support any level of comparison, the patient satisfaction survey would have had to ask veterans whether they were seen within the 30-day requirement." "Because this question was not posed in the survey, the survey results cannot be construed as an indicator of compliance with established scheduling procedures or the accuracy of reported waiting times." Kussman took issue with various definitions and methods used in the study; the IG refuted each charge. Kussman contended that the auditors used the most conservative estimates in order to portray a worst-case scenario. The IG replied that conservative estimates were used not to show worst-case outcomes but to conform with the rules of the Veterans Health Administration, which Kussman heads.

At one point, Kussman served noticed that he intended to hire an outside contractor in order to obtain "a more objective, professional analysis." The IG responded: "We take issue with any implication that the OIG audit was not an objective or professional analysis of the scheduling process," adding that at every step, Kussman's own VHA staff was consulted about methods and procedures and adjustments were made "to incorporate all of their concerns."

This point-counterpoint bureaucratic fight was a new low in the efforts to fix a system that has been so widely condemned. It marked a moment when two Veterans Affairs entities—the inspector general and the undersecretary were battling each other with the sort of intensity that is usually reserved for partisan battles among adversaries, rather than members of the same team.

In the end, the inspector general's auditor had the last word (it was, after all, her report). In the final sentence of her report,

Belinda Finn served notice on the VA: "We will follow up on the planned actions in this report, and those that remain unimplemented from the 2005 report, until they are completed."

For the VA, 2005 turned out to be a newsworthy, but not very noteworthy, year. It was, for example, the year that the VA managed to shock even its shock-resistant critics in Washington. At one of those normally dreary budget review hearings in the House Veterans' Affairs Committee on June 23, the VA's undersecretary for health, Perlin, testified almost matter-of-factly that the VA had fallen just a bit short in its budgeting for 2005—$1 billion short. "We weren't on the mark from the actuarial model," explained Perlin.

Congressional Republicans and Democrats were so stunned by the VA's calm disclosure that they wound up on the same side, making the same arguments to condemn the VA. Among those who found themselves in the roles of bipartisan bedfellows were Senator Patty Murray, a Democrat from the state of Washington, and Senator Larry Craig, then chairman of the Senate Veterans Affairs Committee. "I was on the phone this morning with Secretary of Veterans Affairs Jim Nicholson, letting him know that I am not pleased that this has happened," Craig, a Republican from Idaho, was quoted as saying in an article in the next morning's *Washington Post*. "I am certain that he is going to take serious steps to ensure that this type of episode is not repeated." Murray was especially incensed because she had been a sponsor of a Democratic bid to add $1.9 billion to the VA budget—only to be rebuffed two months earlier by Nicholson. The VA secretary had written her in April 2005, saying: "I can assure you that VA does not need emergency supplemental funds in FY2005 to continue to provide timely, quality service that is always our goal." Her aides had obtained a VA midyear budget review document suggesting that Nicholson knew of the VA's budget crisis at the time he wrote that letter to the senator, reported the *Washington Post*'s Tomas B. Edsell. The *Post* article added that Nicholson's spokesperson, Terry Jemison, refused to release a copy of the document showing what the secretary knew of the budget shortfall and when he knew it. "We don't provide information about predecisional budget passback and midyear reviews," said the VA spokesperson. That gave Nicholson room to scramble for the high ground. "The health care needs of America's veterans are among VA's highest priorities," the secretary said in a statement the VA was pleased to release. "Working with our partners in Congress, I'm confident that VA's budget will continue to provide world-class health care to the nation's veterans."

Government investigators eventually concluded that the $1 billion shortfall occurred because the Bush administration officials did not want to publicly acknowledge the need for more funds at a time when soaring costs of the Iraq and Afghanistan wars had caused them to trim budgets elsewhere. The GAO concluded in a September 20, 2006, report that the VA's billion-dollar budget disaster was due to "unrealistic assumptions, estimation errors and insufficient data." The GAO added:

VA underestimated the cost of serving veterans returning from Iraq and Afghanistan, in part because estimates for fiscal year 2005 were based on data that largely predated the Iraq conflict and because according to VA, the agency had challenges for fiscal year 2006 in obtaining data from the Department of Defense. . . . While VA originally projected, in its fiscal year 2005 budget formulation, that it would need to provide care to about 23,500 returnees from Iraq and Afghanistan, revised projections indicated that it would serve about four times that number. . . . nearly 100,000 returnees for fiscal year 2005.

There were some people in Washington who were not shocked by the VA's belated disclosure of its billion-dollar budget shortfall—the veterans' advocate officials. They had been seeing for months the new problems the budget crisis was causing in VA treatment facilities. As Richard Fuller, legislative director of the Paralyzed Veterans of America, told *The Washington Post:* "You could see it happening, clinics shutting down, appointments delayed." Indeed, the poor treatment of military veterans was becoming yet another of Washington's worst-kept secrets.

10

The Pain of Unseen Wounds

Slow to Learn the ABCs of PTSD

They come home from the wars and often bring the wars home with them.

Home at last from Normandy and Iwo Jima, from Inchon and Pork Chop Hill, from Khe Sanh and Hamburger Hill, from Kuwait and Khamisiyah, from Kabul and Tora Bora, from Fallujah and Baghdad. And yet at times those battlefields are still there with them. In nightmares while they sleep; in flashbacks while they are awake. In the sudden noise of a motorcycle backfiring or a garbage can clanging, or a guy in a car or a guy in a bar, or a cross look by a guy walking down a street or an innocent look on the face of a child playing on the sidewalk.

They had often fought bravely, heroically, even inventively, in nightmare conditions, witnessing horrors of war and making terrible trade-offs that meant some must die so others might live. When they came home from World War II and couldn't lose the demons of war, these military veterans who had helped save the world from Hitler and the Nazis, from Tojo and imperial Japan were officially diagnosed with a seemingly trivial infirmity:

battle fatigue. Indeed, the term itself made the illness sound in-
significant, and many who suffered from it felt a sense of shame at
their very real problem, as though the illness was their fault, their
failing. Family and friends, uninformed and uneducated by the
government or other experts, also often assumed that something
amiss in the veteran's makeup was at the root of the problem.

In World War I, the British had come up with their own term
for the problem: shell shock. Initially they had assumed it was
caused by the concussion of exploding artillery shells. But they
soon discovered that soldiers who had not been near exploding
shells exhibited the same symptoms.

Battle fatigue was not slang; it was an official diagnosis. The
very nature of the term—*fatigue*—led naturally to the wrong assumption that if fatigue from battle was the problem, then
surely rest in peacetime must be the cure. So it was that soldiers
who returned from World War II were often warehoused in military hospitals to rest for a period of time before they rejoined
their families; then they and their families would live often uneasy lives trying to adjust on their own to problems that were
deep-seated. The World War II veterans who returned home
suffering from these effects were rarely given the extensive psychiatric care and counseling they needed. Then again, there was
no official indication that this was needed; they were, after all,
officially diagnosed with a form of battle *fatigue*.

Indeed, the U.S. Army Field Manual Number 22–51, published as recently as 1994, states:

*Battle fatigue is the approved US Army term (AR 40–216)
for combat stress symptoms and reactions which—*

- *Feel unpleasant.*
- *Interfere with mission performance.*

- *Are best treated with reassurance, rest, replenishment of physical needs, and activities which restore confidence.*

The army manual also raises the concern that a soldier with battle fatigue may be, well, something less than a good soldier.

Battle fatigue may coexist with misconduct stress behaviors. However, battle fatigue itself, by definition, does not warrant legal or disciplinary action. . . .

There are four major contributing factors which cause battle fatigue. They are—

- *Sudden exposure.*
- *Cumulative exposure.*
- *Physical stressors and stress symptoms.*
- *Home front and other existing problems.*

Any one factor may suffice if intense enough. Usually two, three, or all four factors can collectively produce battle fatigue.

The manual goes on to explain that battle fatigue may manifest itself in the form of actual fatigue, anxiety, depression, memory loss, and a loss of the ability to perform certain motor, sensory, or speech functions. Disruptive forms of battle fatigue include "disorganized, bizarre, impulsive or violent behavior, total withdrawal, or persistent hallucinations."

While noting that battle fatigue may be caused by trauma such as an explosion, the manual seems to demean soldiers who suffer from it.

The physical symptoms . . . are magnified when emotions cannot be expressed because of social pressure or heroic

*self-image. They are, therefore, most often seen in the
"elite" units or groups who show few other cases of battle
fatigue, such as officers or the airborne and rangers in
WWII. They are also more common in individuals from social classes and cultures that receive less education and/or
do not learn how to express feelings in words.*

By the Vietnam War, experts were using terms such as combat
stress and traumatic stress instead of battle fatigue. In time the
U.S. government caught up with the nomenclature, but it has still
been sadly behind in prescribing the sorely needed treatment and
care for Iraq War veterans, who seem to be suffering in this war
more than ever before from post-traumatic stress disorder. Once
again, the government was slow and even resistant to treating
those who came home with severe psychological wounds.

With limited resources, the U.S. military and VA hospitals
and clinics moved most vigorously to spend their money and resources on the most visible war injuries: troops with horrendous
brain injuries and limbs lost when their vehicles were hit by
roadside bombs.

Hospital staff members are most comfortable doing what
they have always done, treating the war wounds they have always treated, in the ways they have always treated them. The
problems of soldiers and marines and reserves and National
Guard personnel who are suffering from post-traumatic stress
disorder are considered of lesser importance. And no doubt some
VA adjudicators regard some of those claiming PTSD as fakers
and malingerers.

More than one hundred thousand veterans of the wars in Af-
ghanistan and Iraq had applied to the Department of Veterans
Affairs for treatment for post-traumatic stress disorder as of
October 2007. Thousands more were treated in the VA's recently

opened storefront vet centers, and many others who were still in the military were treated for PTSD in military hospitals. *USA Today* reporter Gregg Zoroya noted in an October 19, 2007, article that mental illness had become the second largest treatment category; orthopedic injuries were at the top of the list, but claims for the mental illness were growing at an ever faster rate. A 1988 study found that 31 percent of the 3.1 million Vietnam War troops were treated for PTSD.

But the Department of Veterans Affairs failed woefully to keep up with the rapidly increasing number of veterans seeking treatment for PTSD. Chris Adams of the McClatchy papers' Washington bureau analyzed 200 million VA records, including every medical appointment in 2005, and on September 16, 2007, reported some troubling findings: even though the VA began stressing the goal in the 1980s of having mental health treatment capability in all of its facilities, as of 2005, nearly one hundred VA clinics provided no mental health care at all. The average veteran who suffers from psychiatric problems had one-third fewer appointments with mental health specialists than he or she would have had ten years earlier. Mental health care was treated much differently from state to state. Some veterans saw psychiatrists, others only saw social workers; in some areas the VA would spend $2,000 per veteran under treatment, but in other areas the average expenditure per veteran was just $500. The amount spent on mental health care per veteran declined from $3,560 in 1995 to $2,581 in 2004—and the number of psychiatric visits also declined.

The problem did not appear to be a lack of funds. According to the Government Accountability Office, the VA told Congress in 2005 and 2006 that it was reserving $300 million for increased mental health treatment, but it never did manage to find a way to spend $54 million of those funds.

But one thing was certain: the VA did not lack for enthusias-
tic expressions from the officials at the top.

The secretary of veterans affairs, Jim Nicholson, whose previous job under President George W. Bush was chairman of the
Republican National Committee, bubbled with buzzwords of
reassurance in March 2007, when he said: "Mental health is a
very high priority of ours. The VA possesses—this will sound
boastful, but . . . as we used to say back home, it ain't bragging
if it's true—but we have the best expertise in post-traumatic
stress disorder in the world. . . . So we are ramped upward, and
we have a terrific cadre of experts in that area, and we are adequately funded to deal with it."

And McClatchy's Adams reported on February 11, 2007, that
the VA health official who was supervising mental health efforts,
Antonette Zeiss, had said in an interview: "We feel very well
poised to meet the needs."

But Adams analyzed data from every VA medical appointment in 2005 and discovered an eye-popping disparity in the
way mental health matters are treated in different facilities nationally.

- *Numbers of visits:* In Hudson Valley, New York, veterans being treated for PTSD get an average of 22 visits;
  nationwide the average is 8.1; in Fargo, North Dakota,
  veterans treated with PTSD received a national low of
  just 3.1 visits.
- *Money spent per vet:* In Connecticut, the VA spent an average of $2,317 on each veteran treated as a psychiatric
  outpatient; in Saginaw, Michigan, the average was $468.
- *Wait time:* In some areas, 90 percent of the veterans got
  appointments in less than thirty days; in Loma Linda,
  California, only 39 percent got appointments that quickly.

- *Duration of visit:* Long visits are well over an hour—
  seventy-five to eighty minutes; short visits can be only a
  quarter of that—twenty to thirty minutes. In Amarillo,
  Texas, 87 percent of the veterans got short visits; in
  Butler, Pennsylvania, only 6 percent of the veterans got
  short visits.

Asked about the disparities, Antonette Zeiss morphed into
the VA's philosopher-in-residence. "It's true there are disparities," Zeiss told Adams. "Disparity is a part of health care."

Perhaps top government officials can afford this zen-centered
calm, but it is a bit more difficult to maintain if you are a vet
with PTSD actually experiencing the "disparity."

Disparity is a part of health care. When McClatchy's Chris
Adams checked the VA records for the following year, 2006, he
found that "disparity" was still very much a part of the VA's mental health care. Adams reported on September 16, 2007, that there
were five medical centers that in 2006 spent less than one-fifth the
national average on PTSD treatment programs. The five centers
were geographically dispersed—in California, Iowa, Louisiana,
Tennessee, and Wisconsin. He also found that while most treatment for PTSD was considered effective, close to one-third of the
VA's inpatient and most specialized PTSD centers had not met at
least one of the quality goals of VA mental health officials.

This is one of those topic areas where once again we are faced
with the question, just what does it take to make official Washington take meaningful action that will really solve the problem? Mc-
Clatchy's exhaustive newspaper exposés of the problems in the VA
didn't shake foundations of official Washington—at least not
enough for the VA to actually fix what is wrong. But that is not to
suggest that the journalists' efforts didn't have some official impact.

For years, the VA had published prominently on its taxpayer-funded Web site the twice-yearly reports that the VA's mental health office prepared on how well it was meeting its goals. But after the McClatchy investigation of the VA's 2005 records, the VA did take at least one official action. "The reports used to be readily available to the public, but the VA removed them from its Web site in the past year," Adams reported in a September 16, 2007, article. "McClatchy obtained the most recent reports, for fiscal year 2006, under provisions of the Freedom of Information Act."

On October 18, 2006, Jim Nicholson was in Grand Chute, Wisconsin, touring the John H. Bradley VA Outpatient Clinic. It was a fine fall day in Wisconsin, but not a good day for the VA secretary, what with the news media there and all. Back in Washington, the Democratic members of the U.S. House Committee on Veterans' Affairs had just released a report stating that the VA's mental health counseling centers were not keeping up with the increasing needs of the veterans.

The congressional Democrats looked at 60 of the VA's 207 readjustment counseling centers nationwide and concluded that the number of veterans who requested treatment for post-traumatic stress disorder from October 2005 through June 2006 had more than doubled—from 4,467 to 9,103 veterans. The centers, overwhelmed, told 40 percent of the veterans who needed individual counseling to instead participate in group therapy sessions. With PTSD markedly affecting the ability of returning veterans to adjust to living once again with spouses and families, the report also said that 27 percent of the centers had limited or plans to limit the number of veterans who would be allowed to have family or marriage counseling.

When Jim Collar, a reporter for the Appleton, Wisconsin, *Post-Crescent* asked Nicholson about the problems cited in the House Democratic report, the VA secretary shifted into a gear more appropriate for his previous job as chairman of the Republican National Committee. He assured his questioner that the needs of returning military men and women are a "very high priority" for the department and that his department's budget and personnel numbers are adequate to get the job done. "We are staffed for it," Nicholson said.

And with a touch of immodesty not uncommon in Washington—and certainly quite common during his reign as VA secretary—Nicholson added: "We're dealing with it with great excellence."

11

A New Generation of Vets

Ratings Games and Waiting Lists

The sandstorm whipping across the desert of southern Iraq gave the U.S. Army military policeman driving the rented white Mazda van that was escorting a truck convoy two choices: Drive blind or stop. The tractor trailers speeding along behind his escort van cut it to one choice: Don't stop. The explosion ahead gave the MP no choice but to slow down. That was when his rented van—which like many in Iraq had no seat belts—was rear-ended by the first tractor trailer. The force of the collision bounced the MP around the van; the impact was so strong it bent the barrel of his rifle.

Eric Adams's second war in the service of his country had just come to an abrupt end. We first met him when he was on MP duty a decade earlier, in the Gulf War, at the destruction of Saddam Hussein's chemical weapons depot at Khamisiyah. He had returned to Tampa, Florida, where he was serving as a city policeman and member of the Army Reserve when his unit got called up and sent to Iraq for the 2003 invasion that toppled Saddam Hussein. In his second gig in Iraq, he did protective details and escort details like the one that brought his war to a sudden stop in July 2003. Adams's injuries were internal and mainly to his head and neck. He did not realize that he was about to begin a new long journey, one that would bounce him from base to base, waiting list to waiting list, as he sought treatment for his injuries and then tried to get the coverage he deserved for his service-related injuries.

Adams had joined the ranks of a new legion of combat soldiers—the new generation of veterans who have served in the post-9/11 wars of Afghanistan and Iraq. They have more head trauma injuries than veterans in any other war, mainly from roadside bombs hitting their vehicles. They also have far more diagnosed incidents of post-traumatic stress disorder than ever before.

He was first flown to the Landstuhl Hospital in Germany, the largest U.S. military hospital in Europe. U.S. troops from Iraq arrive each day; it is called the German front of the U.S. war in Iraq. Adams asked for an MRI but was told one wasn't available; instead he got a CAT scan. He was initially diagnosed with swelling of the brain and concussive syndrome. He had severe migraine headaches.

Adams was shipped stateside to Andrews Air Force Base in the Maryland countryside just east of Washington, D.C., a base best known as the home of Air Force One. From there he went to Walter Reed Army Medical Center in northwest Washington. At every stop he sought an MRI exam but one wasn't available. Then he was shipped to the Eisenhower Medical Center at Fort Gordon, Georgia, and finally to Fort Stewart Hospital in Georgia.

"The army hospitals all treated me very well," he told me.

The army also set about giving Adams a retirement rating. He met with the medical evaluation board office at Fort Stewart. "Originally, they were going to rate me at a 10 percent disability rating—they told me it was a one-time settlement offer," Adams said. "But I researched what was required of the army and put it down in a letter. The army asked me if I had hired an attorney. But it was just me. Then they agreed to reevaluate." Reevaluating is not always a good thing, it turned out. "This time I listed everything from head to toe. Knees were damaged, nerve damage on the left side. Then [the evaluator] tried to associate my problems not with the accident but with sinusitis. He said I had polyps in the nose that had caused some of these other problems. He was saying my problem was caused only by dust. Basically, he was calling me a liar, saying the accident had never happened. But then I gave him documentation of the accident and told him I was going to appeal."

Again Adams asked for his MRI; again he was told he could have a CAT scan. "But I told them the army regulations say I am entitled to an MRI," he said. "That's how I got one. A couple of days later I had my appointment for an MRI. A radiologist read my report and said there are real problems." It was April 2004 and Adams was diagnosed with a calcification cyst of the pineal gland in the brain; it controls the production of serotonin, which regulates sleep. He also had a herniated disk in his neck. Adams got his retirement rating changed from 10 percent to 30 percent; this meant he would get more money each month.

He was also placed on the temporary disability retirement list, which meant he would have to be reevaluated every year. In 2005, he was reevaluated at Fort Gordon's Eisenhower Medical Center. "At Fort Gordon they reduced my rating from 30 percent down to 20 percent. The army regulations say that if you are at 30 percent or more they have to hold you on the books for a medical retirement with a pension. For me it would have been about $1,100 a month, income that would be taxable. So they took me down to 20 percent so they would not owe me that pension."

Dropping Adams's rating could be considered a smart business move if the army was in business to turn a profit. But it is a questionable procedure if the army's sole goal is doing what is right and best for its own veterans. Meanwhile, Adams had a rating from the VA of 80 percent; this would give him $1,280 a month tax-free. He took the VA option.

Adams got through the army and VA bureaucracies because he found a new way to apply his survivor skills. "They lost my records three or four times," said Adams. "They'd tell me they lost my records and couldn't help me now and I'd say, 'Oh, that's okay. I have copies of all of my records.' And I had. And then a short time later they would find my records. After every single appointment, I requested a copy of my records."

Adams had one other problem that could not be detected with an MRI or a CAT scan. It is something you don't discover until you talk with him for quite a while, and then it just sort of comes out, quietly—a low-keyed conversation about what war was really like, what he saw, and the invisible wounds those experiences caused that can be so very quick to surface and so very slow to heal.

"The Army wanted to call it 'adjustment disorder'—a mood disorder. But the VA says it is what it is—PTSD—post-traumatic stress disorder. . . . That was the diagnosis of the VA psychologists." Adams knows how this damage was inflicted, but it is not easy to discuss. "Two of my best friends were killed," he says. There is more. He talks about a time when he was escorting those truck convoys. "There were enemy snipers and bombers who would try to ambush our trucks." One of the tactics of the insurgents was to have a child play in the road—and then attack when the U.S. convoy slowed or stopped. The combined U.S. command in Iraq had issued an order that the convoys must keep going, no matter what. Adams understood the

reasoning: "You had to keep going or else your convoy would become sitting ducks and would be ambushed." One of the trucks
in his convoys hit a child. It wasn't his vehicle and he didn't actually see it happen. But, he says, "No one forgets that."

Adams was accepted as an outpatient in a stress treatment
program at Bay Pines, in St. Petersburg, Florida. His counselor
was excellent, and Adams was making excellent progress when
in early 2007 it abruptly ended. His slot no longer existed, he
was told. He was given no reason except that his counselor had
left the VA after giving the department six months' advance notice. Now Adams was getting no treatment for his PTSD. It was
just three months after VA Secretary Nicholson boasted of
his department's "great excellence" in meeting veterans' PTSD
needs.

Adams contacted his member of Congress, Representative
Kathy Castor. Her office contacted the VA. "The VA said they
would call me in a week," Adams said. "They never did." During
an appointment for his neck injury at Bay Pines, he inquired
again. "They told me if I had a stress problem, to go to the ER."
Nights were long and he couldn't sleep: flashbacks filled his
nights. "So I did what they said—I went to the ER. Told them I
had sleep problems. The doctor said to me, 'Were you in combat?' I said I was. Then he said, 'You need to get a referral from
a primary care physician to get back into the program'—the
program that I had never officially left."

In 2007, Adams solved his own problem through some cre-
ative persistent intervention. He learned that a top VA official
from Washington was going to be speaking at a Memorial Day
ceremony in New Port Richey, Florida. Sure enough, he knew
one of the policemen who were handling security. So Adams
called his pal, who agreed to bring him to the VA official and
vouch for his authenticity. "Well, I got to him and told him the

problem. He blew me off—I thought." But as it turned out, the VA official asked a local VA staffer to check into it. He in turn had his public relations office make a call, and Adams got back into the program.

The VA officials made it happen by finding a way to make it happen—a mentality that normally is not associated with the VA or any government agency. They found the counselor who used to treat Adams, then hired her as an outside contractor to come in and do some part-time work. And Adams was back into PTSD counseling, with a counselor he knew and respected.

The case of Eric Adams shows us a lot about how the VA works, often doesn't work, but can be made to work when those with power and influence are willing to break free of their bureaucratic shackles and actually try to solve a problem rather than just passing it along to someone else. Of course, there is nothing in Adams's case that buttresses VA Secretary Nicholson's claim that his department was meeting the PTSD and other medical needs of returning veterans "with great excellence." Great luck and personal pluck were what got Adams the treatment he needed and deserved.

"If I hadn't known that cop who was handling the security in Port Richey, it may never have happened," Adams told me. "The good news is it shows what the VA can do when someone is willing to make an extra effort."

12

Seeds of Dishonor and Disservice

How a System in Trouble
Sows Disrespect

When the world is at peace, the military system is at its politically correct best. But the strains of war, from the ramp-up to the waging of it, can force rigid demands on all who serve, at all levels. Suddenly demands for infinite necessities butt heads with dictates of finite resources. When it happens, all who are masters of people below must still satisfy impatient masters above. It works that way all the way up the military chain of command and also all the way up the civilian chain of command, as even a deputy secretary of defense must meet the demands of the secretary; and the secretary must meet the demands of the president; and the president must (at least theoretically in a democracy) meet the demands of the people.

So it is that the combined military-civilian system sometimes ends up disrespecting, disserving and dishonoring those who serve in time of war. That is why any criticism of those in government who have ill-served our veterans must also take note of how the official mind-set is often shaped—and sometimes misshaped—by the sudden demands of a poorly planned war. In those times of official strain, government officials and their lower-level minions have been known to intentionally deceive young citizens in order to make themselves look good in the eyes of their military-bureaucratic bosses.

It was the autumn of 2006 and plans for the Iraq War military buildup known as the surge were already drafted. Recruiters were under intense pressure to meet their enlistment quotas in the all-volunteer military. A year earlier, the army had failed to meet its quota for the first time in years. The number of recruits had dropped from 250,000 in fiscal 2004 to 215,000 in fiscal 2005, according to a GAO report. The strains of the sustained combat in an Iraq War that had spun out of control meant that the armed services were stretched perilously thin.

This was a time in which resources at all levels of the military establishment were far below what they needed to be. Officials at all levels of military and defense were coming under pressure to meet goals that could not be met. And when the goals were not being met, those who paid the toughest price were not the top policymakers whose misjudgments had led to problems in the Iraq War. It was the men and women of the U.S. military who at times were disserved—from their first encounter at a military recruitment office to their combat ordeal of being sent into harm's way underequipped, lacking life-saving armor for themselves and their vehicles. The responsibility for the ways in which they were disserved extended from the most senior official in the E-ring of the Pentagon to those loneliest of outposts, the recruitment offices in the suburbs that ring our cities.

In some recruitment offices, recruiters were misleading, and sometimes deliberately deceiving, young Americans in their desperation to make their monthly quotas. Journalists at ABC News and WABC-TV in New York City went under cover, using hidden cameras and microphones to record what recruiters were actually telling young prospects in ten army recruitment offices in the New York suburbs of Long Island and Westchester County, in New Jersey, and in Connecticut. WABC-TV investigative reporter Jim Hoffer reported in a November 2006 story that more than half of the recruiters his team videotaped had either stretched the truth or flat-out lied to the youths. More than half. There is no way of knowing just how prevalent this sort of prevarication was, for few news organizations were as enterprising as WABC-TV. But the real value of WABC-TV's exclusive was in what it told us about the desperate state of the military, which was under pressure from its civilian chieftains whose miscalculations had put the U.S. military in such jeopardy in the first place.

In a New Jersey suburb, a student wearing an undercover camera and microphone supplied by WABC-TV walked into an army recruiting office to test the spiel. The student asked about the chances of being sent into combat: Aren't people still being shipped out? "Naw," replied the Army recruiter, "they bringing people back."

Student: "Nobody is going out to Iraq anymore?"

Army recruiter: "Naw, we bringing people back."

In Mount Vernon, New York, a WABC-TV undercover student asked an army recruiter about the prospects of being sent to fight in the Iraq War. "We're, like, we're not at war," said the recruiter. "War ended a long time ago," and added: "The news never said war, they're not lying now, they never said war."

In another conversation, an undercover student asked: "Will I be going to war?" The recruiter replied: "I would say your chances would be slim to none."

In Yonkers, New York, an army recruiter told a youth that it was possible to avoid being sent into combat unless a recruit chose a specialty that was deemed essential: "As long as you don't choose a job in this area, you don't have to worry about going over there."

Of course, some of the recruiters went about their job honorably and truthfully. In Stamford, Connecticut, an army recruiter who was asked about the chances of being sent to war replied candidly: "Every job in the army does include combat. Plain and simple."

But in a number of the other offices, recruiters found ways to shade the truth to make it more palatable. Nearly half of the recruiters found some way of linking the prospective dangers in the Iraq War to life right there in the New York suburbs.

In Patchogue, Long Island, an Army recruiter said: "You have a ten times greater chance of dying out here on the roads than you do dying in Iraq." Also: "We've had more close calls on the Long Island Expressway than we did when we were over there."

In Elizabeth, New Jersey, the recruiter said: "I like Subway sandwiches and salads. I watched the news yesterday, a guy got killed at Subway."

The Army's top officer in charge of recruiting in the northeast United States, Colonel Robert Manning of the 1st Recruiting Brigade, agreed to review the undercover videotapes for WABC-TV and he clearly was not happy with what he saw and heard. "It's hard to believe some of things they are telling perspective applicants," Manning said. "I still believe that this is the exception more than the norm."

That led investigative correspondent Hoffer to ask: "Well, what are you saying, then? That we just got wildly lucky to find recruiters—more than half of the ten we visited—to be stretching the truth or even worse, lying?" Replied the colonel: "I've visited many stations myself, and I know that we have many wonderful Americans serving in uniform as recruiters." But

Manning surely understood that recruiters would be on their best behavior when he was on hand—which does not mean that the recruiters, under pressure as they were to make their quotas, might be a little less proper (that is, less truthful) when the only person in the room was an impressionable student who was thinking about joining the army.

After Manning reviewed a number of the tapes in which recruiters seemed to minimize the chances of being sent into combat, Hoffer asked: "Chances are if you're signing up to the army these days, you have a pretty good chance of going to Iraq, don't you?" "I would not disagree with that," said the colonel. "We are an army and a nation at war still."

The Yonkers army recruiter told the undercover student that if a recruit didn't care for army life, he or she could simply quit and go home: "It's called 'failure to adapt' discharge. It's an entry-level discharge, so it won't affect anything on your record. It will just be like it never happened."

WABC-TV's Hoffer asked Colonel Manning about that: "This recruiter makes it seem it's pretty easy to get out of it if you change your mind. Is that true?" The colonel replied: "I would believe it's not as easy as he would lead you to believe it is."

Hoffer: "It's probably pretty tough, isn't it?"

Col. Manning: "It's tough."

Later, the journalist asked the colonel: "Doesn't this fly in the face of what this military stands for—honesty and honor?"

The chief of recruitment, who was public-spirited enough to volunteer to put himself through this public wringer, replied: "Yes, obviously, there is training that needs to be done." Unspoken but understood is the fact that no amount of training could change individuals who think it is okay to lie or con impressionable and trusting young men and women—just to meet their quotas.

Meanwhile, the government itself looked into these allegations of recruiter cheating and misconduct. According to a GAO investigation, statistics from the Defense Department show that allegations of recruiter improprieties increased dramatically, from 4,400 cases in fiscal 2004 to 6,600 cases in fiscal 2005. The GAO said these improprieties include actions that are "perpetrated by a recruiter or alleged to be perpetrated by a recruiter to facilitate the recruiting process for an applicant. These recruiter irregularities range from administrative paperwork errors, to actions such as failing to disclose disqualifying eligibility criteria or instructing applicants not to reveal medical conditions or prior civil litigation, to criminal violations committed by a recruiter who is subsequently prosecuted under articles of the Uniform Code of Military Justice. Criminal violations may include such actions as sexual harassment and falsifying documents."

According to the August 2006, GAO report, "A 2005 internal DOD survey reports about 20 percent of active-duty recruiters believe that irregularities occur frequently."

The GAO investigators also reported that the Defense Department "is not in a sound position to assure Congress and the general public that it knows the full extent to which recruiter irregularities are occurring."

The old marine is looking troubled. It is 2006 and he has made a lot of money since his days in Vietnam. Construction is his game. Well, actually golf is his game, and now he is flying from his Atlanta office down to his Florida home on a golf course for the weekend. He is my seatmate on this AirTran Airways flight, and he is saying that he has just gotten an e-mail from his son and he is upset about what his son had to say. His son has asked him for his holiday season gift a little early this year—it's always money. But that isn't what has set the old marine's jaw so tight. His son is an army man. He's in Iraq, in Fallujah, and he has e-mailed that he would like his gift early this year so that he can buy himself some body armor. As the old marine talks, the muscle at the back of his jaw starts to clench and unclench rapidly. Of course he'll get the money—at once! But that isn't what is upsetting. He's upset because he is thinking about his son's fellow soldiers. Fine young men, all, but they don't have multimillionaire dads they can hit up for money for body armor. So when they all go into harm's way, some will be safer than others. "Dammit, it's not right. It's wrong. Very wrong. Our government owes it to our troops to give them the best state-of-the-art equipment. Because this is about saving lives."

This was the first I'd heard about the body armor problem. And I was as stunned as my seatmate was. I told him I thought there was something else bugging him: he'd always voted Republican—he was all for President Bush. "Exactly. And Cheney. And Rumsfeld. And now I am mad that they've let this happen—sent our troops into war without the armor they need. It is just plain wrong."

Soon the Pentagon explains that it is getting the best armor it can, as fast as it can. But these things take time, the Pentagon says. Which begs the question: How can an individual soldier in Iraq procure body armor if the Pentagon can't? Easy: the soldier went online, found body armor at a military surplus site, and ordered from that commercial store what Uncle Sam's store could not provide.

On December 8, 2004, Defense Secretary Donald Rumsfeld went to visit U.S. troops in Kuwait, to give them a pep talk as they were being deployed to Iraq. To boost morale, Rumsfeld held a sort of town meeting with the troops. He talked to them mostly about World War II, about saving Europe and the sixty-third anniversary of the bombing of Pearl Harbor, and about the inauguration just a day earlier of Afghanistan's democratically elected president. The secretary wanted to make the troops feel hopeful. He wound up getting an earful, according to the reports from U.S. journalists who covered the event and the DOD's own transcript, available on its Web site.

Specialist Thomas Wilson, an airplane mechanic with the Tennessee Army National Guard, raised his hand and Rumsfeld called on him to ask a question.

> **Q:** Yes, Mr. Secretary. My question is more logistical. We've had troops in Iraq for coming up on three years and we've always staged here out of Kuwait. Now, why do we soldiers have to dig through local landfills for pieces of scrap metal and compromise ballistic glass to up-armor our vehicles, and why don't we have those resources readily available to us?

Wilson's question was greeted by loud cheers and hoots and applause. The specter of American troops having to scrounge through landfill looking for junk to "up-armor" their vehicles in the hopes of saving their lives was shocking. Rumsfeld, a former pilot whose hearing suffers from what he likes to call his "aviator's ear," either couldn't hear or sought more time to sort his answer. Wilson warmed to his task, politely but pointedly.

> **SEC. RUMSFELD:** I missed the first part of your question. And could you repeat it for me?

> **Q:** Yes, Mr. Secretary. Our soldiers have been fighting in Iraq for coming up on three years. A lot of us are getting ready to move north relatively soon. Our vehicles are not

armored. We're digging pieces of rusted scrap metal and compromised ballistic glass that's already been shot up, dropped, busted, picking the best out of this scrap to put on our vehicles to take into combat. We do not have proper armament vehicles to carry with us north.

SEC. RUMSFELD: I talked to the General coming out here about the pace at which the vehicles are being armored. They have been brought from all over the world, wherever they're not needed, to a place here where they are needed. I'm told that they are being—the Army is—I think it's something like 400 a month are being done. And it's essentially a matter of physics. It isn't a matter of money. It isn't a matter on the part of the Army of desire. It's a matter of production and capability of doing it.

As you know, you go to war with the Army you have. They're not the Army you might want or wish to have at a later time. Since the Iraq conflict began, the Army has been pressing ahead to produce the armor necessary at a rate that they believe—it's a greatly expanded rate from what existed previously, but a rate that they believe is the rate that is all that can be accomplished at this moment.

I can assure you that General Schoomaker and the leadership in the Army and certainly General Whitcomb are sensitive to the fact that not every vehicle has the degree of armor that would be desirable for it to have, but that they're working at it at a good clip. It's interesting, I've talked a great deal about this with a team of people who've been working on it hard at the Pentagon. And if you think about it, you can have all the armor in the world on a tank and a tank can be blown up. And you can have an up-armored Humvee and it can be blown up. And you can go down and, the vehicle, the goal we have is to have as many of those vehicles as is humanly possible with the appropriate level of armor available for the troops. And that is what the Army has been working on. . . .

The other day, after there was a big threat alert in Washington, D.C. in connection with the elections, as I recall, I looked outside the Pentagon and there were six or eight up-armored Humvees. They're not there anymore. [Cheers] [Applause] They're en route out here, I can assure you.

The next day, the news accounts would highlight just a few of Rumsfeld's sentences. Rumsfeld would be forever remembered as having said: "As you know, you go to war with the Army you have. They're not the Army you might want or wish to have at a later time." Also: "And if you think about it, you can have all the armor in the world on a tank and a tank can be blown up. And you can have an up-armored Humvee and it can be blown up."

Washington was stoked. Democrats rushed to the cameras: "Callous . . . contemptuous . . . stunning." Republicans were equally appalled, but quieter. A Rumsfeld spokesperson said that, in autumn of 2003, only 156 of these armored Humvees were being made each month. But when the Pentagon needed more, the production rate was jumped all the way to 450. Which makes you wonder why, if they were so conscientious and caring, wasn't it done that way from the outset.

Every few months, for the next several years, the news media would carry another report that read like the same old problem, revisited. Troops lack body armor; vehicles lack protective armor. U.S. men and women were dying and being seriously wounded because the Pentagon had not planned ahead to protect the troops from the harm that would come their way in the war in Iraq.

On September 29, 2005, Associated Press correspondent Lolita C. Baldor reported: "Nearly a year after Congress demanded action, the Pentagon has still failed to figure out a way to reimburse soldiers for body armor and equipment they purchased to better protect themselves while serving in Iraq."

All the while, U.S. troops were being killed by roadside bombs. On January 7, 2006, with body armor still largely undelivered, *New York Times* correspondent Michael Moss reported on a classified Pentagon memo that for the first time put numbers to the human carnage resulting from the lack of proper armor:

> *A secret Pentagon study has found that as many as 80 percent of the marines who have been killed in Iraq from wounds to the upper body could have survived if they had had extra body armor. Such armor has been available since 2003, but until recently the Pentagon has largely declined to supply it to troops despite calls from the field for additional protection, according to military officials.*

The problem was that the ceramic shields that are worn by most of the troops in Iraq only cover the chest and back. The memo said that 74 of 93 marines who had suffered fatal wounds were hit in the side and shoulder areas that remained uncovered. The report said that 340 U.S. troops in Iraq died from wounds to the torso. Moss's exclusive article proved politically explosive: it was the first time the military's medical examiner had revealed the true cost of inadequate body armor.

Although the troops had been urgently requesting improved body armor since the war began, the Marine Corps waited until September 2005 before buying twenty-eight thousand sets of armor that covered the exposed sides of troops, Moss reported. And as of the start of 2006, the army was still trying to make a decision on what type of armor to purchase for its 130,000 soldiers.

According to the *Times* article, the extra armor for the Marines would only cost $260 a set. Military officials had initially decided that the extra protective plates would add too much weight and hamper the free movement of the troops wearing fully equipped vests, so they had opted for the lighter, less protective equipment. But the results of this secret Pentagon study were said to have convinced the Marine Corps to sweep aside those concerns about weight and restrictive movement in the interest of trying to give the troops maximum protection, the newspaper reported. "As the information became more prevalent and aware to everybody that in fact these were casualty sites that they needed to be worried about, then people were much more willing to accept that weight on their body," Major Wendell Leimbach, a body armor specialist with the Marine Corps procurement unit, told *The Times*. It turned out that since March 2003, the Pentagon had been gathering information about the extent of the wounds in order to determine just how significant body armor could be in protecting troops. In 2003, Dr. Craig T. Mallak, medical examiner for the military, told a military panel that the Pentagon's data "screams to be published," according to *The Times*. But two years would pass before the information was made public. Meanwhile, the Marine Corps reportedly asked for the information in August 2004. But—and this is mind-boggling—the Marines balked at paying the medical examiner $107,000 to have the information analyzed. Because of haggling over this paltry sum of money, the study didn't start until December 2004 and the Marine Corps didn't begin getting the analysis until June 2005.

The fact seems so absurd that the mind wants to reject what

the eyes are reading. For want of a measly $107,000 vital information was withheld from the Pentagon thinkers who might have acted earlier to get more armor to the troops. And while these troops were dying for want of armor, thousands of people who work in the Pentagon were going home to their comfortable suburbs in Virginia each night and dining with their families.

The Times noted that the Pentagon had also encountered extensive problems in getting vehicles with better armor. Time after time, official pronouncements about production schedules of these improved armored vehicles would be followed by reports of delays on the production lines.

Early in the Iraq War, the *Times* article reported, the Pentagon experienced shortages in obtaining plates for the bulletproof vests. Not until 2005, two years into the war, did the Pentagon begin using a model with stronger plates that would provide greater protection. Since the first days of the war, soldiers had been seeking added protection to prevent bullets from piercing the sides of their bodies. They hung armor designed to be crotch protectors under their arms to provide greater protection to the side areas that the troops felt were most vulnerable to insurgent attacks. And some soldiers began trying to buy their own armor.

All in all, it was a rather pathetic period in American warfare. Les Brownlee, former acting secretary of the army, had ordered a study of the armor pros and cons. The study, obtained by *The Times*, came to this conclusion: "Our preliminary research suggests that as many as 42 percent of the Marine casualties who died from isolated torso injuries could have been prevented with improved protection in the areas surrounding the plated areas of the vest." Another 23 percent of the marines who died from torso injuries might have been saved with side plates that extend below the arms, while 15 percent more could have benefited from

shoulder plates, the report said. Analyses by military patholo-
gists showed that at least three hundred lives might have been
saved by better body armor.

There was one more outrage to come. It had to do with why the
Pentagon's armor manufacturing contractors were falling so far
behind their production schedules. The reason was in large part
due to the fact that the Pentagon miscalculated its armor needs
because it did not anticipate that there would be a significant insurgent opposition. Also, Pentagon cost-cutting had caused serious disruptions for some of the armor contractors, and some were
on the verge of shutting down because of lack of business.

On February 12, 2007, *Washington Post* correspondent Ann
Scott Tyson reported that thousands of the army's Humvees still
lacked the life-saving armor: "The Army is working to fill a
shortfall in Iraq of thousands of advanced Humvee armor kits
designed to reduce U.S. troop deaths from roadside bombs—
including a rising threat from particularly lethal weapons linked
to Iran and known as 'explosively formed penetrators' (EFP)—
that are now inflicting 70 percent of the American casualties in
the country, according to U.S. military and civilian officials."

After four years of war in Iraq, a pattern had long ago been
established. The media would report that troops were being
killed because they lacked armored protection. Then the Pentagon would explain that it was doing the best that it could. Then
Congress would pound on the Pentagon. Then the Pentagon
would find a way to do much better. Then a new problem would
surface—and the whole series would be repeated.

But that same month, a new sort of body armor story surfaced. It was a very human story about one very inhumane
snafu, courtesy of the U.S. Army.

On February 8, 2006, the Associated Press carried a story by
correspondent Allison Barker that seemed almost to be dark

comedy. The story, written in a straightforward tone, provoked instant outrage just by reciting the barest of facts, accurately and in context:

Charleston, W.Va. (Feb. 8)—A former soldier injured in Iraq is getting a refund after being forced to pay for his missing body armor vest, which medics destroyed because it was soaked with his blood, officials said Wednesday.

First Lt. William "Eddie" Rebrook IV, 25, had to leave the Army with a shrapnel injury to his arm. But before he could be discharged last week, he says he had to scrounge up cash from his buddies to pay $632 for the body armor and other gear he had lost.

Rebrook, who graduated from West Point with honors, said he was billed because a supply officer failed to document that the vest was destroyed as a biohazard. He said a battalion commander refused to sign a waiver for the vest, saying Rebrook would have to supply witness statements to verify the vest was taken from him and burned.

"When that vest was removed from my bleeding body in Iraq, it was no longer my responsibility," Rebrook said Wednesday.

This is the sort of story that gives institutions a bad name, be they the U.S. Army or the Department of Veterans Affairs. It is an example of the blatantly uncaring action that becomes emblematic of bureaucrats in so many organizations, a broad application of guilt by symbolism that is in one sense unfair to those who do their jobs caringly and carefully. But perhaps it is not all that unfair because too many who do their jobs well are too often content to keep their heads down and fail to speak up and stop practices by others that are plainly wrong.

13

An Agent Orange Veterans Day

The skies are gray and so is the mood on this Veterans Day 2007 in Washington, D.C. Just to the west, Abraham Lincoln is sitting in his chair, looking down from his monument upon several thousand veterans who are clustered around memorials to the veterans from a century that was busy with wars. To the east, old soldiers, octogenarians now, many in wheelchairs, are with their families at the sprawling monument to what they fought for in World War II, a big and busy memorial featuring fifty pillars, one for each state, etched with sayings commemorating an achievement that even today seems breathtaking in its success against all odds. Farther west on the mall, just south of the Reflecting Pool that stretches almost from the Lincoln Memorial to the Washington Monument, Korean War veterans, who are septuagenarians now, are moving with their families around the walkway that features statues of soldiers bent by the burdens they carry, not fighting but just trooping eastward, faces weary from their ordeal and the penetrating cold.

On the other side of the Reflecting Pool and just a bit farther

west, closer to Lincoln's perch, is the monument you cannot see
from a distance because it was built on a graceful downward in-
cline; it has none of the attention-grabbing characteristics of
those white granite pillars of World War II or those larger-than-
life gray stone soldiers of Korea. It is just a long low slab of black
granite, engraved with 58,249 names—men and women killed in
the war in Vietnam. The ones who didn't come home alive are
surrounded today by their buddies who did. Many are with their
families today, pausing to point out a name, reaching out to
touch the wall. They remember the battles. They remember being home watching on their television sets as the enemy took the
South Vietnam capital they had been defending. They remember watching as that last chopper lifted off the pad of human
desperation atop what they always thought was the impenetrable U.S. embassy. But that was so long ago, and it is the one
memory no one talks about.

The troops have reconnoitered at the wall, and today they are
remembering so much of what they spent so long trying to forget, those days and nights down in the swamp jungles of the
Mekong Delta or way up at the North Vietnam border. They remembered McNamara's line. The folly masterminded by a defense secretary so enamored of his own brilliance and infallibility
that he confidently stripped the vegetation from a broad swath
of jungle and seeded it with state-of-the-art electronic sensors
that it was said would make it impossible for the enemy to move
south undetected—the same enemy who eventually cakewalked
into Saigon.

Veterans Day is a somber one for all veterans, but especially
for the veterans of a war that was lost, who never came home to
parades and tickertape. On this gray day, hundreds of them have
gathered to hear one of their own, General Colin Powell, give a
speech. But all of them, the general included, know this day is

not about speech making, nor is it even about those who are here to hear it. It is about those names on the wall and what Vietnam took away and never gave back to those who came home. They were the ones who accomplished their missions over there but never got to celebrate a mission accomplished over here.

Today many are wearing a hat or part of the uniform they wore over there; others are wearing jackets from the fraternity of those who served. Among them are four guys in black jackets that are loaded, NASCAR-style, with emblems surrounding lettering that says they are from the Vietnam Veterans of America, Nassau County chapter. They are Long Island guys, which means that they will be straight talkers who will tell you right off what is on their minds. And what's on their minds today, along with those names now on the wall of buddies who were once at their side, is the fact that they still have to fight battles. Not with the Vietcong or the North Vietnamese army (we have made peace and now do business with them). But with a legion of lawyers and bureaucrats who bivouac in daylight just eight blocks east and eight blocks north of the wall, in that gray and beige stone building on Vermont Avenue NW, the Department of Veterans Affairs.

"They try to discourage you from filing a claim for benefits—it's bah-bah this, bah-bah that," says John Rezin, age sixty, of West Babylon, Long Island, a navy guy whose job in the war included ferrying supplies to the Green Berets at the Cambodian border—good training for his later work as a UPS driver stateside. But he insists that the VA give him his medical tests, which he is allowed twice a year. He does so because of what he learned from the guy standing at his side, Joe Ingino, fifty-nine, of Hicksville, Long Island, who was U.S. Army, 1st Infantry Division. Joe, who went on to drive a truck after the war, is now called "the preacher" by his pals because for the last four years he's been preaching at them to get checked out regularly at the VA hospital on Long Island. He did, and it may have saved his life. "I was an infantry guy and I was all over where they sprayed Agent Orange," says Ingino. "So I went in for my test four years ago and—yup—I've got diabetes."

By the time Ingino got tested and discovered his diabetes, the VA had moved from its knee-jerk position of flat-out denial to admitting that Agent Orange did indeed contribute to the onset of diabetes. So Joe applied, got his benefits, and then became a preacher on the Vietnam vets circuit, cajoling one and all to get tested before it is too late.

Gregory Chiappoine, of Levittown, Long Island, was a navy helicopter door gunner who got shot down over the Mekong Delta, in South Vietnam. His buddies got him out of the swampland. He's had a 50 percent disability from PTSD. ("I've got a real bad temper," he says.) Joe had been preaching at Greg about getting tested for so long that one day he went to the Northport VA hospital, got an appointment, and got tested. "I thought I'd get the all-clear. But they discovered nodules in my lung. So now I'm monitoring that."

While Joe, Greg, and John are talking on the steps between the Lincoln Memorial and the Reflecting Pool, they are also on their cell phones trying to find Frank—"he's the guy you really got to talk to, because he's the one who really knows his stuff," says John. Just as he says that, up walks Frank Tobani of Wantagh, Long Island. He is the claims service officer of their chapter, and while he can sling it with the best of them, he can also talk it with lawyerlike precision and specificity.

"In the early days, the government just denied everything, every claim that linked exposure to Agent Orange to physical problems that showed up later," Tobani says. He runs through the short course of how the VA used to have these maps detailing precisely where and when Agent Orange was sprayed—"and you had to show that you were there, in the right place at precisely the right time." It was an absurd procedure, so absurd, in fact, that even the VA jettisoned it after a couple of decades of denials. After all, this was wartime—guerrilla warfare at that—and troops were everywhere, in and out. Agent Orange was sprayed here and there as needed in the rush of combat, and much later, somebody would try to do the paperwork, to make up something resembling what actually happened.

So the VA changed its rules and now, all vets who were in Vietnam during the period when Agent Orange was sprayed are presumed to have been exposed. And they will be covered for service-related benefits if they develop physical symptoms for a specific list of maladies, declared by the National Academy of Sciences to be presumptively caused by exposure to Agent Orange. Tobani talks about the slow pace of the process; claims filed by veterans exposed to Agent Orange were originally denied; years later, when those specific diseases were put on the list, the veterans had to go through the entire process all over again, filling out new forms and so on. (The VA Web site has a section on Agent Orange: "These are the diseases which VA currently presumes resulted from exposure to herbicides like Agent Orange.")

Tobani starts ticking off the chronology of complex medical problems originally denied but now covered; the complex names drawn from his mental list roll easily off his tongue. "Peripheral neuropathy, acute or sub acute," was put on the list relatively early; spina bifida birth defect of children born to Vietnam veterans made the list later; diabetes was included just a few years ago. A liver disease and some cancers are on the list—respiratory cancers, prostate cancer, some brain cancers—"but not glioblastoma, because the VA is dead set against approving it for Agent Orange," Tobani says. "At least not until the National Academy of Sciences approves it." As Tobani speaks, it is easy for a listener to understand why his pals from Nassau County Chapter 82 rely upon his legal and medical knowledge as they try to sort through the complex regulations about what is covered and what isn't. But Tobani isn't a lawyer; he's a phone company representative. Somebody had to step in and help his Vietnam vet pals, so he volunteered and made it his business to become knowledgeable and to stay up to date.

"I just found some ranchers in Canada who have an unusually high rate of cancer after handling some herbicides," Tobani says. He does his research to help his pals, and of course many veterans he may never meet. But the Department of Veterans Affairs should be taking the lead in researching this—and other health issues that have become health crises for veterans.

Yet the de facto position of the VA in so many of these veterans' health matters often seems to be willful denial. For example: the question of whether exposure to Agent Orange in Vietnam contributed in any way to the susceptibility of veterans to contract Parkinson's disease in later life. For two decades the VA watched from the sidelines while highly respected research groups conducted scientific investigations that turned up possible but not definite linkages between herbicides and Parkinson's. In 1994 the National Academy of Sciences' Institute of Medicine issued the first of four studies that were titled "Veterans and Agent Orange." In a section subtitled "Health Effects of Herbicides Used in Vietnam" that 1994 report stated: "In the past decade . . . an increasing concern has developed scientifically over the possible link between Parkinsonism and chemicals used as herbicides and pesticides. . . . These data support the concept that some herbicides and pesticides could possibly be associated with Parkinsonism." The three following studies essentially reinforced the possibility of such a link but found no absolute proof of it.

So the VA chose once again to grasp a scientific loophole and use it to justify not giving the monetary benefit of the medical doubt to Vietnam veterans who had been exposed to Agent Orange and later contracted Parkinson's. The VA continued to list Parkinson's in its list of diseases for which service-related benefits were not warranted due to exposure to Agent Orange. In July 2001 the VA issued an "Agent Orange Review" that stated that the only way a veteran who suffered from Parkinson's could get service-related disability compensation was to provide "evidence that it was acquired in military service." The VA added: "This means that the symptoms began or worsened during active duty or within one year of discharge." Of course, the VA knew well that serious illnesses such as Parkinson's or cancers usually develop long after an exposure to a toxic agent. Indeed, by the end of 2000 the VA reported that only 649 veterans from all wars had been diagnosed with Parkinson's and thus had been granted service-related disability benefits.

In 2005 the Board of Veterans' Appeals issued a ruling in an Agent Orange–Parkinson's case that was indeed significant, ruling in favor of a Vietnam veteran who had contracted Parkinson's and against the VA adjudicators of the regional office in Winston-Salem, North Carolina, who had denied him service-related disability benefits. The case originated with a request for service-related disability benefits that was filed in March 2002 by an army veteran from North Carolina who had been diagnosed with Parkinson's disease twenty-nine years after he came home from the Vietnam War. According to case records filed with the board, the American Legion had worked with the veteran to prepare his case. The case record showed that while the veteran's civilian job after the war had caused him to work with heavy metals, which some studies have shown could be a factor in Parkinson's if large quantities were absorbed in his system, a screening test had shown the metallic traces in his body were within normal limits. The case record noted that in June 2002 Dr. Ellis F. Muther, a private physician who examined the veteran's case history, concluded that there was no explanation for his Parkinson's "except a possible exposure to Agent Orange." The report said it was the examining physician's view that "Agent Orange had been demonstrated to be a neurotoxin" and that it was "highly possible that that was a contributing factor in the etiology of the appellant's Parkinson's disease."

Meanwhile, according to the case record, the Veterans Benefits Administration had initially dismissed the veteran's claim without going into case detail but merely issuing what is called a "Fast Letter" on June 25, 2003, which noted that a National Academy of Sciences study had concluded that "the credible evidence against an association between herbicide exposure and Parkinson's disease outweighed the credible evidence for such an association." But in December 2003 the Board of Veterans' Appeals remanded the case back to the regional office, requesting that the veteran at least be given a VA neurological examination to determine whether he had Parkinson's. Two months later the board also asked a Veterans' Health Administration expert to review the veteran's file and specifically provide an opinion as to whether it was "at least as likely as not that the appellant's Parkinson's disease was related to his period of military service, to specifically include his presumed exposure to herbicide, including Agent Orange, while in Vietnam."

In August 2004 the veteran underwent a VA neurological exam that confirmed he had Parkinson's. The board opinion noted that after a three-day review of existing scientific and medical literature, "the examiner opined that it was at least as likely as not that the appellant's Parkinson's disease may be related to exposure to Agent Orange or other herbicide exposure in Vietnam."

On March 30, 2005, after that apparently significant step forward, the case was shoved one step backward. The Veterans' Health Administration's chief of neurology weighed in, with an analysis based on that 2002 thesis from the Institute of Medicine that a link between the herbicides and Parkinson's was "biologically plausible," but no definite connection had since been established. According to the board's report, "the VHA neurologist stated that he did not find any details of the appellant's particular military service or of his neurologic condition to lead to any conclusion different from that of the Institute of Medicine, namely that there was no definite etiologic link between Agent Orange exposure and subsequent Parkinson's disease." And with that, the pro-veteran rationale that it was "at least as likely as not" was brushed aside as if it were a pesky housefly.

However, in this particular case at least, the Board of Veterans' Appeals had clearly moved away from the VA's reflexively negative, linear mind-set of deny-unless-forced-to-approve that was clearly still dominant in the VA's approach to claims. The board's written opinion carefully built a case, block by block, for supporting the veteran's claim rather than routinely denying it when the cause-and-effect evidence remained in doubt. First the board's opinion noted that the Veterans Education and Benefits Expansion Act of 2001 had required that veterans who served in Vietnam would be presumed to have been exposed to Agent Orange. The board pointed out that the VA had maintained that this presumed exposure to the herbicide did not constitute a reason for service-related disability for a number of illnesses for which scientific studies had found that the herbicide was a plausible but not definitive proof that it caused the illness; and presented the list of health problems (including Parkinson's) for which the VA secretary had not ruled a presumption of service-related connection was required.

In building its case for a ruling undoing the VA's long-standing policy, the board of appeals went on to note that the VA's reviews of the evidence in this veteran's claim had not disproved the statement of the veteran's examining physician, Dr. Muther, who found that the veteran's possible exposure to Agent Orange was the only contributing cause he could identify for the veteran's Parkinson's. Thus, the physician had concluded, it had to be considered highly possible that Agent Orange caused the veteran's Parkinson's.

The board's opinion then observed that "the fact that medicine is still a somewhat inexact science, the Board must resign itself to dealing with medical opinion evidence couched in terms such as 'highly possible,' 'at least as likely as not,' and 'biologically plausible,' rather than absolutes. . . . Under the benefit-of-the-doubt rule, in order for a claimant to prevail, there need not be a preponderance of the evidence in the veteran's favor, but only an approximate balance of the positive and negative evidence. In other words, the preponderance of the evidence must be against the claim for the benefit to be denied.

"Thus . . . the Board finds that the evidence for and against the appellant's claim for service connection for Parkinson's disease is in a state of relative equipoise. With reasonable doubt resolved in the appellant's favor, the Board concludes that service connection is warranted. . . . Entitlement to service connection for Parkinson's disease is granted."

With that, the Board of Veterans' Appeals, which makes the final decisions on behalf of the VA secretary on decisions from the local and regional officers, demolished the rationale that the VA adjudicators had used for routinely denying claims of Vietnam veterans who were presumed to have been exposed to Agent Orange and were later diagnosed with Parkinson's. Indeed, the board's ruling could have become historic, except for the fact that the VA chose not to treat the opinion as precedent-setting. Instead of adopting the board's rationales for reversing the department's long-standing denial policy, the VA viewed the appellate opinion as applying only to that one case—and continued to deny similar claims of other Vietnam veterans.

Meanwhile, medical research made major advances in firming up the linkage between Agent Orange exposure and Parkinson's. Those advances should have caused a VA that truly had the best interests of veterans at heart to move swiftly to grant all claims of Vietnam veterans suffering from Parkinson's—and even take the initiative to contact all veterans whose similar claims had previously been denied.

Researchers at the Mayo Clinic in Rochester, Minnesota, studied all of the Parkinson's cases that occurred in Olmsted County, where the clinic is located, from 1976 to 1995. They concluded that men who used pesticides in farming or for other purposes had an increased risk of developing Parkinson's disease; but there was no increase in risk for women who used pesticides. Dr. Jim Maraganore, Mayo Clinic neurologist and study investigator, explained: "What we think may be happening is that pesticide use combines with other risk factors in men's environment or genetic makeup, causing them to cross over the threshold into developing the disease. By contrast, estrogen may protect women from the toxic effects of pesticides."

And in February 2007, investigators at St. Jude Children's Research Hospital released a study, published online by the National Academy of Sciences, that they said was significant because it "sheds light on the cause of most cases of Parkinson's disease, which currently are unexplained. . . . Although most Parkinson's disease cases have no known cause, experts believe that they are caused by the interaction of genetic susceptibility to Parkinson's disease with exposure to a variety of environmental

factors, such as pesticides and herbicides." The St. Jude an-
nouncement noted: "Parkinson's disease is a disease in which
nerve cells in part of the brain called the substantia nigra die, resulting in the loss of dopamine, a nerve-signaling molecule that
helps control muscle movement. The absence of dopamine from
these cells, called dopaminergic neurons, causes a loss of muscle
control, trembling and lack of coordination." According to the report's senior author, Richard Smeyne, Ph.D., an associate member of the Department of Developmental Neurobiology at St.
Jude: "The majority of these cases of Parkinson's disease appear
to arise because individuals who have a genetic susceptibility to
the disease are exposed to environmental toxins such as pesticides and herbicides, which trigger the formation of free radicals
that kill dopaminergic neurons in the substantia nigra."

VA officials who were truly committed to their department's
statement of its mission—"We have reformed our department
internally and are striving for high quality, prompt and seamless
service to veterans"—could have used the study published by
the National Academy of Sciences to reach an important new
conclusion that could have brought honor and dignity, comfort
and closure, to many Vietnam veterans who had fallen ill with
Parkinson's and were being forced to fight the VA to get the benefits they apparently deserved. The VA could have made the
study its basis for a commonsense conclusion: that (in the par-
lance the VA finds legalistically convenient) it was more likely
than not that Agent Orange contributed to the cases of Parkinson's disease in Vietnam veterans. If seamless service was their
commitment and their mind-set, VA policymakers could have
just said yes. With just a few keystrokes they could have added
Parkinson's to their list of diseases that the VA currently presumes resulted from exposure to herbicides like Agent Orange.

14

Living Monuments

The True Cost of the Iraq War

Monuments to wars exist in just about every city and town in the United States. Some of the monuments are cast from metals; others are chiseled from stone. Some are statues, others obelisks, columns or slabs. But the monuments in every U.S. city and town to the Iraq War and the Afghanistan War are something else. They are alive. They are breathing, thinking, talking, walking (sometimes with manufactured marvels of engineering, science and medicine). These living monuments are men and women who have come home injured but alive from the wars in Iraq and Afghanistan. Most of them would never have come home from any of the wars that came before.

For every U.S. military man or woman killed in the wars in Iraq and Afghanistan, 16 have come home injured. That may read as just another statistical sentence in a book; but when put into context, it becomes a description of a living monument to a killing war, the likes of which we have never seen before. In World Wars I and II, for every military person killed, fewer than

2 came back injured but alive. In Korea, for every military person killed, 2.6 returned injured but alive; in Vietnam, just 2.8.

Many of the veterans who have come home injured in the wars in Iraq and Afghanistan are very badly injured. Others, at a glance, appear relatively unscathed; but they too have suffered severe injuries—wounds that are very real, very painful, but virtually invisible. One of the legacies of the war in Iraq, especially, is that it has produced a signature set of injuries to the head that occurred in two forms: physical and psychological. Each can be devastating.

Traumatic brain injuries were inflicted in numbers far greater than in previous wars by roadside bombs known as IEDs (improvised explosive devices) that were planted by terrorists and insurgents. The IEDs create a concussive hell inside the U.S. enclosed personnel vehicles, throwing human bodies into the metal and steel sides and roofs; soldiers suffer traumatic brain injuries so severe and so extensive that they now are designated by just the initials TBI.

The other form of head injury is the searing psychological damage caused by the horrors that troops have seen inflicted not just on their fellow soldiers but upon civilians, often young children. In the Iraq and Afghanistan wars, these cases have been diagnosed as post-traumatic stress disorder (PTSD), a term that was not used in previous wars when soldiers also returned home from combat with severe psychological impairment. The number of diagnoses of psychological trauma in veterans of Iraq and Afghanistan far exceeds those in previous wars, although that is significantly due to increased awareness within the medical community, not necessarily an increase in combat horrors.

Veterans of Iraq and Afghanistan return to their homes with all of these injuries. Many are quite seriously damaged, and all of them must be treated and cared for and brought back into productive daily life as much as possible. The good news is that in many cases, much is now possible, over time and with proper funding and care.

Meanwhile, in a volume that is mainly taking a historical and often critical look at the way we as a culture, a country and a government have failed to properly care for our war veterans, it is essential that we also take time to pay tribute to those whose daily heroics often get overlooked as we cover the combat news that is mostly accounts of victories and defeats, death and destruction.

The combat hospitals in the war zones of Iraq and Afghanistan have become places where life-saving heroics happen so often that they are more than just routine, they are the job description. The successes of these doctors, nurses, and medics, who do their work in chaotic and dangerous circumstances, have expanded our burdens of war in ways that were never anticipated and planned for by our government policymakers, policy explainers, budgeters, or legislative overseers. Only as the Iraq war grew to be longer in duration than World War II did these public servants, and for that matter the American people, begin to grasp the sweeping extent of our national burden from the wars in Iraq and Afghanistan. Even then, officials in the White House, the cabinet, and Congress were slow to realize the full price the nation must pay to properly heal, care for, and rehabilitate the lives that we have saved. Our wartime burden of lives saved is a burden we are privileged to bear. How we bear it will define what we have become as a country, a culture, a people.

The story of the combat hospital is hardly new. Generations of us grew up getting it from *M*A*S*H*, the movie and then television iconic sitcom set in the Korean War; and as long as there is syndication in television, it will continue to entertain as it explains war to generations to come. More recently, just about every major news organization, electronic and print, has done some sort of story about the heroics performed daily at one of those portable medical centers known as combat support hospitals, or "CASH" in the shorthand of the Iraq and Afghanistan wars.

But every now and then a news organization's reporting proves both enterprising and enduring. In 2006, CNN spent two weeks inside the 10th Combat Support Hospital in Baghdad, covering the nonstop work days and work nights of the five doctors, fourteen nurses, and twenty-two medics in the busiest emergency medical unit in the Iraq war. The result was a one-hour documentary titled *Combat Hospital* that was run and re-run that year and the year after.

In an era in which political bombast passes for analysis, and infotainment often passes for news, and reality television often passes as infotainment, CNN's *Combat Hospital* was compelling reality that is television news coverage at its best. It let the world see just how and why America has entered a new era of wartime reality, one in which the nation has far more troops returning from combat injured but very much alive, living monuments to the war they fought in a distant land. *Combat Hospital* was horrific yet heartwarming and even uplifting; viewers who may have thought it would be difficult and perhaps impossible to watch some scenes found it was impossible to turn away. There were real heroes on the gurneys, covered with blood and sometimes crying out in agony. And there were real heroes surrounding the gurneys, also covered in blood and working so urgently that there was no time to cry for the lives they were struggling to save, especially when they could not succeed. Later the combat hospital teams would also return stateside; at home, some would surely suffer from PTSD. Heroes also suffer.

In May 2006 the 10th Combat Support Hospital was operating in the controlled chaos that was its business-as-usual, as medics brought in a young man who was in bad and bloody shape. Nurses moved immediately to ready the patient, the first step being cutting his clothes off his body. As they cut, one of them asked the injured man his name. "Caleb," he replied.

Caleb's life at that moment was in the hands of Captain David Steinbruner, M. D., whose hospital colleagues called him "Captain Chaos" because of his way of staying cool in a crisis. This had all the makings of just such an occasion. Caleb was in very bad shape. Steinbruner told the doctors and nurses around the table that Caleb looked pale, very pale. Caleb had lost a lot of blood, but not his fight or will.

"Am I (EXPLETIVE DELETED) dying?" asked Caleb. Steinbruner, all business and clearly concerned, asked Caleb if he was having trouble breathing. "A little bit," the young man replied. Seconds later, Captain Chaos summoned a tone and tack that may well have helped the patient help himself. "Don't you dare try to die on me," Steinbruner said. "I didn't give you permission." Caleb responded, "Don't let me die." To which Steinbruner, his voice clearly calm and sounding confident, replied: "I won't let you die. I promise. I promise. Okay? I give you my word. Okay?"

Around the table, the nurses and doctors had to make instant assessments as they worked and that meant talking about the patient's wounds and condition as they worked on him. One asked Caleb if he could move his hand; and when the soldier did, the medic replied: "That's a good sign, bud." Another observed that the injuries were "pretty bad" and could require an "amputation." Caleb heard that, of course and, in a voice that was now stronger, asked: "Hey, am I going to lose my (EXPLETIVE DELETED) leg?"

"I don't know," Steinbruner answered candidly. "That I don't know. Okay? We'll try to save it if we can. I just don't know. I can't give you an answer on that yet." Later, the doctor told CNN's cameras what he had seen and sensed at that moment: "We had a young American soldier, totally alert and awake. He got a near amputation of his right hand and very bad, bad fractures proximally and through the soft tissue of his left leg. He may or may not lose the left leg, too. With any luck, they can keep that going."

After the patient was moved out, Dr. Steinbruner reflected on what he tells patients in those traumatic, chaotic life-and-death moments. As he spoke, the strain of the truth lingers just behind the surface of his words: "He says, 'Please don't let me die.' Sometimes I've said, 'I won't,' but every once in a while, I have, and that's the worst, you know? Some guys come off the battlefield so fresh—not him. He'll do fine. Off the battlefield they're so fresh. They're going to die. We just don't know it yet. That's bad stuff. . . . I think we try not to follow up on the patients and not really think too hard about what happens next. That makes it a little easier to bear. Feels like, Okay, you did something good for that guy. He was in a lot of pain, he got definitive care. And then we kind of—end of story. We did the best we could. Then hopefully his life is okay, but we don't know."

The daily case log of the 10th Combat Support Hospital read like storyboard summaries from a year's worth of M*A*S*H shows:

> *Gunshot wound, left upper arm, chest, pelvis; gunshot wound, different patient, abdomen, chest—and these are pretty much successive patients on a single day, or the next day. Injury from fragments from a terrorist explosion, laceration to head; gunshot wound, left lower arm. Injury from terrorist explosion burns to cheek, burns to nose,*

burns to fingers, partial thickness; gunshot wound to neck;
gunshot left, upper leg; gunshot wound, left upper; burns to
face, head, and neck; injury due to terrorism, arm swelling,
gunshot wound to left hand; injury from terrorist explo-
sion, head, fractured, head, gunshot wound, gunshot wound,
gunshot wound, IED arm, IED face, IED multiple frags;
IED head; IED upper extremity, IED face.

On CNN's documentary about the reality of life and death in
the Iraq War, Lieutenant Colonel Robert Mazur, M.D., from
Brooklyn, New York, the doctor in charge of the emergency
room, read the log of one day's work at his Baghdad CASH and
then talked about the workload at this state-of-the-science mobile medical unit. "In general, 94 percent of the patients that
make it to this cache we save," said Colonel Mazur. A helicopter
engine roared overhead, then got louder as it landed. "Helicopters—you get used to listening for the helicopters. When we
hear the choppers, my heart rate still goes up."

Two soldiers were brought in, one with a traumatic brain injury. Looking at a scanned image of the soldier's head from the
side view, the doctors agreed that what they saw was blood col-
lecting but no penetration wound, which means there was
nowhere for the blood to go. So the blood was pooling inside the
soldier's skull, which can be dangerous. Major Marty Lucenti,
M.D., of Essex Junction, Vermont, explained: "He had a sub-
dural hematoma. Which means he has got some bleeding around
the brain. It was on the right side. And what that does is that
squishes the brain. In severe cases, it can push your brain right
down into your brainstem, right down into your spinal cord and
that will kill you. So what we did was give him stuff to minimize
the bleeding and keep the pressure down, and in the interim he
gets taken to Balad [a U.S. airbase 42 miles north of Baghdad]

by helicopter, where they have a neurosurgeon. And the neurosurgeon will take him urgently to the ER and drill a hole right in his skull to let that hematoma out."

Mazur had worked on the case. "Tough kid," said Mazur. "Very good kid to take care of. Gives me goose bumps when I see how strong those guys are."

For months, Mazur had been one of only a few members of the Baghdad CASH who had not been given a nickname by the staff. But the staff figured he earned himself one in that CNN interview. Ever since, they affectionately called Mazur "Goosebumps."

Sergeant Christopher Flores of Bravo Company, 101st Airborne Division, was wheeled in. He appeared to be the victim of a bomb blast. His face was bloody, his body too. In many ways it looked like a very typical case. But this one would take an unusual twist. Lieutenant Natalie Skates, a registered nurse from Montana, initially greeted him with a soothing "You're doing good, sweetie." Medical personnel tested his extremities to see whether he could feel when his arms and legs were touched. "My toes are killing me," Flores said. Nurse Skates replied, "We're going to give you more pain medication, okay?"

It went on like that for a while until Flores asked: "What's the story, Doc? I mean, give me a brief." Dr. Steinbruner was straightforward: "Your face is going to—if there's no fractures—it's going to require a lot of sewing and wash out in the ER. . . . Your left toe, looks like you're going to lose a little bit of the distal part, the end of it right at the toenails there. Just a tip off the big toe and maybe the second toe in, just the tip."

The sergeant asked: "Will I still be able to walk?" And the doctor replied: "Hell, yes. Of course. Not a problem." At that point, Nurse Natalie Skates began pointing out for the doctor other wounds on the soldier's body. "There's a puncture wound right here, a few punctures." As she spoke, the soldier, although not looking at her, said he recognized her voice—he had been there before as a casualty victim. Like many of the soldiers and marines, Flores tried hard to joke as a way of dealing with his pain and his fate.

"This isn't my first barbecue," Flores said. "It's my second time—actually it's my third time." Dr. Steinbruner, having been this route before, said just that: "Oh, yeah? You've been to this before? You've got to stop visiting us. We appreciate you taking one for the team."

"I hate you guys," said Flores—and the game was on. Nurse Skates: "But we love you." Dr. Steinbruner (aka Captain Chaos): "We love you, too."

"This is the same nurse that treated me before," said Flores. "I didn't notice her by her face, but by her voice." What was occurring at this moment was a moment that sums up all that is great about all that goes on in CASH units—the moment when people connect, not as bureaucratic units but as real people, people who relate in ways that cannot be fathomed by governments that have lost their way, nor by legislatures that cannot care unless some special interest has funded them to do just that.

"I know, sweetie," said Nurse Skates.

"That's how I knew," said Flores, still relying upon his hearing and his memory, not his eyesight, for recognition. "I was here last time. It was not that long ago."

Dr. Steinbruner played along: "You don't want to be a frequent flier with us. That's never a good sign. After that happens, you win a set of steak knives and get to go home. How about that?"

"Send me home, Doc," said Flores, the patient. "Based on your experience, how long do you think it's going to take for me to recover?"

"That's a good question," said Dr. Steinbruner. "Probably, I don't know, maybe a month." To which Flores, a bandaged patient who also knows his red tape, asked, "A month for all this shit to recover? . . . You got to prolong that because I still have three months left." Dr. Steinbruner got it. "Did I say that?" Steinbruner said. "I mean three months. Didn't I say three months?"

Flores has been this route before. "Don't call my mom this time. Last time they called her, she was freaked out." Nurse Skates reassured: "No, no, no. You're the one who's going to call her."

Later, Nurse Skates and Dr. Steinbruner reflected upon what they had brought to this patient in their CASH. "This one is a first for me, having a repeat customer," Skates said. "A lot of them come in just with major injuries and they're joking around, trying to pull through. They just roll with the punches. . . . These guys are great guys. They really are. They have courage that I just would never, ever expect people to have."

Dr. Steinbruner sounded the same theme as his nurse. "That guy has served his country," said Steinbruner. "I mean, wounded twice in action plus the fear of every day going out and not knowing if you're going to get wounded again." The doctor paused, then pointed his right hand in the direction of Flores's gurney. "That guy is a hero," Steinbruner said and walked out the door.

Later, Flores was indeed the one to deliver the news back home. He called on a cell phone and his father answered. "Dad, hey Dad. It's Chris. Hey, I got some good news and some bad news. Well, the good news is probably going to be I'm going home pretty soon. The bad news is I got hurt." Dr. Steinbruner was there, and he got on the phone to offer some reassurance to the sergeant's father. "Sorry about that bad news," said the doctor. "But your son's a trooper. He's been joking and giving us a hard time."

Months later, Flores was indeed stateside. His right cheek that was loaded with stitches was still quite scarred, his toes were mostly gone, and he was talking about the honor he had felt just serving in Iraq: "I don't regret it one minute. I don't regret that my face is like this. I don't regret that my toes are almost gone. As a matter of fact, I embrace the fact that this happened to me and I'm just proud to be in the infantry. . . . I wanted to get out there and I wanted to do something for our country. Being out there it shows you how fortunate we are."

At the 10th Combat Support Hospital, the doctors, nurses, and medics all specialize in quick quality care—and complete candor. An unidentified soldier was rushed in, and he was clearly in bad shape. "We don't lie to them," said Specialist Gina Herrera, a medic from Virginia Beach, Virginia. "We don't tell them, 'Oh, everything is going it be fine, no, no, you'll be fine.' Because that's—that can mess them up emotionally, mentally, and leave them even worse. . . . When you first start out being a medic . . . the first couple of times you see something really gruesome, you go through like an automatic drive, everything comes naturally. You know what you need to do."

On CNN's screen a doctor was talking to a patient lying on an examination table. The doctor was about to put into practice the CASH philosophy that bad news is best given straight—that military men and women who have faced tough combat deserve and can take tough truth. So he began by telling the patient he was going to put him to sleep for a bit; and in an effective way to gauge the patient's state of mind, the doctor simply asked how that sounded. "That sounds good," said the patient. Sensing the patient could take what he had to say, the doctor got right to it.

"Dude, that left leg, it's coming off," said the doctor. "Okay," said the patient. For a few seconds it was hard to sense who was consoling whom. "I'm sorry," said the doctor. "That's fine," said the patient. "All right?" asked the doctor. "I understand," said the patient—but then he asked the question anyone would want to ask: "There's no way to save the leg, huh?" To which the doctor replied: "The left leg, no. Okay? Right leg, absolutely. Okay? I'm sorry, man. I can't lie to you. Okay?" And with that, the doctor turned to a nurse: "Hook me up with the intubator there. Hold on. Give me suction." In a few minutes the patient was under. The operation was on, the leg was off.

Only after the work has been done and the patient has been moved out did Gina Herrera, the medic from Virginia Beach, feel the emotion of what she has been a part of. "If you sit there and you're watching or you sit there afterwards and you think about it and it's like, wow, you know, that guy lost his leg. You know? It can really affect you, so as long as you can detach yourself from the emotions of the situation, then you just do your job and do as much as you can for the patients."

A hardened senior officer hurried into the 10th CASH bringing two of his men, both very badly wounded. Apparently they'd been in a vehicle that was hit by a roadside IED. It soon becomes apparent that there was at least one other in the vehicle who was beyond being saved. The officer dutifully looked on, making sure that his men were put on the tables and were being worked on. Then, his job done, the senior officer passed out, hitting the floor hard.

Later Dr. Steinbruner sought out the officer, who clearly was in need of consolation. "It's hard for me," the officer began, "to think what we're going to do, how fast we're going to do it and everything. It's . . ." His voice trailed, and Steinbruner's filled the void. "It's not an easy war," said the doctor. "No, it's not," said the officer.

Then Steinbruner got to what he sensed was really troubling the officer—what their conversation and the scene in the operating room was really about. "Was there still somebody in the vehicle?" asked the doctor. "Yeah—from here down . . . ," said the officer. "I mean, the arms and—one arm was in one side. The nose was in . . ."

"He didn't feel it," Steinbruner interjected. "I'm sorry. You want to do me a favor? Talk to somebody about this stuff. Because it's going to haunt your dreams for a while. You know what I mean? Which is appropriate. If you just keep it bottled in, it's going to be bad news. And the two guys you saved are coming back here to say [thanks] to you guys on the field. Okay?"

After the officer left, Steinbruner explained to the CNN interviewer: "I think that guy right there, the fact that he passed out on us was the fact—he helped bring them in, collect the pieces and—of his own soldiers that he's responsible for, and that just overwhelmed him. These guys are like fathers to these men out here. Right? Surrogate fathers? So what happens to them happened to their sons, essentially."

FROM HEARTWARMING TO HEARTBREAKING

The reality that so many Iraq and Afghanistan war veterans have come home injured but alive brings with it many tales that are heartwarming. But along with those stories have come reports that are heartbreaking—about increased numbers of homeless veterans of these wars and Iraq and Afghanistan war veterans who committed suicide after returning home.

The statistics for homeless veterans are troubling—and the predictions for future years are downright dire. One out of every four homeless people in the United States is a veteran, while only one in eleven Americans is a veteran, according to an analysis of 2005 U.S. Census and Veterans Affairs data. Analysts estimated that 194,254 veterans were homeless on any given night. Meanwhile, VA officials hastened to point out that 250,000 veterans were homeless on any given night twenty years ago, when the bitter residue from the Vietnam War was still a factor.

But while officials from such groups as the National Alliance to End Homelessness could spar with VA officials over the implications of those old numbers, there was a general consensus that things were surely going to get worse before they got better (if they ever did). Activists even reached an eerie common choice on the preferred metaphor to make the point. "We're going to be having a tsunami of them eventually because the mental health toll from this war is enormous," Daniel Tooth, director of veterans' affairs for Lancaster County, Pennsylvania, told the Associated Press in the fall of 2007. Meanwhile Phil Landis, chairman of Veterans Village of San Diego, a counseling center and residential facility, told *The New York Times*: "We're beginning to see, across the country, the first trickle of this generation of warriors in homeless shelters. But we anticipate that it's going to be a tsunami."

Homelessness is one area where the VA has moved significantly. In 1987 the VA began focusing on the plight of homeless veterans. The VA budgets roughly $265 million a year on programs related to homelessness, plus some $1.5 billion for health care for homeless veterans. Also, Iraq and Afghanistan veterans will receive two years of free medical care. The VA's head of homeless veterans programs, Pete Dougherty, was quoted by the Associated Press as saying: "Clearly, I don't think that's going to

totally solve the problem, but I also don't think we're simply going to wait for 10 years until they show up. We're out there now
trying to get everybody we can to get those kinds of services today, so we avoid this kind of problem in the future."

Sometimes news happens in large numbers, where we can grasp
the dimensions of it. Other times newsworthy things happen in
small numbers, but quite visibly, because they are happening in
public. The sad plight of homeless veterans is in that category.
But there is another category that, in the aggregate, is alarmingly
newsworthy; yet each of these events happens singularly, hidden
away where we really do not take notice of it unless it is brought
collectively and forcefully to our attention. Suicides of veterans
are in this category, especially when they are suicides of veterans
of the Iraq and Afghanistan wars.

In 2005, in the 45 states that provided data to CBS News, at
least 6,256 military veterans committed suicide. That comes
down to 120 veterans who took their own life every week. Military veterans were twice as likely to commit suicide as non-
veterans in 2005, according to Dr. Steve Rathburn, acting head
of the biostatistics department at the University of Georgia, who
analyzed the data at the request of CBS News. The rate of veterans who committed suicide was between 18.7 to 20.8 per every
100,000 veterans; the rate of non-veterans who committed suicide was less than half that, 8.9 per 100,000.

But this report by CBS News chief investigative correspondent Armen Keteyian uncovered a statistic that was far more
alarming: The rate of suicides by young veterans, aged 20 to 24,
who had served during the era of the war on terror, was between
two and four times higher than civilian suicides in that age
group. Non-veterans in that age group committed suicides at a

rate of 8.3 per 100,000; veterans in that age bracket committed suicide at a rate of between 22.9 and 31.9 per 100,000.

"These statistics tell me we've really failed people that served our country," said Senator Patty Murray, a Democrat from Washington State who is on the Senate Veterans' Affairs Committee. "If these numbers don't wake up this country, nothing will."

15

Whip-Cracking Washington

Revelations at Walter Reed

Washington was frozen in suspended animation due to one of the worst ice storms in years on the morning of Sunday, February 18, 2007, as cars were unmovable and the roads and walkways impassable for all but the hardiest, which is not a description that is worn easily by the federal class. At their homes in the frozen slush of the city and the freeze-framed snowbanks of the suburbs, the federal workers who are employed in this city that famously doesn't work were wondering if Monday would be a day trapped at home with the kids, or if they could make it downtown to return to the business-as-usual that is the federal food fight, in which half the political people routinely refer to the other half with out-of-wedlock references and expect in return salutations in the form of references to anatomical apertures. The last thing that had happened in the escalating battles over the Iraq War was that eighteen Republican members of the House of Representatives had joined House Democrats in opposing a further troop buildup—and what made it significant was that this was the first time that those who broke with President Bush included conservatives who had been his staunch supporters and were from safe districts where their reelection was assured.

Among the few who made it through the frozen streets on that Sunday morning were the newspaper delivery people. They were delivering a missive to the front porches and breakfast tables of the nation's capital that would forge fundamental change. On this morning and in the days that followed, the city of the great divide came together as one, united in a common cause.

"The Other Walter Reed: Soldiers Face Neglect, Frustration at Army's Top Medical Facility," said the headline on the front page of *The Washington Post*. The article, by staff writers Dana Priest and Anne Hull, the first in a series that would win a Pulitzer Prize, began by setting a scene so starkly that official Washington did not dare ignore all that would follow:

> *Behind the door of Army Spec. Jeremy Duncan's room, part of the wall is torn and hangs in the air, weighted down with black mold. When the wounded combat engineer stands in his shower and looks up, he can see the bathtub on the floor above through a rotted hole. The entire building, constructed between the world wars, often smells like greasy carry-out. Signs of neglect are everywhere: mouse droppings, belly-up cockroaches, stained carpets, cheap mattresses.*

That was how Washington was introduced to the reality of Building 18 in the Walter Reed Army Medical Center. That was the place where a grateful nation had placed Duncan so he could recover from the injuries he incurred in Iraq—a broken neck, a shredded left ear; he had nearly bled to death from his wounds. He was but one of hundreds of soldiers who had been brought there after suffering major injuries in the wars of Iraq and Afghanistan.

This jarring, classic, journalistic exposé awakened Washington and the country to just one of the many injustices that was being visited upon the young men and women who had sacrificed in distant lands to safeguard their homeland.

Beginning with this first 4,696-word article about the horrible conditions at Building 18, and extending on through the many follow-up articles, the two *Post* reporters pursued the story by telling other stories that told larger truths—stories of squalid living conditions wrapped in reams of red tape, as well as bureaucratic delays and runarounds that were cruel and unusual punishment heaped on those who had fought our battles and come home wounded and expected to be cared for in this facility that is just five miles from the White House.

But the most remarkable thing about it was the meaning behind the words in one sentence: *The common perception of Walter Reed is of a surgical hospital that shines as the crown jewel of military medicine.* The elites of Washington had for years made Walter Reed one of their standard show-and-tell drop-bys. President Bush had been there, as had his presidential predecessors. Defense Secretary Donald Rumsfeld had, too, and so had his predecessors. The powerful members of the Senate and House committees that are officially charged with making sure that everything is just right at facilities such as Walter Reed came regularly to get the full treatment. They had seen what *The Post* called "the hospital's spit-polished amputee unit, Ward 57."

As is the way with official Washington, it is easily conned—and often it is asking to be conned. But the bottom line is that its officials, at all levels, failed to act in our best interest in their taxpayer-funded jobs—sad but no longer news. What was so remarkable about the Dana Priest and Anne Hull pieces was that

they made change happen. By their very presence and promi-
nence on the front pages of *The Washington Post*, these articles
forced Washington to see what had been under its collected nose:
Washington's elite were slumlords to our bravest and most deserving soldiers, who had been so severely wounded in their service of our country.

These articles were but the latest in a series of other journalistic efforts published not in the capital city but in the
heartland—including the work by the Knight Ridder (now Mc-
Clatchy) correspondents Chris Adams and Alison Young—that
had revealed the ways in which Washington had long been failing the nation's military veterans.

When bad news hits the front pages in the nation capital, the
first thing just about every political leader wants to do is discover that it isn't true. Or at least to be handed a few factoid fig
leaves so they can go before the cameras and say that. Especially
when the bad news hits at a time when things are already going
from bad to worse.

The Bush White House was in the throes of a bad news patch
the size of Iraq and Afghanistan combined when *The Washington Post*'s first Walter Reed exposé was splashed all over the
front page on that Sunday morning in February 2007. The war
in Iraq was already going badly, very badly. In Afghanistan,
things were going from better to bad, as the gains of the initial
invasion were being whittled away by a resurgent Taliban that
wouldn't stay defeated once the U.S. focus had shifted mainly to
Iraq. President Bush's premature exultation in his "Mission Accomplished" aircraft carrier photo-op in the Pacific had become
an object of ridicule in comedy monologues and Democratic
stump speeches; perhaps worse, the unrest among his fellow Republicans in Congress was no longer a Washington secret but
page-one and prime-time news. So the last thing that President

Bush needed to see on the front page of his Sunday paper was an exposé about how, on his watch, seriously wounded soldiers were being forced to live in the deplorable conditions at Walter Reed Hospital, just up 16th Street from his comfortable domicile. After all, the president had made repeated visits to soldiers at Walter Reed, assuming it was a model of superlative care for those admirable men and women who'd been wounded in the wars he had sent them to fight. Nobody in his government had ever told him about this latest outrage—but now *The Washington Post*'s Dana Priest and Anne Hull were telling the nation. Even Walter Reed was unraveling? The president wanted his aides to check it out and report back whether it was accurate; his advisers checked and reported back that it was.

"Find out what the problem is and fix it," Bush told his staff, according to his press secretary, Tony Snow. While there was no surefire solution for what was wrong in Iraq and Afghanistan, Walter Reed had to be fixable. Bush ordered his new defense secretary, Robert Gates, whom he'd dragooned back to Washington from a fine job as president of Texas A&M, to find out who was responsible for the shame at Walter Reed and make some heads roll; and lo, it would soon come to pass. But not before official Washington rushed to perform its ritual of high outrage.

Senators and representatives fell all over themselves to get to the TV cameras and promise immediate action. Army Secretary Francis Harvey and Vice Chief of Staff Richard Cody rushed to tour the facility they should have known all about. The *Post* also reported: "Walter Reed's commander, Maj. Gen. George W. Weightman, said in an interview that the Army leadership had assured him that all the staff increases he had requested would be met. 'This is not an issue,' he said. 'This is their number one priority.'" But while the staff was being increased, a few jobs were being summarily lost; for example, his.

Days later, Weightman was fired by Secretary of the Army Francis J. Harvey, who stated that he "had lost trust and confidence" in Weightman's ability to fix what was wrong. Two days later, Harvey was fired by Defense Secretary Robert Gates because, said Gates, "I am disappointed that some in the Army have not adequately appreciated the seriousness of the situation pertaining to outpatient care at Walter Reed. Some have shown too much defensiveness and have not shown enough focus on digging into and addressing the problems."

The extent to which some officials just don't get it is always surprising. So it was that the *Post* article on Harvey's firing also reported: "Later, in an interview, an emotional Harvey appeared both apologetic and defensive. 'It's unexcusable to have soldiers in that type of building,' he said, explaining why he resigned. But he also said that the *Post* stories lacked balance. 'Where's the other side of the story?' he asked, his voice rising. 'Two articles in your paper have ruined the career of General Weightman, who is a very decent man . . . and the secretary of the army. If that satisfies the populace, maybe this will stop further dismissals.'" Of course, two articles didn't ruin their careers. They ruined their careers when they permitted impermissible conditions to exist for years—either because they didn't find out about the problems or didn't make sure they were informed of the problems.

Where's the other side of the story? There simply is no other side, except to say that these officials may not have willfully condoned the abuses, but merely lived their public lives in willful ignorance.

On March 3, 2007, thirteen days after the *Post* article, President Bush used his regular Saturday radio address to tell Americans how he felt about the news from Walter Reed. It was not the sort of weekend uplift that citizens were accustomed to hearing from him.

> *Good morning. One of my most solemn experiences as President is visiting men and women recovering from wounds they suffered in defense of our country. Spending time with these wounded warriors is also inspiring, because so many of them bring the same courage they showed on the battlefield to their battle for recovery.*
>
> *These servicemen and women deserve the thanks of our country, and they deserve the best care our Nation can provide. That is why I was deeply troubled by recent reports of substandard conditions at Walter Reed Army Medical Center. Most of the people working at Walter Reed are dedicated professionals. These fine doctors, nurses, and therapists care deeply about our wounded troops, and they work day and night to help them. Yet some of our troops at Walter Reed have experienced bureaucratic delays and living conditions that are less than they deserve. This is unacceptable to me, it is unacceptable to our country, and it's not going to continue.*
>
> *On hearing the reports about Walter Reed, I asked Secretary of Defense Bob Gates to assess the situation firsthand and report back to me. He confirmed that there are real problems at Walter Reed, and he's taken action to hold people accountable, including relieving the general in charge of the facility. Secretary Gates has also formed an independent review group that will investigate how this situation was allowed to happen, how it can be fixed, and how we can prevent it from happening again. Walter Reed has a long tradition of outstanding medical service, and*

*my Administration will ensure that the soldiers recovering
there are treated with the dignity and respect they have
earned.*

Good things can indeed come from painful and poignant revelations, especially when they appear on Sundays on the front page
of *The Washington Post.* So it was that, the following autumn,
Washington and the nation learned a lesson that is sweet yet
also infuriating about what it takes to make the VA do the right
thing. This is the story of the sad life of an Iraq War veteran
who returned home to humble surroundings in tiny Romney,
West Virginia, and a most admirable and remarkable wife who
helped him cope as best he could, in an existence that seemed
forever frustrating. Until they got some help from an unex-
pected source.

The Washington Post's Anne Hull and Dana Priest latched on
to the very moving and powerful tale of former U.S. Army Scout
Troy Turner, his wife, Michelle, and their ten- and eleven-year-
old children from previous marriages. On Sunday, October 14,
2007, the story of their lives was on every porch, in every parlor,
at every breakfast table of everyone in official Washington. It
was another of those stories that is impossible to miss and, once
started, impossible to put aside.

The Turners' story opened in Romney with Troy, who has
suffered from post-traumatic stress disorder ever since returning
from Iraq, sitting in a recliner and his wife on the phone plead-
ing with the electric company to keep the power on.

"Can't you tell them I'm a veteran?" Troy asks. To which
Michelle replied, "Troy, they don't care." Gently, painstakingly,
the *Post* reporters painted this portrait of a family in misery. One
car repossessed. An answering machine screening for bill collec-
tors. The $860 monthly disability check from the VA doesn't

cover life's necessities. The sad story of this once-capable young man who now sits and watches hours of children's cartoons, interwoven with the heroic efforts of a young mother who is aging before her time as she tries to balance all of life's ordeals and still keep the family whole.

Troy's career in Iraq was painted starkly: "His platoon sergeant was decapitated by a rocket-propelled grenade, and others he knew were obliterated." Then we learn that he was also exposed to a number of bomb blasts that could have left him with brain damage, and we wonder why he isn't getting total care. But he wasn't even getting any counseling and the VA hospital in Martinsburg, West Virginia, had all fifty of its PTSD counseling slots filled, with a waiting list of twenty-five more. This of course indicates that the VA should have long ago added more counselors to accommodate the needs of the veterans—but many bureaucrats and bean counters like to play within their boxes, looking not to solve problems ahead but to cause themselves no problems today. So Troy Turner was trapped in a VA hell, which meant no rest for Michelle, no resolution, no salvation. Yet these days Michelle was the one who must soldier on.

Just when we think it can't get any worse, along comes one more small thing that becomes the unbearable last straw: when Michelle goes to the VA office to get reimbursed for this round-trip drive, she is paid at a VA rate of 11 cents a mile, a rate that has not been changed since 1977. The federal workers of the VA and all other agencies get reimbursed 48.5 cents a mile but a disabled military veteran gets only 11 cents a mile. Then she gets her receipt for $14.52 and goes to the next window to cash it—but first the government takes out $6 for "deductibles" and the federal clerk hands her $8.52.

Think of all those senators and all those representatives on all those committees that approve all those amendments. And think of all those self-important subcabinet swells who are always hot to trot along their personal upwardly mobile pathway to a cabinet job (for clout) or a corporate job (for cash). Any one of them could see this injustice and promulgate a regulation that would make it right. A federal worker fighting rush-hour traffic on the Beltway has it bad, but a soldier fighting terrorists and roadside bombs has it worse. Even at the top levels of the VA it suddenly became clear that this was a governmental wrong that could not be ducked, dodged, dismissed—or ignored.

Just a few days after that article ran in Sunday's *Washington Post*, the VA was moved to act big time. It turned out that the VA makes house calls. None other than Antonette Zeiss, the VA's deputy director for mental health services, was moved to leave Washington and travel to Romney. She spent ninety minutes at the Turners' mobile home, along with a PTSD counselor from the Martinsburg facility (the one that had no slot for Troy). They assessed Troy's needs and those of his family and made a decision: the VA doubled Turner's disability benefits check, reassessing his disability rating at 100 percent. That also meant his wife and two children were eligible for medical insurance and educational benefits.

Two thoughts occur. One is about this demonstration of Washington in action (as opposed to Washington inaction): Was Zeiss motivated to leave the Beltway and visit the Turners because those two top army officials who had been less that energetic in response to *The Post*'s first exposé wound up fired? (We can never prove it, but I believe one of the healthiest things that can happen in Washington is that all officials get the message that bad things will happen to them if their people permit bad things to happen to good people—and they seem to not really care.)

Then there is this second thought: If isolated exceptions can be made for a PTSD patient such as Eric Adams in Tampa, who refused to meekly accept a VA bureaucrat's statement that help is impossible and skillfully finagled a way to reach the ear of a Washington official who quickly made something good happen, and if a huge isolated exception can be made for Troy Turner and his brave wife, Michelle, because *The Washington Post* chose to feature them on the front page, then a truly caring VA can make those exceptions the rule for thousands of veterans who are every bit as deserving.

But that cannot happen until all of us—the politicians and the nation—change our ways in an era when our leaders have not called upon us to sacrifice. For this change requires commitment and the money to pay for it. Money to pay for the additional counselors and for the benefits that will bring the veterans' benefits to a level that is genuinely fair.

Troy Turner was grateful to get his new rating and doubled benefits. But when asked, he spoke to *The Washington Post* not about himself but the others. "I just hope they do it for the rest of them," Turner said. "Not just for me, but for all of us."

PART THREE

Solutions

16

Blue Ribbons and Red Tape

Commissioning Change

When Washington officials set out to fix a publicly exposed problem, the first thing they do is create a blue-ribbon panel—unless it is a really big problem. Then they create a blue-ribbon *commission*. Sometimes it is a presidential commission, other times a congressional commission. In 2007, as the firestorm mounted over the way America's veterans have found themselves under siege as they tried to obtain government benefits they'd earned in wartime, we had one of each. At the very least, this showed that Washington understood it had erred so severely in its treatment of veterans that the usual explanations would no longer suffice.

The track record on blue-ribbon commissions is that what they usually propose is: tweak this, tighten that, test something else—and, of course, create a new bureaucracy to review and analyze it all again next year. Indeed, some of that happened this time too. But these two commissions—one appointed by the president, the other by Congress—approached their tasks in very different ways and produced entirely different recommendations.

President Bush appointed a commission that would be clearly

seen as bipartisan, picking as its cochairs two high-profile figures with blue-ribbon credentials: former senator Bob Dole, a Republican from Kansas who had been awarded two Purple Hearts and a Bronze Star with Oak Leaf Cluster for heroism in World War II and had been his party's standard bearer in the 1996 presidential campaign, and former secretary of health and human services Donna Shalala, a Democrat who was now the president of the University of Miami.

The official name of the commission they headed was a mouthful: the President's Commission on Care for America's Returning Wounded Warriors. Not even the city of acronyms could get its ample mouth around PCCARWW; a White House lettersmith gamely tried to trim it to just "PCCWW"; but official Washington just called it the Dole-Shalala Commission, which worked, except that White House image protectors were not thrilled to see the president disappear from his own commission.

Serving on the Dole-Shalala Commission were two wounded veterans of the Iraq War, army captain Marc Giammatteo and navy hospital corpsman 3rd class Jose Ramos; Tammy Edwards, an advocate for families of wounded service members ever since her husband, Staff Sergeant Christopher Edwards, had been severely burned by a bomb blast in Iraq; Kenneth Fisher, founder of the truly innovative and impressive Fisher House Foundation, a not-for-profit organization that builds housing for families of hospitalized military personnel and veterans; Dr. C. Martin Harris, chief of information at the Cleveland Clinic Foundation; Edward A. Eckenhoff, founder of the National Rehabilitation Hospital; and Gail Wilenksy, an economist who had formerly headed the Medicare and Medicaid programs.

The congressional Veterans' Disability Benefits Commission was a military-minted commission headed by retired army lieutenant general James Terry Scott, and all but one of its thirteen members had prominent military credentials. This commission, which had been created in 2004, had been dutifully plodding through a laborious fact-finding exercise for more than two years. It held hearings, studied relevant data, and heard relevant experts in Washington. Occasionally it had left Washington to hold town hall meetings in the heartland. All the while, it had attracted very little attention from the news media and was virtually unknown to the general public.

As we look at what the two commissions did in their overlapping pursuits, it is instructive to keep in mind what they did *not* do. They did not drill through the Department of Veterans Affairs to determine where and why the VA was failing the veterans it was supposed to be serving. They did not look at the claim adjudication and appellate process with an eye to discovering why so many reviewers seem so intent on denying veterans' claims for service-related benefits—sometimes seemingly disregarding evidence that supported the veteran's claim. They did not look at why so many of these denial decisions were overturned on appeal—sometimes several times for a single case—in a cycle of wasted time and money. They did not investigate whether top officials at the VA had ordered or urged this apparent just-say-no policy. They did not ask whether the underfunded VA is seeking to systematically reject as many veterans' claims as possible to save money. They did not look at the core question of whether—and why—the VA had, in fact, become the veterans' adversary rather than their advocate.

Bob Dole and Donna Shalala said at every opportunity, starting on day one, that they were determined to do something more than just tinker and tweak. And to some extent, they succeeded in that goal. Still, in their early public sessions they went out of their way to make it clear that they were going to give the VA bureaucrats a pass. Indeed, their commission wound up giving them the benefit of the doubt that had so often been denied the veterans.

At an early commission hearing on April 23, 2007, at Walter Reed, Shalala's opening remarks were conciliatory: she seemed to suggest that everyone was operating with good intentions—it was the system that was at fault.

"I think we have to be extremely careful," she said. "Though red tape in this country has a bad name, often there is legislation layered on legislation as people try to fix problems, and trying to sort through that for an individual trying to use the system is not easy. But I want to be very careful that we don't beat up bureaucrats who are trying themselves to navigate the rules that they have to administer something by, and that we're positive about everyone right through the system trying to do the right thing, though dealing with very complex systems that have grown up over the years and that often aren't user friendly because of the complexity of what was designed over the years."

She added: "Now, I'm not naïve enough to think there are simple fixes, but both the senator and I are both strong-willed and positive enough to know that fixes can be found and that fixes can be made. We're very solution-driven on this commission. We know the problems exist, but our task is to turn problems into solutions and we'll focus on what is wrong only as a means to determine how to make it right. So we all look forward to the hearing today from our witnesses, both about the challenges we're facing and the recommendations to help guide us in this very solution-focused mission."

Then it was Dole's turn. He began by saying that as a young man home from the war, he had been a service representative for the American Legion, the Veterans of Foreign Wars, and Disabled American Veterans. "Obviously there are problems," he said, but added: "They're not quite as bad as sometimes reported in the press. We're looking for solutions. We're not trying to nail any-body, as Secretary Shalala said. There are a lot of good people try-ing to implement these programs and sometimes it's very difficult to do because of the regulations and because of what those of us in Congress might have said in our legislative history or somewhere in the legislation itself."

That meeting in Washington provided major insights into where the Dole-Shalala Commission was going and how it planned to get there. The first person the commissioners heard that day was retired command sergeant major Michael Lopez, of the army's 10th Mountain Division, 2nd Brigade, who is now with the Military Order of the Purple Heart, a veterans advo-cate organization. In Iraq, in May 2005, Lopez had been hit by a roadside bomb and woke up four days later at Walter Reed Army Medical Center in Washington. He had nothing but praise for the way he was cared for there. His injuries healed to the point that a few weeks later, he was shipped back to Fort Drum, New York. He was able to resume his duties as a sergeant major even though he had lost the vision in his left eye.

"I'm one of the lucky ones," Lopez said. One of the reasons he said that was that he had learned—but only by happenstance—about the existence of an insurance program that was totally paid for by the government for which he was eligible.

"When I returned to Fort Drum, I learned through one of my first sergeants, who was injured earlier in the conflict and had al-ready been sent back to Fort Drum, about the Traumatic Service members' Group Life Insurance program, TSGLI. I wasn't real knowledgeable about it because I've never heard about it before, but he gave me the website. I went to the website, downloaded the forms, filled them out, and after sending it in two or three times, once I got it straight, I did receive compensation under the program."

The problem, he said, was that he only knew about the program because he'd been lucky enough to stumble into it by chance. "I think there are a lot of soldiers, servicemen, airmen, sailors, Marines that return that just aren't aware that the program exists," Lopez said. "And I'll give you one example. Last Friday, a young soldier named PFC Albright from the cavalry unit at Fort Drum came to see me about membership in the Purple Heart Association. As I was helping him fill out the paperwork, I asked him about his right foot. Every single bone in his right foot had been blown up—crushed by a roadside bomb. The doctors did everything they could at Walter Reed to fuse what bones they could together, but he's never going to run again. He's never going to walk properly again."

PFC Albright had not been told about the insurance program when he was at Walter Reed, but Lopez was able to help Albright sign up. TSGLI is an insurance program that is free; all soldiers have to do is take the initiative and fill out a form to sign up for it. But if soldiers don't know it exists and the government doesn't care enough to tell them about it, they miss out.

Fact-finding commissions sometimes find facts where they least expect to. It turned out that some of the commissioners didn't know about the insurance program either.

SEN. DOLE: Could you just tell us what TSGLI means?

CSM LOPEZ: Sir, I didn't go into details as far as what it means—

SEN. DOLE: What do the initials mean?

CSM LOPEZ: Traumatic Service Group Life Insurance.

SEN. DOLE: Pardon?

CSM LOPEZ: Traumatic Service Group Life Insurance. It pertains to injuries that the service men and women received during combat and it allows them to receive compensation once they return from the combat theater, whether it's on active duty or whether they separate from the service.

SEN. DOLE: It's an insurance program?

CSM LOPEZ: Yes, sir.

SEC. SHALALA: The government carries for—for active-duty soldiers.

CSM LOPEZ: Yes, sir. They added this to the SGLI, which was the typical life insurance policy. Several years ago when they added this policy. I believe it's under Prudential, because those that come back and are severely wounded could use some compensation in that regard.

SEC. SHALALA: And many soldiers coming back don't realize that they're insured in addition to whatever the services response was?

At that point, commission member Martin Harris stepped in to explain to Dole and others not in the know that this program had been enacted in 2005 and gave a short course on how it worked. Then Harris added: "I think the problem is that some of the guys that were injured prior to the program coming out weren't aware of the program because they were already out of the system. But at Walter Reed at least, they have people there from physical and occupational therapy that do inform you about the TSGLI."

Lopez couldn't let that one pass. "I wish that was always the case, but that's—I gave the example of PFC Albright who came through Walter Reed in September of last year and still [had] not received any information about it."

Lopez also addressed other matters in his testimony before the commission. He discussed the vast amount of paperwork soldiers and veterans have to fill out and the long waiting time that it takes just to get a claim processed. Then he added, almost as an afterthought, the story about his tooth.

"I've been waiting myself a year to get a tooth replaced from the roadside bomb, and just waiting on resources and funds to become available," Lopez said. "And I'm sure eventually I'll get taken care of it."

Shalala, quite appropriately, asked him to explain the story of the tooth. It turned out a tooth had been badly damaged in the blast; at Walter Reed a dentist had properly tried to save it. But when Lopez was at Fort Drum it became clear that the tooth was close to shattered and had to go. "Initially I was told that funds were available to get it taken care of up near Fort Drum, but they didn't have the funds," Lopez testified. "Then I was told there was an oral surgeon in Syracuse, so I went for an appointment. He said it would be taken care of. Six months later, I called them back and they said they didn't have the resources and they were going to hire a different oral surgeon to do the surgery. . . . Since I'm 80 miles north of the VA center in Syracuse, if they had the funds available, they would have allowed me to get that done through a civilian contractor, but since they didn't and they had an oral surgeon in Syracuse, they told me I would have to go there and get it done there. And I did do that.

Unfortunately, they said that they didn't have, I guess, the resources or the proper tools, and then they lost the oral surgeon who was there for whatever reason, and they said that I'm on the waiting list. So eventually, I'm sure, it will get taken care of."

Everyone on the commission listened and everyone seemed sympathetic, but no one voiced the obvious: this situation was botched through institutional idiocy. This is just the sort of problem that is so small that it becomes totally understandable. But in truth what happened was unconscionable because it is so easily solvable. A soldier whose tooth was shattered by a wartime bomb blast shouldn't have to wait politely and patriotically for months for treatment he was owed by Uncle Sam. The government could so easily create something akin to a Medicare card for veterans and service members. That way they could simply make an appointment with any private physician, show the card, and have the work done in a timely manner. The government would of course pay for the procedure.

Next to testify was Robert E. Wallace, executive director of the Veterans of Foreign Wars. He gave the sort of clear-eyed, commonsense view (mixed with the straightest of straight talk) about how easy it would be to make a real difference—*if* the leadership at the top really insisted that it be done. Wallace testified about the mandate of the commission in his subtle and diplomatically nuanced way: "It's totally about those who were involved in the outpatient treatment, scheduling, and processing of our wounded being discharged and then returned to duty. It's about the pathetic lack of leadership of senior U.S. Army officials who lost their focus of mission. Your job, as we see it in the Veterans of Foreign Wars, is to make the system better, less bureaucratic, more streamlined, and seamless."

He also offered one solution that top officials at the Defense Department and the VA could have made happen years ago but never did—perhaps because the real focus of the top guns at the Pentagon and the VA is waging bureaucratic turf wars. They even fight over paper, which is why the VA often finds it so hard to get records from the Defense Department when a veteran's military record needs to be reviewed as part of a benefits claim.

"The VFW's vision is very simple: it's one unified record," said Wallace. "When a man or woman signs their enlistment papers or takes [the] oath of commission, an electronic file should be created. This file should contain all important personnel information, deployment information, but also their medical records, indicating any illnesses or injuries the service member might suffer. On separation, we want this file to be transferred to the Department of Veterans Affairs where it can be assessed quickly and routinely updated with later medical issues. The up-to-date, easily assessed file is critical for the quick adjudication of any disability claim the individual may file."

Wallace put his support behind a plan that has always seemed like common sense but hadn't ever been done: members of the military should be given a complete physical examination when they are leaving the service.

"An important area that needs improvement also is separation physicals. The VFW would like to see one single separation physical and one single disability rating. Combining these two would greatly improve access to VA care for our veterans, but also give them a head start in the disability claims process, thus reducing the burden of VA's claims processing system. Not only would this physical determine any existing disabilities, but it would also serve as a baseline for future ratings decisions, greatly improving the accuracy and efficiency of these decisions. . . . If the person was going to be medically discharged, the VA rating schedule would determine the individual's military and VA disability rating. One physical, one rating, everyone treated fairly across the board, less red tape, and less waiting time."

Wallace sounded a conspiratorial note as he observed two co-incidental facts: Soldiers with an army disability rating of 30 percent or higher are entitled to government-paid health care, while those with lower ratings are not. Many of these soldiers with ratings below 30 percent get re-rated by the VA, which generally gives much higher ratings. His point was to suggest that the army has found that it can save money by giving lower ratings and thus not have to pay for the added benefits that come with higher ratings. This begs the question, is the Army being disingenuous (read: dishonest) in its rating system?

"Today we have people getting out of Walter Reed at 10 and 20 [percent disability ratings]," he said, "and you . . . read a lot about staying under that 30 percent because 30 percent gives them healthcare, et cetera, et cetera. Well, they're getting out at 30 percent, let's say, and we're handling their case and we're getting them 90 percent from the Department of Veterans Affairs. Now, something's wrong. Something's wrong. What's wrong? The Department of Defense looks at one disability, the VA looks at the whole person. And the whole person is the disability. Post-traumatic stress could be with a leg injury. The Department of Defense will look at the leg, not at posttraumatic stress."

Wallace ended his appearance before the commission by firing an assessment salvo that was on target. He said that none of these important changes have been made at the VA because VA secretaries haven't pushed for them and their bosses, our presidents, haven't demanded them.

What is the biggest reason this hasn't happened? It's a total lack of leadership. It's a lack of leadership and determination. I could come in as secretary of defense or secretary of veterans affairs and I could have my best interests at heart, but [it is as though I'd] become the director of FEMA all of a sudden, and I'm putting out fires and every-thing, and I just . . . put this on a side and I just don't move it. There's going to be a push to Congress. Senator Dole, you're probably on many pieces of legislation that's been pushed over the last 20 years to make this happen and it hasn't happened. And it's got to—I think it's now reached the point where the president's got to make it happen.

When it became Dole's turn to ask questions, he followed up on Wallace's point about the disparity in the ratings between the military and the VA. Dole said that there must be some compli-cated reasons why something that seemed so simple had not been done years ago. "It's got to be pretty complex," said Dole, "I mean, or somebody would have done it."

"I think the complexity is a mind-set," Wallace replied, adding that things can be made much simpler, rather than plac-ing the burden "on the poor individual." But Dole still wondered if there aren't people in high places who thought this streamlin-ing just wouldn't work.

"If there is, they haven't come out of the woodwork," said Wallace. "And we suggested and recommended seamless transi-tion and it's never gone anywhere. The VA meets with DOD and we're going to do this and we're going to do that. I think just last month they started to talk about the fact that they're going to start sharing medical records. . . . Why we should give millions of dollars or billions of dollars to DOD to create a healthcare system—a medical record system—and VA's got one that's touted in every magazine in the country. That's the best. Why duplicate it?"

Next the presidential commission came to a moment that could only make sense to someone who spends his days tying red tape into bows and calling it a job well done. The commission heard from the director of the Compensation and Pension Service, Bradley G. Mayes. He had a finely honed PowerPoint presentation, which he supplemented by explaining at considerable length that veterans all are informed about the pension and other programs awaiting them on their departure from the military. Because they get a pamphlet explaining it all to them when they first enlist!

"A lot of people don't know that we actually send out a pamphlet at enlistment," Mayes said. "We get data from the Department of Defense. It's a data transfer, so we know when service members go on active duty, and we have this pamphlet. It's a summary of VA benefits that's sent out to service members basically at enlistment."

Shalala wanted to make sure she was hearing this right.

SECRETARY DONNA SHALALA: But basically you send the pamphlet out at enlistment, which is not exactly the time in which someone's thinking about their exit. Is that correct?

MR. MAYES: Yes, Secretary, that's correct. In fact, it probably ends up in a—

SEC. SHALALA: Sounds like the admissions material we send out: no one reads it at that point.

MR. MAYES: (*Laughter.*) Right. Yes, ma'am.

SEC. SHALALA: As long as they're in, they're not reading anything.

In the afternoon, the Dole-Shalala show featured a diverse playbill. First came a military whistleblower, then a retired general, and finally a Government Accountability Office analyst.

First was a National Guardsman from Pennsylvania, Michael B. Kozlowski III, who had served in Operation Iraqi Freedom, reenlisted, and volunteered for a second tour—only to be injured in maneuvers at Fort Dix, New Jersey. He was cared for first at Fort Dix and then at Walter Reed, and when he and his fellow patients found conditions and treatment unacceptable, he spoke up. "I complained of poor treatment and conditions for myself and my fellow soldiers," he said. He contacted his Pennsylvania senators and representative. "I suffered severe retaliation and was forced to file a whistleblower's complaint with the Office of Inspector General of Walter Reed Army Medical Center," he said. He did not specify the nature of his injury or the retaliation he experienced. But his complaint proved to be precisely what the commission had heard about that morning.

My complaint dealt with a directive or policy that required the medical case managers to limit soldiers to not more than 10 percent disability rating to save the Department of Army from having financial responsibility resulting of the denial of service members' disability retirements. The case managers then referred all veterans to the Veterans Administration to request that the disability be upgraded so that the Veterans Administration would be responsible for the care of all injured veterans. Case managers routinely refused to give the veterans copies of their medical records so that they could file legitimate claims at the Veterans Administration.

Further, the case managers would misfile or misplace from the veterans' medical records vital information that would have been helpful to the veterans in the pursuit of proper disability benefits after leaving military service. Routinely, the case managers of cases involving traumatic brain injuries and posttraumatic stress disorder would attempt to create a preexisting condition of a learning disability and/or some type of bipolar diagnosis or personality disorder to further deny legitimately earned disability benefits to soldiers with a traumatic brain injury or posttraumatic stress disorder. Also, for soldiers suffering debilitating injuries involving their limbs, head, back and/or respiratory problems, the case managers would again attempt to establish preexisting conditions to deny these soldiers any earned disability rating and/or disability retirement.

Kozlowski said that because he and his fellow soldiers had contacted members of Congress and because those contacts resulted in investigations being launched, he faced what he called further retaliation. He and his fellow soldiers were "ordered to submit to unnecessary and unlawful medical evaluations in blatant disregard of a Department of Defense directive and public law prohibiting this unlawful action." He added: "Because of my advocacy for myself and my fellow soldiers, I was given a general discharge under honorable conditions rather than an honorable discharge."

What came next was a rather poignant moment for this commission. Sitting there in front of a former presidential standard-bearer, a former cabinet secretary, and assorted success stories from the world of business, Kozlowski said: "Today, I find myself one of the one in four military veterans who have been homeless as reported by the Veterans of Foreign Wars, VFW. And I am one of more than 8,000 returning veterans from Operation Iraqi Freedom who find themselves without an opportunity to return to their former employment they had left in order to volunteer for active duty."

No one on the panel had anything they wanted to ask of the young man sitting in front of them. Nor did they have any warm words. "Thank you," said Shalala and, turning to the older, more prosperous and proper witness in the next chair, "General?" Lieutenant General Dennis McCarthy, now retired after forty-one years in the Marine Corps, currently executive director of the Reserve Officers Association, had the floor.

Gail Wilensky began asking about reports of differences in care that was being given to reservists who were sent to fight in Iraq, were injured, and then discharged out of active duty.

"Frankly," said the general, "we've heard that some are improperly or inadequately counseled and told that if you want to go home and get care at home, you're going to have to leave active duty to do it, which is not true."

Then came Daniel Bertoni, of the GAO. He too had a PowerPoint presentation, only his was a presentation of things that had gone wrong. He was a whiz at it and soon the commissioners found themselves in a blizzard of acronyms. As in: "In terms of timeliness, the bottom line here is that the services are not meeting DOD's timeliness goals for the MEB and PEB process."

SEC. SHALALA: Mr. Bertoni, I'm going to stop you for just a minute. Could you just slow down a little? Because you've got a lot of material here and we want to absorb it. So normally, we tell people to speed up. I'd like to tell you the opposite.

MR. BERTONI: I'm normally in front of the congressional committees that, you know, they want me on five minutes, so— okay, no problem. I can slow down.

SEC. SHALALA: Yeah. We've got plenty of time for you. We'd like you to slow it down a little bit, so we can really absorb this.

Soon, Bertoni, now in slow motion, was explaining: "Basically DOD really is not monitoring this information and holding the services accountable." Then he got to one of the central problems with the VA—the VA's slow-motion processing of disability benefits claims: "We have reported on ongoing problems with VA disability claims processing, especially in regard to timeliness, accuracy, consistency. We've reported on the need to obtain better medical service records, especially in regard to servicing PTSD claims, and also the need to improve the quality of medical exam reports that are going to ultimately . . . be very essential for the final decision."

Next, Bertoni served up this gem of a sentence, leaving no room for misinterpretation: "In terms of their ability to make accurate, complete, and timely decisions, VA has had real problems making timely, accurate and consistent decisions."

Bertoni continued: "From '03 to '06, we had pending claims ballooning to almost 400,000. The average processing time has grown to 127 days, and appeals are taking 657 days on average. Accuracy rates and consistency still remain problematic. I think the bottom line here is that we have a system that is extremely strained and will be further strained in the future as more . . . veterans enter into it. In going forward, we have reported that VA really has to find ways to work smarter, leverage its resources and increase productivity to deal with these increasing workloads."

Finally, Bertoni explained that the VA "lacked the quality assurance process to ensure that key evidence needed to make disability decisions was being gathered and included in reports."

This meant that veterans were "potentially being denied benefits when there was a key record in the file that could corroborate the disability."

He said it was taking more than a year for the VA to make decisions on veterans' claims for PTSD—and those claims had increased by 80 percent in the past decade. Turning to VA medical exams, he stated: "We found that VA exam reports often did not contain that key information and this lack of information could result in bad decisions, increased appeals because people who feel they do have a legitimate claim will likely appeal, and increased pending claims, further straining an already strained system."

It was at that point that perhaps the most compassionate question of the day was asked. It came from Kenneth Fisher: "The report says that PTSD claims is about one year in terms of waiting for them to be processed," Fisher began. "What happens during that one year? . . . Are they receiving any kind of counseling during that period or are they just waiting? Did you find that out?"

"I don't know," said Bertoni. "I mean, I think if an individual, who perhaps was out of the service for several years, walked into a VA office, applied for a PTSD claim, I don't believe that that individual would receive any services prior to the determination of disability." Bertoni thought about that and added: "You know, an individual spends a year of his life trying to prove that they're disabled, and then after that year we tell them you need to go back to work."

"If he's still around," Fisher interjected.

"If he's still around," Bertoni agreed.

San Antonio, May 4, 2007: The Dole-Shalala Commission has hit the road. The commissioners want to hear the views of experts in the heartland—experts who include a number of veterans at the other end of the VA funnel.

Brent Masel, director of Transitional Learning Center, a facility that treats individuals with brain injuries, is speaking to the commission. He started by saying that what he is about to say was not a lie.

"The story sounds so phony, I wouldn't dare tell you this story unless it was really true," said Masel. "Last night while I was in the office, I heard a conversation amongst my cleaning crew, and usually I tell them just to be quiet, but I came out. And one was telling the story of her best friend whose son had sustained a brain injury during his second tour in Iraq and was now getting services in Virginia. . . . She commented on the incredible burden it was for the family to travel to Virginia and couldn't understand why he couldn't be treated closer to home, closer to friends and closer to family. The incredible burden on the family, the friends and on the soldier. Well, I went out into the hallway and I said, 'You're not going to believe what I'm doing tomorrow.' And we talked about that, and she said, 'I beg you, please tell the Commission of the hardships that have been created by such a limited number of treatment facilities geographically for traumatic brain injury.' And I know it sounds like I'm making this up but I'm not. On my mother's grave, it's a true story."

He urged that the Defense Department and Veterans Affairs expand the number of private-sector rehabilitation providers that can be approved for treating veterans, especially those with traumatic brain injury. It was a theme long sounded by Bob Dole.

SENATOR ROBERT DOLE: I just wonder if it makes economic sense, Dr. Masel, the point I've been making, for the VA or the DoD to go out and build all these centers when you already have them available in the private sector, and we were talking earlier about the four polytrauma centers, the first tier, I guess, and it is a long way from here to, well, any of those, and I don't know, I've been wondering from the standpoint of economics if it wouldn't be better, not only better but easier for the families to deal with it to get expert treatment within say a hundred miles instead of a thousand miles.

DR. BRENT MASEL: Absolutely, sir. The big issue is geography and families want to be close and the patients want to be close. The other issue is there are private-sector facilities that are available right now and there is absolutely positively no question about it, the sooner the individual gets services, the sooner they get treatment, the better they do. In the state of Texas, there's a waiting list for those who are indigent to get funded and for them to receive services, and it's quite clear, the longer that they have to stay on that list, the more difficult it is to get a good outcome, so the answer is absolutely, the facilities are available right now, today, to take these men and women.

Dr. Andrew Moore, recently back from Baghdad, where he commanded a mobile surgery team, gave the commissioners a good news–bad news assessment. An orthopedic surgeon at the air force's Wilford Hall Medical Center and a 1993 graduate of the U.S. Air Force Academy, he began with fulsome praise for the trauma centers and health-care delivery to those in battle. "There is tremendous and near seamless integration of the three medical services at every echelon of care in theater," he said. "It's become almost cliché now to hear about a wounded Marine having initially been treated by a Navy corpsman, find themselves medivacked by an Army helicopter crew, undergo emergency surgery in an Air Force theater hospital. The system works well."

"Now for the bad," he continued. "Essentially the problems faced by America's wounded warriors and their families are not unique to them. All patients and all family members attempting to navigate the bureaucracy of the military medical system . . . face the same problems. . . . The problem is the system itself. Again, the bureaucracy faced by wounded warriors is not unique to them. Within the stateside of military medicine, everyone suffers from it. [A]ddressing only the care of the wounded in the system to me is a bit like mopping up one room in the *Titanic*.

"Why is this system broken? . . . There's problems with socialized medicine. It has inherent flaws. We have made too many promises to many beneficiaries. We have decreased funding and manpower during the war. . . . It doesn't make sense to decrease funding in a time of war to me.

"How do I recommend you fix the problems?

"One, I know it's a political hot topic but I think the civilian health-care model, especially when you look at centers of excellence—like the Cleveland Clinic, like the Mayo Clinics or hospitals for special surgery—do better than we do and we should continue to try to transfer noncombat and contingency essential medical care out to these facilities and integrate military staff within our civilian counterpart institutions. . . .

"Congress needs to pay for what they've promised to all beneficiaries or trim back on benefits or raise copays.

"Correct pay disparity between military providers and their civilian counterparts or at least their counterparts in other governmental agencies like the VA. Work to retain physician gray-hairs and then work to incorporate better communication from electronic medical records between the services between the VA.

"Now I would very briefly elaborate on a few of those points. Communism does not work well as a government model and it should be no surprise it does not work well in the medical delivery model either. Barring those individuals who have a professional or personal stake in patient care, there's no motivation to work harder, longer or more efficiently."

San Diego, May 24, 2007. The commission divided into a number of subcommittees in order to inspect a number of different sites. Lieutenant Colonel Leslie "Chip" Pierce reported back to Dole, Shalala, and the other commissioners a troubling account of what a subcommittee discovered during a visit to the Camp Pendleton Marine Base.

The subcommittee visit to Camp Pendleton began with a briefing about traumatic brain injury and post-traumatic stress disorder treatment at the behavioral health clinic. "In the past year, Camp Pendleton has cared for 296 TBI patients," Pierce reported. "The clinic's frustration is in the provision of care sensing that line commanders are not always committed to PTSD identification and treatment once they return home. Other staff concerns were raised over two issues, the first being current staffing levels forcing the health-care providers to conduct administrative functions, thus taking away from primary care. The second concern was with the timely hiring of qualified personnel in a competitive market. The inability to compete in the job market creates an increase in the patient-to-provider ratio, which is compounded by the supported unit's multiple deployments."

That was followed by Pierce's candid and troubling report about a visit to six Wounded Warriors, as the army group calls itself.

The second forum was with Wounded Warrior which took place at the wounded warrior barracks. Present were 6 Marines, all of whom felt that they were being somehow punished for being wounded. Their perceptions were based on the stark environment in which they lived and with certain rules of their Medical Hold unit. The interior of the building appeared to be sterile and uninviting as a place to live and recuperate. The recreation rooms did have nice furniture, TVs, pool tables, and game systems. However, the rules of the unit do not permit residents from using these facilities during duty hours. Nor do the rules permit residents from resting in their rooms. Those wounded warriors who could perform light duty were given menial tasks rather than jobs which could give a sense of contribution and self-worth. It was also noted by these Marines that when visitors come to Camp Pendleton to see the Wounded Warriors, they are taken to a location in the barracks area known to these warriors as "The Petting Zoo."

On July 25, 2007, some four months after its creation, the Dole-Shalala Commission delivered its report to the president. From the very first day, Dole had emphasized that he was not about to preside over a quilting bee that would produce a patchwork, no matter how colorful and comforting it might be, and the final report emphasized that very point.

We don't recommend merely patching the system, as has been done in the past. Instead, the experiences of these young men and women have highlighted the need for fundamental changes in care management and the disability system. Our recommendations address these fundamental

changes. We believe they will help military service mem-
bers and veterans of today and of tomorrow, as well.

Making the significant improvements we recommend re-
quires a sense of urgency and strong leadership. The ten-
dency to make systems too complex and rule-bound must be
countered by a new perspective, grounded in an understand-
ing of the importance of patient-centeredness. From the time
injured service members are evacuated from the battlefield
to the time they go back to active duty or are discharged
home to complete their education, go to work, and be active
family and community members, their needs and aspira-
tions should inform the medical care and disability systems.

The Dole-Shalala Commission saw its mandate as a limited
one: their focus was on troops returning from Afghanistan and
Iraq, not veterans from previous wars and eras. This would lead
to a controversy that would later develop after the commission
issued its proposals.

The commission made six recommendations that were indeed
broadly within their charter as they saw it:

1. Immediately create comprehensive recovery plans to
   provide the right care and support at the right time in
   the right place. (A recovery coordinator would oversee
   each patient's care.)
2. Completely restructure the disability determination and
   compensation systems. (Defense Department would determine a service member's fitness to serve; the VA
   would establish the disability rating, compensation, and
   benefits.)
3. Aggressively prevent and treat post-traumatic stress disorder and traumatic brain injury. (The report of the

President's Commission on Care for America's Returning Wounded Warriors said: "VA should provide care for
any veteran of the Afghanistan and Iraq conflicts who
has post-traumatic stress disorder [PTSD]. DoD and VA
must rapidly improve prevention, diagnosis, and treatment of both PTSD and traumatic brain injury [TBI].
At the same time, both Departments must work aggressively to reduce the stigma of PTSD.")

4. Significantly strengthen support for families. (The report
   called for expanding Defense Department–provided
   respite care and extending the Family and Medical Leave
   Act for up to six months for spouses and parents of troops
   who are seriously injured.)

5. Rapidly transfer patient information between the Department of Defense and the Veterans Affairs Department.

6. Strongly support Walter Reed Army Medical Center by
   recruiting and retaining first-rate professionals through
   2011, when it will close.

It was the second provision that proved controversial. Veterans' advocacy groups were virtually unanimous in objecting to
the details behind the bold concept—because the recommendation was only being applied to veterans of the Iraq and Afghanistan wars. The commission proposed setting up a new system
of rating disability benefits and compensation for all who were
in the military at the time of the invasion of Afghanistan or af-
terward. Veterans groups warned that it was unacceptable to, in
effect, pit today's veterans against those from previous wars. An
injury is an injury—and the compensation for it should be the
same, the veterans' groups argued.

The Senate Veterans' Affairs Committee chairman, Daniel

Akaka, a Democrat from Hawaii, also declared that he had "serious concerns" about some of the recommendations, especially the second one.

"This recommendation has two key components that would fundamentally alter the manner in which the Pentagon and the VA administer those systems," Akaka wrote in a *Washington Post* op-ed article. "The first component—merging the departments' existing systems—has strong appeal. If enough obstacles can be overcome, it is possible that, for some subset of those leaving the military, it may prove feasible to have the two systems function collaboratively, with one physical exam and one disability rating for those who leave the service for medical reasons.

"The second component, that the VA's compensation system should be fundamentally restructured, is far more problematic. The legislation that the White House drafted to carry out this recommendation would have Congress cede responsibility for the proposed retooling of the VA's compensation system to the secretary of veterans' affairs, and it would require the secretary to accomplish this monumental task in just a few months."

Akaka's reaction was classic Washingtonia. His concern about that second provision downplayed the fundamental concerns voiced by veterans' groups and spoke first about his own power and clout. He didn't want to see Congress ceding any of it to the secretary of the VA. But he got there in the end, saying it was wrong to give new disability benefits and compensation to Iraq and Afghan veterans alone: "Congress should focus on creating a system that is equitable for all of our veterans—young and old."

On October 3, 2007, some two and a half years after its creation, the Veterans Disability Benefits Commission delivered a lengthy report to President Bush and fourteen members of Congress. In contrast to the Dole-Shalala commission's six broad recommendations, this congressional commission made 113 recommendations in all. These were its central conclusions:

Some important cross-cutting themes emerged from the study. VA does not devote adequate resources to systematic analysis of how well it is providing its services (process analysis) or how much the lives of veterans are being improved (outcome analysis), the knowledge of which, in turn, would enable VA to improve the effectiveness and impacts of its benefit programs and services.

VBA does not have a program of research oriented toward understanding and improving the effectiveness of its benefit programs. Research efforts in the areas of applied process research, clinical outcomes, and economic outcomes should be undertaken. VA is missing the opportunity to take a more veteran-centered approach to service provision across its benefits programs.

VA has the services needed to maximize the potential of veterans with disabilities, but they are not actively coordinated and thus are not as effective as they could be. The disability compensation evaluation process provides an opportunity to assess the needs of veterans with disabilities for the other services VA provides, such as vocational rehabilitation, employment services, and specialized medical services. This process would coordinate VA's programs for each veteran and make it a more veteran-centered agency.

The commission's rather impenetrable report tinkered and tweaked—it was a masterpiece of incremental modification. No doubt there were many important alterations tucked in there, but it was all about the trees and not the forest. It got virtually no news coverage. Copies of the report are gathering dust on some of the finest shelves in the U.S. government, at both ends of Pennsylvania Avenue.

In late October, President Bush implemented most of the Dole-Shalala recommendations by executive order and sent the rest to Congress as priority legislation.

17

Reality Check, Gut Check

An Interlude in the Search for Solutions

*"We owe a wounded soldier the very best care and
the very best benefits possible."*

—PRESIDENT GEORGE W. BUSH, JULY 2007,
ACCEPTING HIS VETERANS' COMMISSION RECOMMENDATIONS

Midway into an unusually warm and rain-light autumn of 2007, President Bush had no shortage of recommendations on his desk to guide him on how to fix what had gone so wrong with the way we treat our veterans. He had the 29 pages and 6 recommendations of the report from the President's Commission on Care for America's Returning Wounded Warriors, presented to him by cochairs Dole and Shalala in a grand photo-op White House ceremony back in July. And he had the 562 pages and 113 recommendations of the report from the congressional Veterans Disability Benefits Commission, which were presented to him by the not-famous commission heads in a considerably less grand, modestly sized ceremony that was inversely proportional to the size of the package of proposals.

But the president did not have a couple of powerful data points that could have proven crucial to his ability to understand all that was wrong before he made his decision and announced his proposed solutions.

The president did not have a copy of a mind-boggling letter of October 26, 2007, that the Department of Veterans Affairs sent to Eric Adams of Tampa, the former Army military policeman who fought in two wars in Iraq. The letter was the VA's response to his request for benefits for the post-traumatic stress disorder that VA doctors had diagnosed and for which they were treating him.

And the president did not have a copy of the video that CNN technicians were still editing in Atlanta that autumn, reporting the plights of former Marine Ty Ziegel and national guardsman Garrett Anderson. Both were treated unconscionably by the VA when they sought compensation for their tragic, crippling injuries in the Iraq War.

When we last left Eric Adams, things were going rather well, considering the alternatives that had been staring him in the face. After various VA psychologists had agreed upon the diagnosis that the former army military policeman suffered from PTSD, he had pushed hard and had successfully landed himself in the stress management counseling treatment program at the Bay Pines VA facility in St. Petersburg, Florida. In the tradition of better late than never, the VA has devoted considerable resources to developing PTSD programs for Iraq and Afghanistan war veterans, and Adams found his counseling most helpful. His counselors had him recounting the traumatic incidents he had witnessed—incidents that would suddenly appear in flashbacks, both when he was sleeping and when he was awake. He talked of his two good friends getting killed in Iraq, and he showed photos he had taken of dead bodies, Americans and Iraqis. He had quit his job as a Tampa cop (due to his physical and PTSD problems) and had gone to work for the VA at the same facility where he was being treated. He still suffered problems from the traumatic brain injury caused when his van without seatbelts was smashed from behind by the lead tractor trailer in the convoy he was escorting along perilous roadways in Iraq. And the painful disc problem in his neck.

It was in December 2006 when Adams filed his first appeal for changes in his VA service-related benefits ratings. He waited 180 days, and when he couldn't find out what was causing the delay, he contacted the office of his local member of Congress; an aide called the VA and reported back that the government had lost his records. But Adams, now wise to these matters, had kept copies of all of his records; so he made a new set at the local Kinko's and paid about $50 of his own money to have them bound so that individual pages could not disappear again; and sent the two-to-three-inch-thick bound volume of records to the VA regional office in Atlanta, which was handling his case because he worked for the VA in St. Petersburg. Then he waited anew.

After a couple of months, he received a telephone call from a woman who identified herself as working on his case at the Atlanta regional VA office. Adams cannot remember her name and didn't write it down, but he remembers far too vividly the conversation—especially the part where she said she couldn't find any evidence that he had been in combat. "That was unbelievable!" recalled Adams. He said he told her his DD 214 form from the Defense Department clearly stated that he had been deployed in Operation Iraqi Freedom, and he explained that was combat and that his job was leading those convoys through areas known for insurgent attacks, and he told her about the explosion that occurred in front of his van and how it was rear-ended by the huge truck following him. She thanked him and ended the call.

In early November, almost a year after his first filing, Adams got his reply from the VA. The letter, dated October 26, 2007, contained specific decisions on each of the thirteen points in his original request for rating adjustments. He had requested that, in view of the records showing that VA psychologists had diagnosed him with chronic PTSD and were treating him for it, his old rating of a relatively minor 30 percent disability for "service connected adjustment disorder" should be reclassified to "chronic PTSD," with the benefits adjusted accordingly as provided by the VA's rules.

Shockingly, the VA denied Adams's request for classification as suffering from PTSD—despite the diagnoses of the VA's own doctors. The VA decision, signed by Thomas O. Sanders, Veterans Service Center Manager, stated:

> *The evidence from your outpatient treatment records and VA compensation and pension examination now confirms that you have been diagnosed with Post Traumatic Stress Disorder and this diagnosis does, indeed, meet the diagnosis criteria. This evidence, however, while new, is not material because although you currently are diagnosed with this mental disorder, service connection remains denied because we cannot confirm your in-service stressor.*

Understand the unconscionable: This VA adjudicator, sitting in an office in Atlanta, had taken the position that even though Adams was now proven to have PTSD, the VA still wouldn't pay him the service-related benefits he was due on the grounds that the VA insisted it needed documented proof of a specific incident that occurred during his military service and could be proven to be the stressor that caused his PTSD.

"I was stunned," Adams recalled. "It was just like a slap in the face. Here I've done everything I could to serve my country in combat in two wars. And this is the response from the bureaucrats who hide behind their desks. I can't believe these VA people did this. They're not just letting me down, they're letting our country down when they do things like this. It is so wrong."

That, if anything, is an understatement. The VA's unyielding position was more than mind-boggling, it was mean-spirited. It is hard to imagine President Bush, sitting in the Oval Office, being able to make a fully informed decision on reforming the VA's treatment of veterans if he did not know the specifics of at least some of the many cases like that of Eric Adams. It is even harder to imagine him thinking that his Department of Veterans Affairs was doing all it could to do what was right for those who had borne our battles.

Indeed, just re-reading the details of all that Adams had gone through and the VA's callous slapping down of his request, you might think the government could not have reached a decision that was colder or crueler than what it had done in Adams's case—unless you happened to be in a video editing booth in Atlanta, when CNN editors were piecing together the stories of a former Marine and a former National Guardsman who had come home from the wars only to discover they had to launch major new battles against the Department of Veterans Affairs.

Either one of the stories of Ty Ziegel or Garrett Anderson could stand as a powerful reminder of the wrongs our government has been known to inflict upon those who served in the military. Taken together, their stories also stand as clear evidence that the president and the blue ribbon commissions had not gotten around to addressing the real fundamental core problems of what is wrong at the VA. New rules, new regs, new reforms of all sorts cannot compensate for the damage that can be done when some in the government see themselves as the adversaries of those who are seeking service-related benefits. For there can always be a way to deny or at least delay for years benefits that deserve to be paid at once. Budgeters might prefer to see more benefits denied. But fairness to those who fought is part of the cost of war.

CNN's documentary, *Waging War on the VA,* made a powerful impact when it first aired in November 2007. At no point did the documentary argue that the promised veterans' program reforms could not succeed without a reform of the mind-set that was at the heart of these case decisions. But it was impossible to watch the documentary—hosted by CNN's chief medical correspondent, Dr. Sanjay Gupta—after reading the commission recommendations and not come away understanding that you had just seen what the commissions had apparently not seen at all, or at least not addressed.

On the screen, Ty Ziegel is a presence you can never forget. When you see the photograph of him as a young marine going to the war in Iraq, you are struck by the fact that he is a handsome young man with a handsome face and a look about him that is very U.S. Marine. When you see him on the screen today, you are struck by the fact that his face is, well, it is not really a face at all, at least not as we have come to know faces. A suicide bombing in Iraq just a few days before Christmas 2004 has left him with no nose, no ears, no hair, a mouth that is swollen and misshapen, all of it in a head that is swollen large—and he has all of that thanks to miracles made by doctors in two years of operations.

"It's all just one big scar pretty much," he says to CNN's Gupta. "Few breaks in my jaw, got holes from shrapnel, five, six, seven holes throughout my face here, burns, neck, face, and head. This left arm ended up having to amputate first middle finger and my thumb, and I later got my big toe put on there for my thumb."

The doctors had to open up the entire top of Ziegel's skull to try to fix what was destroyed inside; he lost one-quarter of his brain. He keeps a model they made of his skull, complete with the five holes in it that remain forever open. But when Ziegel speaks you know what the suicide bomber had not taken from him—his personality, his wit, his courage, and his love for his family. The Ziegel family is from Metamora, Illinois, a small town northeast of Peoria. Shortly after Ziegel returned from the war, his younger brother, who is also a Marine, shipped out to Iraq.

His military retirement comes to $1,200 a month, but of course he was counting on his VA disability benefits to allow him to have a life that was no frills, but decent. He'd filed his claim and got his first check in April 2007. It was very small—no note or explanation with it. So he began calling to get an explanation, and finally a letter arrived in which the VA told him what it had decided about his injuries.

They rate disability from zero, which is the lowest, to 100 percent, which is totally disabled. A VA adjudicator had decided that Ziegel had:

- Facial disfigurement at 80 percent
- Head trauma a paltry 10 percent
- Left lobe brain injury, right eye blindness, and jaw fracture at zero percent!

Head trauma at 10 percent? Brain damage, eye blindness, jaw fracture at zero? It is impossible to look at Ty and what has happened to him and then look at the VA and say that this is tolerable. Based upon his own estimate of the disability ratings that would naturally follow from his various, visible horrendous injuries, Ziegel calculated he'd be getting something like

$4,000 a month. But he was only getting $2,700. When Ziegel began making the rounds of the news media in the spring of 2007, including going to the VA with a television crew following him, the VA caved. VA Secretary Jim Nicholson waved his wand and the 10 percent head trauma became a 100 percent traumatic brain injury. But not everyone home from every war can spark the sort of political panic that will cause a VA secretary to jump in and right the wrongs committed by his hired hands.

CNN told Nicholson that it wanted to interview him about Ziegel's case and Nicholson said he'd be happy to do so next month. The next day, Nicholson resigned.

On October 15, 2005, national guardsman Garrett Anderson, of Champaign, Illinois, was driving a truck near Baghdad. Things looked not quite right and so he reached for his rifle with his right arm when suddenly an improvised explosive device shattered the day. "At that point, my arm was hanging there, lacerated." He lost his arm.

He had a broken jaw and a body riddled with shrapnel. Back home, he could not fill out his own paperwork because he was right handed and he had no right arm. His wife, Sam Anderson, then in law school, did the ream of paperwork.

When his VA claim decision came back, it was literally unbelievable. You could not read the words and believe your eyes. Sam Anderson read the conclusion on camera for CNN: "Shrapnel wounds all over body not service connected." I can try to write it louder but it will not make any more sense—because the VA adjudicator wrote that Anderson did indeed have "shrapnel wounds all over body"—but that the shrapnel wounds were "not service connected." As in the VA won't pay any benefits compensation for those wounds.

Where did the VA say those wounds came from? Well, the VA never said. "That was a great question because I wouldn't know that either," said Garrett Anderson. He had also filed a claim for post-traumatic stress disorder—but the VA reviewer decided he only had a "panic disorder," which was not as severe.

There is evidence that this was not an inadvertent thing that was somehow overlooked by the VA reviewer. Because when the Andersons received Garrett's paperwork, the place where the reviewer had signed the form was, by then, a rectangular hole. Somebody had gone to a lot of trouble to carefully cut out the signature so that Anderson would not know who had made these decisions that were costing him money he had earned.

But it turned out that was not the most outrageous of VA wrongs committed against Garrett Anderson.

During one meeting with a doctor at the VA, the doctor left the room and Anderson's mother-in-law glanced over at a paper on the doctor's desk. It turned out that Anderson had also suffered a traumatic brain injury—but the VA was not telling him about it. He was married, expecting their first child, and had a serious condition that could worsen at any time—and the VA was withholding the information from him, apparently so Uncle Sam could save a few bucks at the expense of his life.

Anderson was getting only $1,800 a month from the VA, nowhere near the $3,000 he'd earned in Iraq. Of course, he filed an appeal; but he learned that the backlog could take six months or more. So he contacted the office of Senator Dick Durbin of Illinois for intervention and got his money.

"It upsets me that the VA system operates in a way that it takes people with power and who you know and what you know to get what you want," Anderson said. And of course he is right.

That was the first point that CNN's Sanjay Gupta raised when he interviewed the acting secretary of the VA, Gordon

Mansfield, about these two cases. One might think that Mansfield would be among the first to be openly outraged by cases such as these; after all, he is a Vietnam War veteran who does his work from a wheelchair, due to a spine injury. But instead, he was quite defensive and protective of the VA.

Asked if someone has to do what Ty Ziegel did—contact the news media and have his father call the secretary of the VA—to get fair attention to right a terrible injustice, Mansfield quietly said, "Of course not, no, of course not." He is a quiet-spoken number two who had been temporarily promoted to an acting number one. When Gupta noted that Ty Ziegel and his father had to call the secretary's office because no one else at any level of the VA was responding to him, Mansfield became all about defending the VA: "Well, let's be real, you know, about the 224,000 that have applied versus the anecdotal evidence. I think most of them are moving through the process and being taken care of. . . . I can tell you any veteran with the same issue, if it's a medical disability, you know, if it's a loss of a leg below the knee, is going to get the same exact result anywhere in our system." When Gupta asked the VA's acting secretary if he was confident of that assertion of consistency in the VA ratings, Mansfield quickly replied: "I'm confident of that."

At that point, CNN's Gupta quite properly noted the VA's fluctuating rulings on Ziegel's disability. "But remember Ty's own case got inconsistent results," said CNN's medical correspondent. "He was first rated for head trauma at 10 percent before the VA changed it to traumatic brain injury rated at 100 percent." The VA official responded by blaming not the current VA adjudicators for decisions that were so contrary to what viewers could plainly see for themselves, but the schedule of ratings the VA officials were using. "The rating schedule itself is a creature of the economy that was in place during World War II," said Mansfield. Gupta pressed once more.

GUPTA: It might be a little mind boggling for people to know that our rating system we're sort of predicated on a system from 60 years ago.

MANSFIELD: That's a creature of statute and regulation and the bureaucratic process.

GUPTA: I think a lot of veterans don't want to hear that, that their rating system is predicated on a system from 60 years ago.

MANSFIELD: Again, you don't have an awful lot of veterans complaining about the package of benefits they get once they get it.

When Gupta asked Mansfield about Garrett Anderson's case, the interview took just a slightly different turn and sounded a slightly different tone. Gupta began by showing the acting secretary where the signature had been surgically removed from the document—the one that said "Shrapnel wounds all over the body not service connected."

Mansfield just sort of shrugged, extending his hands upward, palms toward the ceiling. Then when he spoke, he seemed nonplussed and not sure of what he should do. But in his own way, as Gupta drew him out, the acting secretary acknowledged his own displeasure with the VA adjudicator, speaking as always in a very soft voice.

MANSFIELD: I can go check for you. If he was blown up, so to speak, and he's got shrapnel from it, I don't know how you would get shrapnel without having it be service connected, quite frankly. I'm sorry. I haven't seen that document.

GUPTA: What kind of system would allow a kind of mistake like that to happen?

MANSFIELD: It makes you angry.

GUPTA: It does.

MANSFIELD: Yes. It makes you more dedicated to changing the system, to do what it's supposed to do, which is to take care of these people.

Bob Filner has reached the station in life where he is a prestigious House committee chairman, and on this autumn afternoon in 2007 he is sitting in his office, which is located in the prestigious Rayburn House Office Building, but at the most unprestigious south end and in a dead-end corridor at that, which means it is about as far away from the Capitol dome as you can get and not be out on the sidewalk. The chairman of the Veterans' Affairs Committee is at his desk, in his shirtsleeves, wearing no tie. Power and prestige do not seem to be what Bob Filner is about. Indeed there is nothing about Chairman Filner that resembles a central casting prototype of a powerful and prestigious committee chairman, and that seems to be just how he likes it. He is a Democrat from San Diego, California, who has also cultivated one other habit that sets him apart from so many of the smooth talkers of Capitol Hill: when you ask him a direct question, he gives a direct answer.

As in this: What is the most important thing that you would change about the Department of Veterans Affairs?

"The key point I would change at the VA is that we have set up an adversarial system between the Department of Veterans Affairs and the veterans," Filner told me. It is, he said, a "cultural thing." He goes on to describe precisely the mind-set that we have seen in so many examples in this book. It is a mind-set that has become completely entrenched in the VA, from the top political appointees down to those who deal directly with the veterans' claims.

"Inside the VA they see their sole job is to say to the veteran, 'You are a liar and we are going to prove that you are a liar and that you didn't deserve your benefits that you have claimed.' We have to get rid of the adversarial way of thinking at the VA. If we were to get rid of the adversaries, we'd get rid of tens of thousands of positions there."

That is why we are talking to Bob Filner. America has spent decades failing to acknowledge the central problem faced by veterans who are under attack from their own VA. Some three hundred thousand veterans are now returning home from Afghanistan and Iraq. Bizarrely, their needs were unanticipated and unbudgeted by those in charge of big thinking and budgeting for the Department of Veterans Affairs. And this is why there is a need for solutions far bolder than those proposed by the two government commissions. We have already run out of time. We can't wait for a president and a Congress to tinker and tweak and lather new layers of micro-improvements on top of the adversarial mind-set that is spread far below the surface of the VA.

It might seem a bit odd that we have wound up at the office of one of Washington's titular tinkerers and tweakers, which is what most chairman tend to be, especially those of the less famous and influential committees. But because this was a no-tie, no-blather sort of chairman, perhaps he had seen enough to have a perspective worth sharing about how things should work— even if the Capitol is not a place that can ever make it actually happen. At least not without pressure from an infuriated public.

When asked what had gone so wrong, Filner focused first not on a single tangible thing but on the mind-set. The House chairman noted that in example after example the first reaction of the Veterans Affairs Department when confronted with big service-related problems affecting huge numbers of veterans is to issue a blanket denial. It was that way when the veterans of the Gulf War began to complain of unusual symptoms that were later labeled Gulf War syndrome. It was that way when the Vietnam War veterans first complained of a host of symptoms that were later linked to Agent Orange. When the VA finally reversed itself, it granted benefits for only a small number of specific maladies. For others, it continues to resist.

"We still are not where we need to be on Agent Orange," Filner volunteered. "Five hundred Vietnam veterans got Parkinson's in their fifties. And they were denied benefits." He paused when asked why. "This is where your cultural thing comes in," Filner said. He was focusing on the men and women who are hired to adjudicate the veterans benefits claims. "They'll say they were committed to the veterans and that they were just doing their jobs. Individually they were probably all nice people. But as bureaucrats, they deal with the papers and the laws. And they never see the people!"

When asked what he thought of the recommendations of the presidential commission, Filner replied: "The Dole-Shalala Commission danced around the big picture."

He then switched to what he called a more "mundane" problem—the budget and the way that presidents and the Office of Management and Budget calculate the real costs of war. "Part of the cost of war is dealing with the veterans. The administration gives us these budget supplementals and all of this crap and never mentions the veterans," Filner said.

Filner's bottom line is that when budgeting for war, the

executive branch must include the cost of all the war-making implements. That includes the procurement and maintenance of weapons and other hardware during and after the war. It also includes the procurement and maintenance of troops during the war and after, when they will be eligible for various service-related benefits. Said Filner: "When you give me a budget for the war, you must give me a budget for taking care of the warriors."

Although the White House and Office of Management and Budget were unable or unwilling to provide a true picture of the cost of war, Professor Linda Bilmes, of Harvard University's Kennedy School of Government, has done just that.

In an important 2007 study, "Soldiers Returning from Iraq and Afghanistan: The Long-Term Costs of Providing Veterans Medical Care and Disability Benefits," Bilmes estimated that the lifetime cost of providing disability benefits and medical care to the veterans of the Iraq and Afghanistan wars would range between $350 and $700 billion, "depending on the length of deployment of US soldiers, the speed with which they claim disability benefits and the growth rate of benefits and health care inflation." Bilmes's calculations were based on the huge increase in the ratio of troops-wounded to troops-killed in Afghanistan and Iraq in comparison to prior wars. (There are sixteen wounded for every fatality in the Afghanistan and Iraq wars, compared with just over two that were injured for every fatality in the Vietnam and Korean wars, and just under two for every fatality in World War II and World War I.)

More than 1.4 million veterans have served in Iraq and Afghanistan and are eligible to apply for benefits for service-related injuries. Indeed, the number of veterans of these two concurrent wars is more than three times what had been projected. The average benefits being paid to Vietnam War veterans is $11,670. The number of veterans of Iraq and Afghanistan who return home with PTSD and traumatic brain injury is greater, by an order of magnitude, than in any previous war. These are health problems that are costly to treat and could push the long-term cost toward the high-end estimate.

The Washington headquarters of the Disabled American Veterans is located in a setting that is more picturesque than political, on Maine Avenue just across from the capital's marina. Inside the organization's Washington office, representatives are focused on a big picture that is the politics of the veterans' affairs budgeting. The DAV, which has 1.3 million members, is among the most active of the veterans' advocacy organizations. One of its most important reasons for being is that it helps its members negotiate the VA's labyrinth of policies and procedures. The DAV has counselors who help veterans prepare their claims for service-related benefits and lawyers who help veterans work on their appeals. If the VA were perfect, and no veteran ever needed any help, the DAV would have little reason to exist. As things are, however, the DAV, American Legion, Veterans of Foreign Wars, and so many other veterans' advocacy organizations remain desperately needed by veterans.

Inside, the DAVs Dave Gorman, the Washington executive director, is asked the same core question that was put to the chairman of the House Veterans' Affairs Committee: What is the most important thing that you would change about the Department of Veterans Affairs?

"We believe the system still is fundamentally sound," says Gorman. "But the process for [deciding claims] . . . is screwed up." He goes on to explain that as the VA increased its claims staff, it hired many young adjudicators who simply don't appreciate veterans, who don't know veterans and find it easy to become adversarial toward veterans.

"They hire thirty-two hundred new people to come into the VA and they just don't know any veterans," said Gorman. "Then some guy who's been there twenty years tells them, 'These guys are all fakers, all malingerers. These guys get a problem and they fake it and file a claim.' And that is what these new young VA hires believe." Gorman is talking about the mind-set and how it is developed at the VA. "A big part of the problem is the training. How do you train these people to do that job?"

The way the claims adjudication process works is that the veteran and the VA adjudicator almost never meet. So Gorman, who plays a credible game of golf these days, which is remarkable considering that he lost both of his legs in Vietnam, tries to see the world as the young VA adjudicator sees it when yet another claim comes in and is stacked with all the rest in his inbox. "When you see this paper come across the desk, it's not just a paper. There is a face behind it—a face like mine. But they don't ever see that face or meet the person behind it. What do they do all day? They look at paper. They look at more and more paper. We've got to train them as to who these people are."

The end result is that at the VA, the burden of proof is entirely on the veteran. It is up to the veteran to scour all the medical books and study the scientific data and make the best medical and scientific case that a certain problem is indeed a service-related disability. Otherwise the VA will continue to do what it seemingly prefers to do—reject veterans' claims and not spend the money.

"If I were to walk down K Street and ask people: 'Do you think this country is taking care of its veterans?' perhaps nine out of ten would say yes."

Asked what he and the DAV think of the recommendations of the Dole-Shalala presidential commission, Gorman says: "The Dole-Shalala Commission was a classic example of pulling together good people and then doing something that is politically expedient." There is something else he wants to say, or maybe something he doesn't want to say; so he ponders it for almost two whole seconds, and then adds: "Bob Dole, in Congress, never did a . . . thing for vets."

He continues: "They made six recommendations, and we are okay with five of them—and the VA is already doing most of them."

The recommendation that the Disabled American Veterans and many other veterans' organizations oppose is Number Two in the commission's report: "Completely restructure the disability determination and compensation systems." Under the existing system, or more properly a hodgepodge of two systems, both the Defense Department and the VA conduct physical examinations and set disability ratings, and benefits compensation rates and schedules. The Dole-Shalala Commission recommended, essentially, that these two parallel, overlapping, and sometimes contradictory systems be ended, and a single system be put in its place. Dole-Shalala recommended that, starting with the veterans who were serving in the military as of October 7, 2001 (roughly all who were in the service as of the start of the Afghanistan invasion and beyond), the Defense and Veterans Affairs departments should agree on one medical exam (instead of two) for all military personnel ending their service. Also, once that individual was discharged, the VA should establish the veteran's "disability rating, compensation, and benefits." The original draft report said it would cover those members of the service who were in combat; but then, as veterans' organizations and others objected, it was broadened to include all those serving at the time of the Afghanistan invasion.

But veterans' organizations strongly objected that this would be trading one dual system for another, and pitting veterans from previous wars against veterans from Afghanistan and Iraq. A two-tiered system would be created: veterans who served at the time of the invasions of Afghanistan and Iraq would be rated and compensated according to the new schedule, but those who fought in earlier wars would be compensated according to the old schedule. "It is like saying that those veterans from the current wars would be compensated from the new system but those other vets will still be covered under the old antiquated lousy system, I guess," said Gorman. "So the DAV asks: I lost a leg in Vietnam and you lost a leg in Iraq. I want to be sure that you will get at least as much as I would have gotten for the loss of income."

A bold proposal from Harvard professor Linda Bilmes has provoked new thinking about what has become an old and cruel VA reality—that huge backlog of claims for service-related benefits. It deserves thoughtful consideration.

We know the story so far: veterans have been forced to wait many months, often years, and at times even decades, while their claims either languish or move glacially through the layered system.

We also know the familiar wasteful and adversarial pattern: adjudicators at regional VA offices wait for months, then return claims for insufficient documentation. Later they reject the claim on the narrowest of grounds; many veterans become discouraged and stop there, but some get legal help and file appeals. The VA's review board frequently sends the case back to the regional adjudicators saying they must look at further evidence, and the case goes back and forth for a while. Or the appeal is also denied and then the case goes to the Court of Appeals for Veterans Claims and it is often bounced back with instructions to consider more of the evidence supporting the veteran's claim. The bottom line is that after months, years, and more, almost 90 percent of all veterans' claims wind up being approved.

The VA's proposal for dealing with the backlog is typical governmental small-think: hire a thousand more claims adjudicators at a cost of about $80 million. They could help ease the backlog or they could act just as their colleagues have acted, which is to say, they could perpetuate and even exacerbate the backlog.

In her 2007 paper, "Soldiers Returning from Iraq and Afghanistan," Professor Bilmes proposes a bold alternative.

The best solution might be to simplify the process—by adopting something closer to the way the IRS deals with tax returns. The VBA could simply approve all veterans' claims as they are filed—at least to a certain minimum level—and then audit a sample of them to weed out and deter fraudulent claims. At present, nearly 90 percent of claims are approved. VBA claims specialists could then be redeployed to assist veterans in making claims, especially at VA's [storefront] "Vet Centers." This startlingly easy switch would ensure that the US no longer leaves disabled veterans to fend for themselves.

You might think that this would have instant appeal to the folks who run the veterans' advocacy organizations, but not really. At the Washington headquarters of the Disabled American Veterans, Dave Gorman said he was troubled by a potential repercussion from the Bilmes proposal. "The integrity of the system is the key," he said. "The system can't be seen as being tainted or it will lose its public acceptance." Skeptics might also add that if Bilmes's proposal goes into effect, it could significantly reduce the compelling need for all of the superb work done by the veterans' advocacy groups, which have become more than just a cottage industry. But the only loss Gorman talks about is public trust. "It can endanger the system by endangering the integrity of the system."

Gorman raises a concern that must also be considered: A day might come when the majority of Americans who never served in the military feel that military veterans are getting government benefits that are greater than what they earned and deserve. If there is no VA adjudication, many Americans may come to believe that some veterans might be claiming benefits they haven't really earned. Such a backlash must be avoided in a democracy, especially one that has no military draft and safeguards itself only with an all-volunteer military.

Weighing the two arguments, there is significant merit to the concerns raised by both Bilmes and Gorman—and there is a reform proposal that can address both. The backlog of cases awaiting adjudication at the VA is intolerable and getting worse. Thus, as a temporary measure, the VA should immediately adapt Bilmes's proposal in order to swiftly clear the backlog in less than a year. The government should treat all of the backlogged claims filed with the VA the way the government treats all tax returns filed with the IRS: select a sampling of the claims for review—and simply process and pay the rest. Do that until the backlog becomes negligible or at least manageable.

But after the backlog has dwindled appropriately, the VA should at least try another approach, one that will take into account the very real concerns of system integrity voiced by

Gorman. It will be unhealthy for all if the public comes to think veterans have a license to just reach out and take as much as they want from the U.S. treasury; it is imperative that Americans hold positive and compassionate views of veterans. Thus, for the long term, I would prefer to see if the VA can achieve the sort of minimal backlog outcome Bilmes envisions but do it by staying with the framework of the existing benefits claims concept—while greatly reforming the way it works. That would preserve the integrity Gorman seeks to preserve. The goal of these reforms would be to transform the system into a veterans' advocacy process, rather than the backlog-creating adversarial process it has become. Codify the de facto outsourcing of advocacy representation—the veterans' groups—to help veterans make sure their claims are flawless at the outset. Bring the veterans' organizations into the VA process and fund their assistance with claim preparation and document gathering to assure that a veteran's claim is complete with all records that can make his or her case. If this is done, adjudicators can move swiftly, especially because this would all be occurring in a new era that genuinely gives veterans the benefit of the doubt. Adjudicators could determine that the facts are there and grant the claim at once; or determine that the facts just don't support the claim (which is something the veteran's advocate support representative would presumably already know). Accuracy and fairness would be stressed from the get-go. The emphasis would be on paying veterans the benefits they earned and deserved. The burden of responsibility of proof would fall equally among the veterans and their representatives who marshal the facts, and the VA adjudicators would have to show why a veteran's case is not being approved.

This system ought to at least be tried, because if it does prove itself, it would probably turn out to give veterans the best of all possible bureaucratic and political worlds: quick decisions based solely on the merits of the veteran's record and public confidence in the integrity of the system. It would fulfill our obligation to those who served in our all-volunteer military.

There is of course one other factor that some, such as those who run the Office of Management and Budget, might consider a negative outcome: for decades, the federal budgeters have benefited grandly because veterans have been shafted by their government. Payments have been denied or delayed for years. Sometimes the money veterans earned was never paid. Other times it was paid belatedly—which meant the veterans did not get to use that money for, say investment purposes, but the government did. Professor Bilmes has calculated the cost to the government of reducing the backlog and paying the veterans quickly: "If 88% of claims were paid within 90 days instead of the 6 months to 2 years currently required, the additional budgetary cost is likely to be in the range of $500m [million] in 2007," she wrote in her 2007 Harvard paper.

The federal government will have to get real about the cost of war. The cost of paying veterans what they have earned in benefits, when they have filed their claim for it, is the price of war—and also the price of democracy. The government was wrong when it delayed paying promised bonuses to the veterans who fought in World War I until the outbreak of World War II. The government is wrong when it profits by delaying and withholding benefits owed to veterans who have fought in all the wars since. And the government has been worse than wrong—it has been cynical and even evil—when it has deliberately out-waited the veterans who either gave up their claims or died waiting for a decision on their claims, as their chosen beneficiaries never got to see the money the veterans had tried to save for them.

Meanwhile, some seven decades after the infamous march on Washington of the Bonus Army, the VA has finally gotten quite good at paying bonuses. Not to veterans but to its own senior career officers.

In 2006 the Department of Veterans Affairs paid $3.8 million in performance bonuses to VA senior career officials in addition to their regular salaries, according to a May 3, 2007, investigative report by correspondent Hope Yen of the Associated Press. Yen, who has been among the handful of enterprising Washington journalists who has pursued significant work on the problems at the VA, obtained a list of the bonuses paid in 2006.

Some of the VA officials who were given lucrative bonuses had prominent roles in the $1 billion budget shortfall just a few months earlier in 2005, Yen reported. "The bonuses were awarded even after government investigators had determined the VA repeatedly miscalculated—if not deliberately misled taxpayers— with questionable methods used to justify Bush administration cuts to health care amid a burgeoning Iraq war," Yen reported.

The Associated Press account reads like a script for a satirical skit on *Saturday Night Live,* but it was all too real. "Among those receiving payments," Yen reported, "were a deputy assistant secretary and several regional directors who crafted the VA's flawed budget for 2005 based on misleading accounting. They received performance payments up to $33,000 each, a figure equal to about 20 percent of their annual salaries." One of those top bonuses was paid to a deputy undersecretary who helped direct the benefits program that was clogged by a backlog that approached four hundred thousand claims from veterans who faced waits averaging 177 days. Others who received top bonuses were a deputy assistant secretary for budgeting and a deputy undersecretary for health.

At a time when the VA's backlog of benefits claims was soaring, the VA's bonuses for top officials were also soaring. Between 2002 and 2005 the VA's average bonus payment doubled. It rose from being one of the lowest among government agencies to an average of more than $16,000—the highest of any federal department or agency.

18

A Department of Veterans Advocacy

Renaming the VA, Rededicating Ourselves

More than a few forests have been sacrificed in dedication to the proposition that something has gone very wrong with the way we have been treating our military veterans. Government investigators, civic investigators, journalistic investigators, have spread the word and the experts have produced reams of recommendations that, if laid end to end, would stretch to somewhere but still get us nowhere.

So our purpose here is to come up with a few bold solutions that will actually get us somewhere by focusing on the central and overarching problems. Our goal is to come up with a few solutions that are so basic that they actually make sense not only to the experts who analyze the system but to those who actually must use it.

A good place to start is at the front door of the Department of Veterans Affairs, that grayish beige stone building at 810 Vermont Avenue NW that stretches the full block between H and I Streets. Actually, not at the front door but at that plaque that is just beside it, the one with the raised gold letters quoting from

President Abraham Lincoln's second inaugural address: ". . . to care for him who shall have borne the battle and for his widow, and his orphan . . ."

Lincoln's noble mission statement must stay. But what is behind the plaque, and also what is in front of it, has to change in a very basic way. In other words, we need to change the VA, and also ourselves. We need to change the mind-set that is at the core of the way the VA operates. And we need to change the mind-set that is at our cultural core, our appreciation for the sacrifices made by our veterans who have indeed borne the battle so we won't have to. We must face up to the hard realities every day that our politicians profess on just two days—Veterans Day and Memorial Day, but not on most days when they issue their presidential orders or cast their congressional votes. We must be prepared to tell ourselves the things that our political leaders don't have the guts to tell us and follow through with deeds that would match those (unspoken) words. We must be prepared to pay the price and shoulder the burden of providing for those who fought for us in the worst of circumstances while we were comfortably at home, reading and watching the news reports of their ordeal.

Now we come to the VA. The reshaping of a departmental mind-set ought to begin with the meaning of its initials. VA has come to mean Veterans' Adversaries. It must come to mean Veterans' Advocates.

This sounds facile, but it's not—it's fundamental. It gets to the core of what is wrong. Presidential and congressional commissions don't go there. Congress doesn't go there—officially. They tinker and tweak; they wonk and wink. They can find lots of ways to change lots of things and still change nothing— because no real change will occur at the VA unless this basic mind-set within is changed throughout.

This new mind-set must be forged at the top and forced through the bureaucratic pipelines, all the way down to the VA's lower levels, where reviewers mindful of bottom-line bonuses and incentives make decisions on veterans' claims and cases, decisions that can rejuvenate or ruin veterans' lives. Holding down costs has always been a priority of budgeters and bureaucrats alike, so at one level we can understand why VA claims reviewers operate as if their mission is, first and foremost, to crack down on waste, fraud, and abuse. Indeed, with a veritable tsunami of claims now rolling menacingly toward the stone fortress on Vermont Avenue NW, it is an inconvenient time to insist that we pay the full price of war. But that is what must be done.

Interlude: When you leave the VA headquarters, turn right, walk south on Vermont Avenue, and turn right again, you are on H Street. And if you walk one block west, you come to the Hay-Adams Hotel, just across Lafayette Park from the White House. It is a posh place with a cozy bar and on one recent evening at about six o'clock, I found myself there, talking to a gregarious fellow with a gravelly voice, a stocky man, not tall, who was recounting to me a triumph at work that had obviously just made his day. He reviews benefits claims cases down the block and around the corner at the VA, and he had just spent the afternoon researching the medical literature relating to a veteran's claims, to see if the experts had conclusively established that the veteran's cancer was most likely caused by something that happened during his military service. Finding no definitive connection in the literature had been his absolute triumph, which he told me about with bureaucratic exultation. As he got to the key moment of his story, he announced his victory in a voice well oiled by the afternoon's alcohol, the decibels so loud that even lobbyists stopped boasting and turned to look as the VA man declared his adjudication triply: "De-nied! De-nied! De-nied!"

Now, maybe the veteran who filed that case was indeed one of these fellows who had tossed a spurious spiel at a VA bureaucrat in the hopes of coming away richer than he deserved. But the VA reviewer's unabashed glee as he shoveled through medical volumes and dug out a factoid that cast doubt on the validity of the veteran's claim should make us wonder about the sort of mind-set we want our VA claims reviewers to have when they approach these cases. Do we want them to be intrepid investigators out to find some thread of doubt somewhere, anywhere, no matter how long it takes to research—so they can then shout "De-nied!" three times? Even if it is only on the basis of an inexact assertion that it is *less likely than not* that the cancer was caused by something that happened during the veteran's military service? Do we want our reviewers to be forever looking for the bad apples in the baskets? Or do we want them to move those baskets, which contain so many good apples, quickly and fairly to market—understanding that in the process we may let a few bad apples get through as well?

One last question: What do we really think Lincoln had in mind when he spoke that phrase that is now emblazoned at the VA entrance? Was Lincoln interested in creating a federal system of zealous pursuers of veterans who are wasters, defrauders, and abusers of the system? Or did he really mean the words he spoke? We know the answer. This was, after all, just a phrase from the passage he so carefully crafted to conclude his second inaugural address.

With malice toward none; with charity for all; with firmness in the right, as God gives us to see the right, let us

*strive on to finish the work we are in; to bind up the na-
tion's wounds; to care for him who shall have borne the battle, and for his widow and his orphan . . . to do all which
may achieve and cherish a just and lasting peace among
ourselves and with all nations.*

If the people and government of the United States are truly
serious about honoring, serving, and respecting their military
veterans—and ending the policies that are dishonoring, disserving, and disrespecting them—there are a number of solutions
that can be accomplished virtually at once. Most can be implemented under existing laws. All it will take is a president who
cares enough to order his VA secretary to get it done.

Here are a few proposals that are based on big bold objec-
tives that are very much a part of the VA's stated mission
of providing "high quality, prompt and seamless service to
veterans":

**Adopt as an emergency short-term solution the basic proposal advanced by Harvard profes-
sor Bilmes to quickly clear the VA's huge claims backlog.** Treat all of the VA's
backlogged claims in the manner similar to the way the IRS
treats all tax returns—by selecting only a sampling of the
claims for detailed review and immediately processing and
paying the remaining claims. The review sampling size should
fall within a range of 10 to 25 percent, with the size determined by how long it will take the VA to reduce its backlog to
a level that is negligible or at least manageable. Then the VA
should implement a new, comprehensive claims processing
procedure that emphasizes the VA's mission to serve as veterans' advocates, dedicated to assuring that veterans receive the
benefits they have earned.

End all official delays and dodges involving official records. On the day a service member is discharged from the military, his or her records should be discharged too—transferred automatically from the Department of Defense to the Department of Veterans Affairs. It is time to end forever the system that sometimes takes months for the VA to get a veteran's records from the Pentagon so that a claim can be processed.

The president should order the two departments to quit their turf fighting and supply all necessary documents promptly. Indeed, former VA official Paul Sullivan, who is now a staunch veterans' advocate as executive director of Veterans for Common Sense, noted that existing law already requires that this must be done if the VA secretary requests it—and that the Defense Department must pay for the cost of transferring the records. (Title 38, section 5106, of the U.S. Code, requires that: "The head of any Federal department or agency shall provide such information to the [VA] Secretary as the Secretary may request for purposes of determining eligibility for or amount of benefits, or verifying other information with respect thereto. The cost of providing information to the Secretary under this section shall be borne by the department or agency providing the information.")

Provide same-day service to veterans seeking care or consultation. Veterans seeking medical care anywhere in the VA system—hospitals, clinics, regional VA headquarters, or community store-front centers— deserve one basic customer courtesy: same-day service. They deserve to be able to meet with someone who can talk to them about their problem. The VA's mission statement proudly proclaims on the department's Web site: "Our goal is to provide excellence in patient care, veterans' benefits and customer satisfaction." So do it.

Outsource expertise to achieve same-day service for veterans filing claims. Veterans must be able to call their closest regional or local VA facility and make an appointment for a consultation. They must then be able to go to the facility and meet with a VA-certified representative who will take the initiative for gathering all of the veterans' VA and military records and data to make the best possible case for the veterans' claims of service-related benefits.

On day one, if a veteran shows up without a service representative to provide assistance and counsel, the VA should assign to each veteran, someone who knows the rules and the ropes. The VA likely will not have sufficient staff for the task, so the job should be outsourced to veterans' advocacy groups, such as the American Legion, Veterans of Foreign Wars, Disabled American Veterans, Veterans of the Vietnam War, Vietnam War Veterans, AMVETS, Military Order of the Purple Heart, Blinded Veterans Association, and Paralyzed Veterans of America. Actually, these groups often provide these services to veterans now. The VA licenses those who help veterans. What is needed is for the federal government to structure and streamline the process so that it works on day one to provide the service each veteran needs. Proper funding to assist these outsourced veterans' organization advocates would be money well spent. The representative must have the knowledge and cooperation of the VA staff to be able to submit a complete package of material to a VA adjudicator so that the claim will not be sent back for lack of documentation. Veterans should not have to hire lawyers to pull together their evidence, research legal precedents, medical and scientific studies.

Make medical facilities flexible so they can meet the needs of veterans. Veterans in need of prompt medical attention must be able to go to a VA hospital or clinic and receive care even if their case is not an emergency.

The concept of receiving care does not mean receiving a fistful of forms that must be filled out so that an appointment can be scheduled months later. Someone with medical experience must be available to consult with a veteran and prioritize the veteran's need. A doctor must be consulted and must sign off on the scheduling of an appointment, certifying that there is no excessive delay that endangers the health of the patient.

VA hospitals are becoming state-of-the-art facilities in many, but not all ways. They lead the industry in using electronic record-keeping. When patients move to other regions, their complete records are instantly available. Bar codes on patient IDs impressively reduce the danger of wrong medications being provided to patients. VA hospitals are praised by veterans for medical care of serious wounds. But very few hospitals in the nation can boast that they are state-of-the-art in treatment of all medical problems, and VA hospitals are no exception.

Create a "Vet-med card" so that veterans can have access to timely care even if they do not live near a VA facility. This is an idea the VA and Congress need to consider: issuing veterans a "Vet-med card" that would serve their medical needs just as a Medicare card serves a senior citizen's. A Vet-med card would allow veterans to seek the best and quickest care available at any hospital, with the government paying the bill. Veterans should not be required to make difficult trips, just to get from their hometown to the nearest VA hospital—especially if their medical problems can be better handled by other hospitals much closer to their homes. A veteran with cancer deserves to be able to be treated at a hospital that is top-rated for its cancer treatment and has the best equipment to test and treat the veteran's case. The veteran should be able to go to this hospital, show a Vet-med card, and be treated, with the U.S. government paying the bill.

This sort of flexibility provides advantages that extend beyond the veterans to the VA hospitals; it makes little sense for VA hospitals to spend millions on equipment and facilities that merely duplicate what is available nearby at other hospitals.

Give veterans the benefit of the doubt in adjudicating claims for service-related benefits. It is the existing law but it is not the existing practice. The VA, as true veterans' advocates, must be willing to apply all existing laws to give veterans the benefit of the doubt when a service-related connection to a problem cannot be proven conclusively through military records and medical studies.

It would seem unnecessary and even insulting to suggest that we need a bold new reform that says the VA must obey the laws that have already been enacted by Congress and signed into law by presidents. But the truth is that the VA has, in effect, routinely ignored the instruction by using the narrowest interpretation, a vindictive way for the government to keep benefits payments low. Title 38, section 1154, of the U.S. Code, states: "The [VA] Secretary shall accept as sufficient proof of service-connection of any disease or injury alleged to have been incurred in or aggravated by such service . . . notwithstanding the fact that there is no official record of such incurrence or aggravation in such service, and, to that end, shall resolve every reasonable doubt in favor of the veteran."

Cases in which the science remains inconclusive must not be routinely decided against veterans by means of flimsy legalese— that it is "less likely than not" that a certain chemical or radiation exposure caused a certain illness.

Stop rewarding VA officials with lucrative bonuses for overseeing, tolerating, and failing to fix a system with soaring case backlogs and fast but erroneous denials of veterans' claims.

The fact that the VA has paid the highest bonuses in the U.S. government while performing its mission in such a flawed manner is a failure of top-down decision-making that starts with presidents and VA secretaries who either didn't see what was happening or saw but didn't care. Claim denials that are repeatedly overturned, in lengthy and costly appellate proceedings, are cruel to veterans and no service to taxpayers. VA bonuses should be paid to encourage accuracy and promptness in the benefits claim decisions, with measurable accuracy being defined as decisions that are right the first time, are not remanded and countermanded in appeals. Encouraging prompt and accurate judgments is the best and most decent way to reduce that unconscionably long case backlog.

Finally, none of these proposed solutions can ever resolve the problems that have become so pervasive within the VA until a new mind-set of veterans' advocacy is cultivated and disseminated throughout the entire department. So we come to a final proposal that is probably the only way to banish forever the era of veterans' adversaries and replace it with a new positive mentality—an official name change.

Rename the VA: The Department of Veterans' Advocacy. The new name would make the VA's mission unmistakable to all. It would foster a positive new mind-set and instantly re-badge the bureaucracy in a way that best serves the government and the people.

A reunion of spirit needs to be promoted between America's military veterans and the government department that is their point of contact and potential lifeline. It is the sort of advocacy bonding that comes too late for Bill Florey, Michael Stanco, Jack Leavitt, Alfred Brown, Belie Bowman, and George Wilkes, and so many others who died knowing that they had been dishonored, disserved, disrespected by their government. But there are thousands upon thousands of veterans who deserve a better fate.

Veterans home from the war need to know that their battles are finally over—that they can indeed get what they have earned. Our military veterans must not be forced to battle in peacetime the government they served in wartime. Peace need not be hell.

Index